A Rabbi Reads the Psalms

A Rabbi
Reads the Psalms

Jonathan Magonet

scm press

British Library Cataloguing in Publication Data
A catalogue record for this book is available
from the British Library

0 334 02953 8

First published in 1994 by SCM Press
9–17 St Alban's Place, London N1 0NX

Second Edition published in 2004

Typeset by Rowland Phototypesetting Ltd,
Bury St Edmunds, Suffolk
Printed and bound in Great Britain by
Biddles Ltd, www.biddles.co.uk

Contents

Preface to the Second Edition

It is good to see this book reappearing. It is the one from which I have had most 'feedback', usually from students of the Psalms – European and American, Jewish and Christian – who have found it to be a useful introduction not only to a Jewish reading, but to the text itself and the methods of biblical poetry.

For this new edition I have added two chapters, on Psalms 51 and 118, and an epilogue that requires an explanation. In many of my books I refer to the annual Jewish–Christian Bible Week that has been running in Germany at the Hedwig Dransfeld Haus for 35 years. It remains a unique occasion for the intensity of study and encounter, and the mixture of Jews and Christians, clergy and lay people, who have been regular participants. In the summer of 2003 we finally reached the Psalms on our journey through the Bible. But at the same time we learned that the Haus that had hosted us for so long was in serious financial difficulties and may close. It has been my personal tradition to preach the sermon on the *shabbat* morning of the Week, linking the texts we have been studying to some current issue. The result was the sermon that is printed here, since it does link to at least one of the Psalms we had been studying. It leaves open a challenge, one frequently offered by the Psalms – to learn how to sing to the Lord a new song.

Jonathan Magonet
September 2003

Dedicated to the memory of
Dr Ellen Littmann
Rav Shmuel Sperber
Rabbi Dr William Braude
Andreas Hinz

For Doro, Garriel and Avigail

Preface to the First Edition

Writing books seems to become addictive. There is no more daunting experience than sitting in front of a blank computer screen trying to find the opening words. But it is very exhilarating to chase down an idea, plough through the appropriate references, and pull the whole thing together yet again. And something curiously exciting and sad as the final parts begin to fall into place, an end is in sight and one is already getting prepared for the sense of loss that will inevitably follow – the writer's equivalent of the postpartum depression.

When I had the possibility of a second two-month stint as a guest Professor at the Kirchliche Hochschule in Wuppertal, it seemed like an excellent opportunity to do some more writing on a biblical topic. But what subject? I had been toying with the idea of doing something on Psalms – since each one is discrete and could be handled in a single chapter it seemed like a useful way of tackling a series of individual subjects, rather like the characters I had explored in *Bible Lives*. When I approached John Bowden of SCM Press with yet another suggestion of a book for him to publish, he replied casually that 'books on the Psalms always do well' and left it at that. Given John's rather low-key approach to things I took this as an enthusiastic endorsement of the project.

In the event my time in Wuppertal was much more busy with guest lectures and seminars than I had anticipated and it was much harder to get on with the book. But I completed about a third of the writing and had the opportunity to make useful notes on a number of Psalms I wanted to explore. To my surprise the rest fell into place quite quickly despite the demands of Leo Baeck College on returning to London. Which suggests that too much leisure is not good for my creativity.

I would like to thank the Kirchliche Hochschule for giving me the opportunity to begin this work, and thank in particular the

Ephorus, Siggy Kunath and Professor Berthold Klappert whose friendship I was delighted to renew. A special thank you is also due to Dr Guy Rammenzweig, the Director of the Predigerseminar in Essen, for his various invitations, company and friendship. I am happy to acknowledge an award from the Deutscher Akademischer Austauschdienst (DAAD) that made the trip financially possible.

Once again I owe a debt to the staff and students of Leo Baeck College who carried on gamely without their Principal. Dr Joanna Weinberg generously took on the additional academic responsibilities and John Olbrich the administrative ones.

As always the last word must go to my wife Dorothea who suffered yet again the 'single parent syndrome' in my absence, and Gavriel and Avigail who somehow forgive my absences – the physical ones abroad and the mental ones when I'm tied to the computer. Without their support none of this work would be possible.

1

Why Another Book on the Psalms?

When King David had completed the Book of Psalms he felt very proud and said: 'Lord of the universe, have You a creature that proclaims more praises of You than I?!' So God sent him a frog which said: David, don't be so proud of yourself. I chant the praises of my Creator more than you do. Moreover, I perform a great virtue in that when my time comes to die, I go down to the sea and allow myself to be swallowed up by one of its creatures. So even my death is an act of kindness. (*Yalkut Shimeoni* 2.889)

This Rabbinic Midrash, a parable that emerges from commenting on the biblical text, does not record David's answer. But it belongs to a number of such tales that either debunk or at least qualify David's literary achievement as the composer of the Psalms.

Perhaps the Rabbis were suspicious of art for art's sake. Artistic inspiration had to be kept within very clear limits, bounded by Torah, the teachings and laws of God. When David organized the return of the ark to Jerusalem and a man called Uzzah touched it and was struck down, the Rabbis blamed David for not even knowing a very basic law: the ark should have been carried on the shoulders of the Levites, not put into a wagon! But what can you expect from someone who writes, in Psalm 119.54:

Your statutes have been my songs in the house of my wandering.

To consider the laws of God as mere 'songs' was quite unacceptable! And yet, for the Rabbis, David is also the great composer of most of the Psalms – and the collector and editor of those ascribed to earlier people. Just as Moses gave the Five Books of the Torah, so David gave the Five Books of the Psalms to Israel (*Midrash Psalms* 1.2). Nor were the Rabbis entirely unsympathetic to the problems of artistic creativity. They noticed that there are two Psalm headings which are identical except that the word order is reversed. Some have the caption '*mizmor l'david*', 'A Psalm of/to David'; while others state '*l'david mizmor*', 'To/of David, A Psalm'. What is the difference between them? When it says '*l'david mizmor*' it teaches that the *shechinah*, the presence of God, rested on him and at once he composed a song; when it says '*mizmor l'david*' it teaches that he began to work on his song and only afterwards the *shechinah* rested on him (*Pesachim* 117a).

I began with two negative evaluations of David precisely because they are so unexpected – which is part of my own justification for writing this book. The Psalms are so much part of the common religious world of Judaism and Christianity, and so many books have been written about them, that to produce yet another one requires some explanation. Of course any author thinks that he or she is saying something 'new', or at least giving a different perspective on something old. But having taught the Psalms to students at Leo Baeck College and other audiences for almost 30 years, I am aware that within the vast literature of commentary and exegesis there is very little that introduces the kinds of interpretations brought by the Rabbis – whether ancient, medieval or modern. Moreover, there are very few books which provide a 'user friendly' introduction to how one actually sets about working with the Hebrew text itself, or give access to the richness and complexity of the language of the Psalms to the non-Hebrew reader. So this book is organized to provide a way in to this special world through:

- an introduction to the nature of biblical poetry,
- a guide to some of the poetic structures that recur in the Psalms,
- a look at some different Rabbinic approaches to the Psalms,
- studies of a number of Psalms as a way of illustrating these various aspects – and for the fun of exploring their individual dynamic and meaning.

At this point I must make an awful confession. I was not very fond of the Psalms when I first began consciously to read them – in the services at the West London Synagogue when I was a member of the youth club. To put it bluntly, they all sounded very much alike. (A friend put it even less kindly by describing them as 'chewing gum'!) That is to say, the language, terminology, repetition of themes and sentiments, made each Psalm seem very much like the previous one. Of course there were some that stood out – most obviously

Psalm 23, for example. But there was a 'sameness', which was not helped by the monotone with which they were read in English, or the hesitancy at unfamiliar words when they were read in Hebrew.

All of which induced a certain amount of guilt. After all, the Psalms were a central part of our liturgy. They were, everyone assured me, the most sublime expression of human spiritual aspirations, reaching to the depths of the soul in torment and to the heights of ecstatic joy. Well yes, but they still sounded pretty much the same to me.

The transformation came about for me when I had to begin translating the Psalms for a prayerbook. Precisely because I began to understand their complexity, the interconnections between the words within them, the levels on which each part could be understood, and the problem of seeing the parts within a coherent whole, my translations were quite impossible! 'Pregnant', was one comment, 'overstuffed' was another. That is to say, I had tried to convey in English all the nuances I kept coming across in the Hebrew, and the result was incomprehensible. For the prayerbook something much more simple and direct was needed, and where there was ambiguity in the text some kind of solution had to be found that made sense even if it meant that a lot was left out. It is a pleasure to have the opportunity here of introducing and exploring the sort of complexity that must otherwise be left out.

Thirty years on I still have many questions about the Psalms. As with so many such things the problem is learning how to own a particular passage – to enter its inner world and somehow find ways of linking it with our own personal history and experience. Which means avoiding two extremes: being bullied into feeling that it *ought* to speak to us when it does not, or giving up, simply because the idiom or the language is remote. Perhaps writing this book is my own way of staking a claim on at least some of the Psalms – but it is only the beginning of such a process and by no means the end.

To whom do the Psalms belong? This may seem like a silly question. In a very real sense they have become part of universal culture, available in a myriad languages and embedded in so many religious traditions. Most obviously they are an essential part of Christian religious practice and experience. So much so that at a lecture once a nice Christian lady sounded quite pleasantly surprised when she asked, 'Oh! do Jews have the Psalms as well?' The answer is, of course, a resounding 'Yes!' – to the extent that no part of Jewish religious life or liturgy is without the full text of particular Psalms or extracts from them as essential parts of later liturgical compositions. But, as with so much biblical material, Jews sometimes feel that much of their tradition has been hijacked by Christianity so that it is difficult for us to look at particular texts without somehow experiencing them as 'Christian'! Certainly that is the case when the Psalms are read, or chanted, in English. In Hebrew it is a different matter. The Hebrew name for Psalms, *tehillim*, is derived from a verb *halal* meaning to praise, and there is a wealth of musical tradition and particular associations that places them very firmly within the familiar world of Jewish prayer.

This is not the place for a comprehensive listing of the Jewish liturgical use of the Psalms, but some indication may be of interest.

Psalms 113–118, the 'Hallel' ('praise') Psalms are read at every Jewish festival, as well as on the New Moon and during the Passover evening home service, the Seder (when Psalm 135 is also read). Though these same Psalms are sung for all the Pilgrim Festivals, the melodies used vary to give a unique flavour to each occasion. Why were they chosen for this purpose? According to one Rabbinic view, because they refer to five essential aspects of Jewish religious experience and belief; the Exodus from Egypt; the crossing of the Sea of Reeds; the giving of the Torah at Sinai; the resurrection of the dead; the birth pangs of the Messiah (*Pesachim* 118a).

Psalms 95–99 and 29 form a unit at the beginning of the Friday evening service, a tradition inaugurated among mystical circles in Safed in the sixteenth century, in addition to the traditional use of Psalms 92 and 93 that goes back to Temple times.

Psalms 24 or 29 accompany the return of the scroll to the ark after the reading of the weekly portion in the synagogue on *shabbat* morning.

A whole range of Psalms, initially 145–150 but later many others, were used by individuals as part of their private preparation before the daily morning service and were gradually incorporated into an expanded morning liturgy.

During the Temple period the Levites used to recite a special 'Psalm of the Day' and this now forms part of the morning service. For the first day (i.e. Sunday, the first day after the *shabbat* – Jewish days are not 'named', but rather counted in relation to the *shabbat* towards which they point) – Psalm 24; second day: Psalm 48; third day: Psalm 82; fourth day: Psalm 94; fifth day: Psalm 81; sixth day: Psalm 93.

Since the twelfth century Psalm 104 and the fifteen 'Songs of Ascents' (Ps. 120–134) have been recited on *shabbat* afternoons during winter.

The daily afternoon service is preceded by Psalm 145 which is also read on two other occasions during the daily services.

The Grace after Meals is introduced by Psalm 126 or 137.

Psalms 90 and 91 accompany funerals.

Psalm 84 is part of the Wedding Service.

In addition to these 'formal' situations there are any number of private occasions when individual Psalms or groups of them are read. There is a tradition of reading through the entire Book of Psalms on a regular basis and there are 'Societies of Reciters' in traditional Jewish circles who maintain this practice at the Western Wall in Jerusalem.

Particular Psalms are believed to have healing or other powers and belong to a folk tradition of their use. A colleague once visited a small Jewish community in a remote part of the world and was startled to be asked the following question by a woman congregant. It seems that she had experienced difficulties in her marriage some years before and had asked a visiting Rabbi what she should do to make her husband love her again. He had suggested that she read a particular Psalm regularly and that her difficulties would be cleared up. She had done so and it had indeed been effective. However, in recent months things had been going badly again, so could my colleague recommend a new Psalm she could recite? My colleague was somewhat nonplussed but after a long talk managed to get into a more familiar and comfortable 'counselling' situation. Someone commented to him later that he should have suggested a Psalm that was twice the number of the one she had been using, on the basis that if it was no longer working one should double the dose!

There is a long folk tradition of the use of biblical verses for magical purposes, particularly for the warding off of evil spirits or dangers, though the Rabbis struggled against the practice.

Psalm 29.3–10 contains seven references to the 'voice of God', so it was thought to protect someone who must drink water on a night when evil spirits were active.[1]

In the Middle Ages the book *Shimmush Tehillim*, 'The [Magical]

Use of the Psalms', was highly popular and often translated.
The following illustrations from it of specific Psalms to use in par-
ticular circumstances are taken from a list given in the *Jewish
Encyclopedia*:[2]

Psalm 1.1	– against miscarriage.
Psalm 1.3	– against trees shedding their fruit.
Psalm 6	– against diseases of the eye and danger on land or water.
Psalm 8	– against crying children.
Psalm 14	– against defamation, and when one's veracity is doubted.
Psalm 19	– against evil spirits; difficult labour; and to awaken intelligence.
Psalm 23	– in interpretation of dreams.
Psalm 33	– for a woman whose children die young and against epidemics.
Psalm 34	– to secure the favour of princes and governments.
Psalm 35	– against mischievous busybodies.
Psalm 58	– against vicious dogs.
Psalm 63	– on accounting with one's business partner.
Psalm 73	– against compulsory baptism.
Psalm 84	– against sickness.
Psalm 93	– for support in a law suit.
Psalm 105	– against a quartan ague.
Psalm 106	– against a tertian ague.
Psalm 108	– to have happiness in one's house.
Psalm 110	– to make peace.
Psalm 121	– when travelling alone at night.
Psalm 128	– for an expectant mother.
Psalm 130	– to escape arrest by the night watchman.
Psalm 138	– for love.
Psalm 146	– against sword wounds.
Psalm 149.6	– against pollution.

This belief in the efficacy of Psalms in times of distress is very
deeply embedded in Jewish thought. It leads to a Yiddish phrase,
'Don't wait for a miracle, *zog tillim*, recite Psalms!'

Faith in the power of the Psalms has invaded even the most secular
Jewish consciousness. My colleague Rabbi Tuvia ben Chorin of
Jerusalem found himself on military service in a tank during the

October War. He had his Hebrew Bible with him and was reading through the Psalms for comfort in this terrifying situation. His words were picked up on the intercom and the other soldiers asked him what he was reading. When he said it was the Psalms, these 'secular' Israelis said: 'Don't keep them to yourself!' and he carried on reading them out loud.

Having described my own initial difficulties about relating to the Psalms, and seen how central a role they play in Jewish religious life, it may be appropriate to say a little about how I set about writing this book. First, much of it is based on notes acquired over many years of teaching these texts and attempting to formulate a more coherent approach to them. But I also used the opportunity of a two-month visiting professorship at the Kirchliche Hochschule in Wuppertal to start examining some less familiar ones.

As to technique there is an aspect to my study of biblical texts that I am almost embarrassed to acknowledge. As well as working in my own booklined study as scholarly custom demands, there is nothing nicer than sitting in a café with a photocopy of a Hebrew text in front of me and sort of 'doodling' with it – in fact that is a useful first stage before looking at what other commentators have made of it.

This is a practice I learned from a novelist friend in Jerusalem who used to sit for years in the same café, writing and correcting his manuscript, often outliving the existence of the café and moving on to the next one. I find such an atmosphere pleasant and more alive and human than an empty study. There are sufficient distractions to grab my attention from time to time – and to encourage me to concentrate enough for them to be blotted out. It is also nice to munch on the chocolate cake and slowly sip a cappuccino.

In some ways this is the 'vulgar' part of the exercise of exploring a new Psalm. The text presents itself to me as a puzzle, much as I imagine crossword puzzles appeal to other people. It is a challenge, a contest between the author and me to find out what he is 'really' saying. Now whether or not one can get to the 'authorial intention' is one of the great debating points of modern literary criticism. Somewhere between recognizing the impossibility of doing so, and getting a pretty good idea about what the writer was up to – particularly in terms of the structures and strategies he was using – there has to be a middle ground, and I would stake my claim for a fairly commonsense idea of what that may be in many cases. Certainly that preliminary 'run through', without benefit of other commentaries, is the most exhilarating, and often the most frustrating, of exercises. It really is a kind of struggle with the author, long before such refined questions as the religious ideas to be drawn from the Psalm can be addressed. The writer is playing his (or her) own game and I am challenged to use my experience of Hebrew writing to take him on. I suppose that this is a kind of intellectual macho exercise, though the chocolate cake may dim the heroic image somewhat.

I am aware in the above description that I have assumed that the writers of the Psalms were men. This is most probable, given the nature of Israelite society and the association of most of the Psalms with a cultic setting. Nevertheless, in writing about individual Psalms in this book I have tried to be careful in the way I express the gender of the author. It is part of a sensitivity that has grown over the years. 'Man' is supposed to be a generic term for 'people', regardless of gender, but that assumption has to be questioned today. However, this issue does raise problems in the translations I have done of the Psalms. If the Hebrew says *ish*, 'man', does it mean 'person', irrespective of gender, which requires one kind of translation, or is it intended as a male in the particular context? I have tried to differentiate as the distinction is real in many passages.

A similar problem arises with the translation of the name of God. According to Jewish tradition, the tetragrammaton, the 'four-letter' name of God, YHWH, was not to be pronounced aloud. Instead a substitute word *adonay*, 'Lord', was used. However, this is not entirely satisfactory and already Moses Mendelssohn in the eighteenth century, in his German Bible translation, sought to go back to the original four-letter name in finding an appropriate term. Based on the assumption that this name was derived from the verb *hayah*, 'to be', he used the term '*Der Ewige*', 'the Eternal', presumably seeing the name as referring to the timeless existence of God.

In more recent times Martin Buber and Franz Rosenzweig in their German translation took the sense of 'to be' as more existential and instead of using an actual name translated it as He or Thou, as appropriate to the context. Today the term 'Lord' raises a number of problems. Because of its masculine associations it does reinforce the perception of God as a 'Man' (despite our theological awareness that this is not the case) and thus strengthens those hierarchical structures that give men a greater dominance in society, and especially, all too often, within our religious communities. Though the title 'Eternal' is not entirely satisfactory it is more neutral and it has a venerable history (James Moffatt used it in his celebrated Bible translation), so I have used it throughout – except when quoting writers who used 'Lord'.

There remains, however, the problem of the personal pronoun when it is used for God. I have had to go through the difficult exercise of translating some of the Psalms for a new prayerbook where the intention was to use inclusive language in a consistent way. With a lot of ingenuity and a degree of circumlocution it was possible to get around those places where God is referred to as 'He', for example, by using 'who' or simply repeating 'God', or recasting the sentence entirely. When really stuck it was decided that it would be legitimate to change into the second person and address God as 'You'. But for the purposes of this book I have wanted to stay as close as possible to the word order and detail of the Hebrew text so that those who have no Hebrew could more or less follow what is going on. The result is something of a hybrid as I have had to stick to 'He' on a number of occasions when I would have preferred a different solution. But this problem exactly reflects the challenge of understanding the world of Ancient Israel. The revolutionary nature of biblical religion lies in its perception of God as utterly different from the nature gods with which Israel was surrounded, the discovery of a God who was at the same time a transcendent cosmic force and a distinctive personality intervening in the history and private life of a people. In a patriarchal society that 'personality' must inevitably be addressed in masculine terms (though female imagery could also be used on occasion (Isa. 49.15; 42.14; 66.13). Nevertheless, the refusal to accept any graven image of God constantly subverted that conventional terminology. The same tension remains an issue till today.

Some technical notes are in order at this point. The first has to do with transliteration. Writing Hebrew letters and words in English characters is always a bit problematic. First, there are two major systems of pronunciation of Hebrew – Ashkenazi, associated today in particular with East European Jewry, and Sephardi, associated with the Jews of Spain and North Africa, and now adopted by the State of Israel. The Sephardi pronunciation has come to dominate but many Jews have had to switch between one and the other with a resultant mix that used to be called 'Ashkephardi' – a sort of Jewish equivalent of Franglais. I will try to use a consistent Sephardi system, but it is important to remember that we do not know how Hebrew might have originally sounded in the biblical period. I recall that some 'classically' trained Hebraists taught that the letter *vav*, should be pronounced like a 'double-u', as 'waw' – rather like I learned Latin at school – 'civis', a citizen, being pronounced 'kiwiss'. The dominance of spoken Hebrew, *ivrit*, seems to have established the Sephardi norm for most Jews today.

But there are other difficulties. Some letters have no English equivalent; the *alef* and the *ayyin* may both be silent, so apostrophes, curved in different directions, have been used to differentiate them – though actually the *ayyin* is a kind of glottal stop and is 'grunted' in the best Sephardi circles and even transliterated as 'ng'. Further-more there are all sorts of exotic printing attempts to illustrate the 'mobile *shva*', a pause in the middle of a word – for example, an upside down 'e' hanging in mid-air. In short, it is easier to learn Hebrew letters and pronunciation sometimes than to read the translit-eration! Finally, of course, it depends on the language into which you transliterate – since the letter *shin* in German, would have to be written 'schin' to conform with the conventions of spelling.

So I have tried to use a sort of commonsense English method that more or less allows the reader to make the sounds of the Hebrew itself. For this I have abandoned a number of distinctions between letters that a scientific transliteration would require. Thus the letter *kaf* can be pronounced 'hard', like the letter 'k', or 'soft', like the 'ch' in 'Loch Lomond'. The former is usually transliterated as 'k' and the latter as 'kh'. (By the same logic the hard *bet* should be written as 'b' and the soft *vet* as 'bh'.) For convenience I prefer to write 'ch' (as in the Scottish Loch). However, there is another letter, *chet*, which is a softer sound though today it is rarely differentiated from the *kaf*. Again conventions include writing it as 'h', with a little dot underneath – to distinguish it from the letter *hey* 'h'. You can see the problem in the English transliterations of the Festival of Chanukah, which is also spelt as Hanukah. I've elected again for the 'ch' (Loch) on the assumption that readers who know Hebrew will go to the original to read, and those who do not will want to hear the sound. For the troublesome *shva* I've usually used an 'apostrophe' ('). The letter *quf* I have transliterated with a 'q'.

One more technical matter that can prove an irritation. The Hebrew numbering of Psalm verses includes the heading to the Psalm as verse 1. In the RSV these readings are not included in the numbering, so Hebrew Psalm verses are sometimes one number ahead of the equivalent English verse. I have kept to the Hebrew numbering for my own translation.

I treat 15 Psalms in some detail in this book. Since this leaves over 130 unexplored this study is hardly comprehensive and no basis on which to make definitive statements about the nature or purpose of the Psalms as a whole. Fortunately there are any number of excellent commentaries and monographs, works of scholarship and works of spirituality, to turn to. I like to take my time, live with each Psalm, tease out the most obvious elements and, like a good brandy, let it mature so that it can always be rediscovered afresh. The diversity of even the few that are examined here is a reminder of the richness and subtlety of biblical writing, and of the vast gaps we still need to fill in order to understand the context, political, social, cultural and existential, of so much that has been handed down to us. We have a long journey before us.

All journeys begin with a few first steps, and one of these is to have some idea of the conventions of writing and literary expression that are part of the biblical culture we are entering. So our next chapter begins to address that subject. Another essential is to learn Hebrew, but since most readers have not *yet* done so, I have tried to indicate through the transliterations what is going on on that level as well. For those with some Hebrew who would like to follow the argument more directly I have provided at the back of the book the complete Hebrew texts of the Psalms under discussion.

The Hebrew Bible has three divisions and the Rabbis distinguished their nature. The first part, the core around which the others are overlaid like the layers of an onion, is the Torah, the Pentateuch, which is seen traditionally as the direct word of God to human beings. The second division, the Prophets, extending from the beginning of Joshua to the end of the Minor Prophets, is likewise revelation, but mediated, and therefore transformed to some extent, by the individual experiences of the prophets themselves. But the third division, the Writings, the one that contains the Psalms, is 'inspired by the *ruach hakodesh*, the holy spirit of God'. Rather than being the revealed word of God to humanity, it is the self-revelation of human beings

to God, the expression of every aspect of human life, joy and suffering, pain and exaltation, addressed to the source of life. In such a
collection the Psalms, because so much personal material is recorded
there, have a very special role to play.

As I suggested at the beginning of this chapter, it is not always
easy to enter their world, to identify and understand what they are
saying. But they have nourished and sustained communities and
individuals on their own spiritual and life's journey for over two
thousand years, so each reader is challenged to go ever deeper into
them. There is a teaching of the Chasidic master, Nachman of
Bratslav that serves as a preface to the collection of Psalms in a
prayerbook I co-edited. It seems appropriate to quote it here as well,
as a reminder of the many dimensions of the Psalms to be discovered
and the experience of the generations that each of us has something
to gain from, but also contribute to, them.

> Every single person, according to what he or she is, is able to find
> himself or herself within the book of Psalms, and earn repentance
> through reading the Psalms.

2

Biblical Poetry for Beginners

Before approaching individual Psalms, it is helpful to have some idea about how biblical poetry works. As with all such matters certain elements are very easy to grasp, though the whole topic gets more complicated the more you study it. There are a number of important books[1] on the subject, especially as the literary approach to the Bible has gained ground. Insights have been refined and, alas, to some extent 'jargon' has increased. So the following brief outlines are meant only as helpful starters to understanding some basic patterns and structures that seem important for understanding the composition of the Psalms.

There is a very convenient starting point in a little poem that appears at the beginning of Genesis. In my more fanciful moments I suspect that the compilers of Genesis included it here for precisely the same purposes as this chapter – to enable those starting to read the Hebrew Bible to have a sample of biblical poetry at the beginning to cut their teeth on!

In Genesis 4 we are introduced to the family of Lemach, one of the descendants of Cain, whom you will recall was the first to kill another human being, his brother Abel:

> Lemach took for himself two wives, the name of the one was Adah and the name of the second was Tzillah. Adah gave birth to Jabal who was the ancestor of those who dwell in tents and have cattle. His brother's name was Jubal, who was the ancestor of all who play the lyre and pipe. Tzillah also gave birth to Tubal-Cain; he was the forger of all instruments of bronze and iron. The sister of Tubal-Cain was Naamah. (Gen. 4.19–22)

Sounds like a nice, gifted family. But Lemach is about to break into song, perhaps accompanied by Jubal on pipe, to show that some of the problems associated with Cain are still very much present in the world.

	Lemach said to his wives:	
Adah and Tzillah	hear	my voice
wives of Lemach	attend	my word,
for a man	I killed	for my wound
and a lad		for my bruise.
for sevenfold	was avenged	Cain
but Lemach		seventy-seven times.

(Gen. 4.23–24)

adah v'tsillah	*sh'má'an*	*qoli*
n'shei lémech	*ha'zéinah*	*imrati*
ki ish	*harágti*	*l'phitzi*
v'yéled		*l'chaburati*
ki shivatáyim	*yukam*	*qáyin*
y'lémech		*shiv'im v'shiv'ah*

In the translation I have followed the word order of the Hebrew to illustrate more directly how the pattern works. The most obvious thing that emerges is that everything is said twice – or rather that each line is followed by a second line that either echoes it very closely or provides a minor or major variant, or even strongly contrasts with it. The classical term for this pattern is 'Parallelismus Membrorum' and it was coined by Bishop Lowth in his pioneering study of this phenomenon, *De sacra poesi Hebraeorum* (1753, 1763). In his important re-evaluation of the understanding of biblical poetry, and parallelism in particular, James Kugel (see note 1) has pointed out that Lowth's term means 'the parallelism of the clauses', but that many of his successors have misunderstood it to imply that every single element ('member') in the first part should have its exactly corresponding element in the second part, though this was probably not Lowth's intention. Moreover, Lowth tried to classify the different kinds of parallelism – as synonymous, antithetical and synthetic (for cases that did not fit the other two categories!) – and again his followers have made the mistake of trying to fit everything into this over-rigid scheme. (And when they did not fit, sometimes amending (improving?) the Hebrew original so that they did.) For our purposes we will stay with the term 'parallelism', since it does indicate that the second part of the line may echo the first in some way, but we will try to be cautious in our use of examples and our application of the term.

Another problem that Kugel raises is that having found 'parallelism' people have tended to use it as a way of defining what constitutes biblical 'poetry'. But then new problems emerge. First, because parallelism occurs in any number of passages, for example legal collections, proverbs and 'prose' passages, that would not normally be classified as 'poetry'. Conversely, can we even talk of 'poetry' as a separate category within the Hebrew Bible at all? Or rather, where does the borderline lie between passages that are obviously prose and those places where the rhythm, or some form of repetition, or use of metaphor or other kind of 'heightening' of the style, suggests that we are moving into a more 'poetic' form? Since our sense of what 'poetry' is may be determined by models derived ultimately from Greece we may actually be imposing all sorts of artificial categories on the Hebrew texts of the Bible that come from a different cultural milieu entirely. Instead we should really be trying to understand biblical modes of literary expression from 'within' the biblical tradition as far as we can.[2] After all, biblical Hebrew comes out of an environment in the Ancient Near East where there is a long history of literature and literary forms, so the existence of a developed awareness of style among the biblical writers is pretty much self-evident. But how one sets out to define it or classify it is very complicated. Fortunately such a task is beyond the scope of this chapter – and anyone who wishes to read further in this problem could well start with Kugel's *The Idea of Biblical Poetry* and some of the other books listed in note 1.

Curiously the 'fact' of biblical parallelism seems to have been 'forgotten' in the later tradition of Rabbinic interpretation of the Bible. Or rather the Rabbis did not often make statements about literary structure but instead addressed the contents directly. Furthermore they tended to treat passages where some parallelism was involved as if it was not there – that is to say, they would treat the two half-lines as if they were completely separate, each one needing to be interpreted quite independently. But this was part of a wider debate on interpretation that runs throughout the history of Jewish Bible exegesis. Should each word, even letter, of the Hebrew Bible be understood as a separate word of God to be interpreted by itself, or should one recognize that repetitions might be there for 'stylistic' purposes, to add 'colour' to a text or emphasize a particular aspect?

As Rabbi Ishmael put it: Words of Torah were couched in human language, or, to put it more crudely, God too has to work within the conventions of Hebrew grammar and syntax. I have discussed this problem at some length in *A Rabbi Reads the Bible*,[3] so I do not want to enter into it again here. Instead it is worth noting that the phenomenon of parallelism was recognized in some early Rabbinic commentaries even if they never attempted to classify it in a systematic way. Take, for example, the following passage:

> For the Eternal listens to the needy
> and despises not *His* prisoners. (Ps. 69.34)
> Rabbi Benjamin ben Levi said. The beginning of this verse does not [correspond to] the end, nor the end to the beginning. It should have read either: 'For the Eternal listens to the needy and does not despise prisoners.' Or else: 'For the Eternal listens to *His* needy and does not despise *His* prisoners.' (*Genesis Rabbah* 71.1)

Scattered throughout the studies of the medieval Jewish commentators are similar observations about the patterning we associate with 'parallelism'. Abraham Ibn Ezra (1092–1167), who lived in Spain at the time of the first scientific exploration of the nature of Hebrew language and grammar, had this to say on Genesis 49.6:

> Into their (Simeon and Levi) council my soul (*nefesh*) will not enter,
> to their company my 'glory' (*kavod*) will not be joined.
> Rabbi Moshe haCohen Ibn Giktala [the grammarian] has said that *k'vodi*, 'my glory' actually means the same thing here as *nafshi*, my 'soul' [both terms could be rendered as 'self'], and that there are many such examples in the Book of Psalms. And he has indeed explained well, for the same meaning is here being expressed twice as in similar examples of 'prophetic' language, such as the Song of Moses (Deuteronomy 32.7): 'Ask your father and he will tell you, your elders and they will say to you.' Also Balaam's statement in Numbers 23.8: 'How can I curse whom God has not cursed, and how can I denounce whom the Eternal has not denounced?' So in this case, 'in their council' is equivalent to 'to their company', 'enter' is equivalent to 'be joined', and 'my soul' to 'my glory'.

His contemporary Rabbi Shmuel ben Meir (Rashbam) (1085–1174) living in France commented in a similar vein on a sentence in the Song at the Sea, Exodus 15.6:

> Your right hand, O Eternal,
> glorious in power,
> Your right hand, O Eternal,
> shatters the enemy.

This passage is like a number of other examples: 'The floods lift up, O Eternal, the floods lift up their voice' (Ps. 93.3); 'How long will the wicked, O Eternal, how long will the wicked rejoice!' (Ps. 94.3); 'For see Your enemies, O Eternal, see Your enemies perish' (Ps. 92.10). The first half does not complete his statement until the latter half comes, repeats it and then completes his statement. But the first half mentions the person about whom he is speaking.

Despite some reservations the terminology of 'biblical parallelism' remains helpful since it draws our attention to the two 'half-lines' that are interacting with each other. The disadvantage arises in cases where the second 'half-line' seems to have nothing whatsoever to do with the first half, beyond a general sense of a shared rhythm or the advancement of the ideas it contains within the composition as a whole. It is important to be aware of these problems of classification and terminology, but in the end each piece of biblical poetry must be evaluated by itself since there are infinite variations possible on this basic pattern. Rather than generalize any more, it is best to look in more detail at the Lemach song.

The first part is actually a classical example of Bishop Lowth's 'synonymous parallelism' – that is to say, the words in the second half are 'synonyms' for those in the first half – and indeed it would be possible to switch them between the two halves without affecting the sense in any way.

adah v'tsillah	*sh'má'an*	*qoli*
n'shei lémech	*ha'zéinah*	*imrati*

Adah and Tzillah	hear	my voice
wives of Lemach	attend	my word

We know that Adah and Tzillah are the wives of Lemach; the verbs 'hear' and 'attend' are likewise interchangeable, as are the closing 'my voice' and 'my word'.

The whole can be shown schematically as follows:

a   b   c
a'   b'   c'

When we move down to the next part of the poem things start to get a bit more complicated:

| *ki ish* | *harágti* | *l'phitzi* |
| *v'yéled* | | *l'chaburati* |

| for a man | I killed | for my wound |
| and a lad | | for my bruise. |

Schematically we could show this as:

a   b   c
a'   c'

The most obvious feature is that there is a gap in the second half where we would expect the verb 'killed'. But a moment's reflection shows that the verb is not really needed to understand the second phrase. Since we are operating within this 'parallelism' framework, we *know* that there should be a verb meaning 'kill' in the second part and so we can supply it ourselves without the author having to do so. This is called 'incomplete parallelism' and becomes a potent source for subtle variations, because the readers are forced to 'fill the gap' out of their own imagination. Moreover, it becomes one of the ways in which the readers are actually drawn into the text and engaged with it, instead of merely being passive 'observers' of what is going on, a pattern to be found throughout the Hebrew Bible in different ways.

In this particular example it is the verb that has 'dropped out' in the second half, but it could be any one of the other elements as well. Nor need it be something from the second half of the verse that is missing once we are working within a parallel structure. Look at the following structure from Psalm 20.8 (English v. 7). I will give it in Hebrew first and then a literal translation as the usual translations inevitably obscure the problem faced by the reader – that is to say, they make the decision for us as to how to fill the 'gap'.

éileh v'réchev
v'eileh vassusim
va'anáchnu b'sheim adonai elohéinu nazkir

some	in chariot
and some	in horses
but we	in the name of the Eternal our God speak out.

We can also show this schematically:

a	b
a	b'
a'	b''	c

The 'a' column is repeated in the second line, referring to the same 'some people' who do something with either chariots or horses, i.e. the weapons of war. The third 'a' is not a synonym in this case but a contrast – as opposed to 'some', we, Israel, do something different. Similarly the 'b' column contrasts the two weapons of war, chariot, horses, with the 'name of the Eternal our God'. Finally the third part supplies the verb that has been missing all along – the verb *nazkir*, from the root *zachar*, usually translated as 'remember' Here in the *hiphil* form it means something like 'proclaim' or 'speak out', or even 'boast' – a reminder that the Hebrew idea behind 'remembering' is literally to 're-member', to give that which is recalled a reality again, a tangible, physical renewed existence.

So what is the effect of this particular construction? In the first place it creates a marvellous tension as we wait for the missing verb in the first two lines – what is it that these people intend to do with their chariots and horses – we both know and do not know at the same time. Only with the final verb do we understand the degree to which they boast of their power through these tangible symbols of war, in contrast to our reliance on God. But this tension, that it is possible to sustain in the Hebrew, runs into problems in translations – so that they inevitably supply a verb to fill the gap – as in the RSV, for example:

> Some *boast* of chariots, and some of horses;
> but we boast of the name of the Lord our God.

Others use the word 'trust' instead of 'boast' to provide for the first missing verb.

But there is also a second effect of this 'absence' in the first two phrases – for it points literally to the emptiness of such 'trust' in chariots and horses when contrasted to the real strength to be derived from trust in God. The missing verb underlines the missing reality.

A similar construction can be found at the beginning of Psalm 115:

lo lánu adonai
lo lánu
ki l'shimcha tein kavod

Not to us, O Eternal,
not to us,
but to Your name give glory.

We will look at the implications of this startling introduction to the Psalm in a later chapter, but it is worth noting once again that the idea that no glory should be ascribed to 'us' (in contrast to the glory that should be ascribed to God) is reinforced by withholding the operating words till the end – even the 'something' that we do not deserve is not mentioned, a kind of doubling of the negative.

But if we now return to our Genesis verse, we are confronted with two further issues. The first is relatively simple, but opens up a Pandora's box of problems. Since a word has 'dropped out' in the second part its rhythm is obviously affected. Here begins the enormous range of problems associated with the nature of Hebrew metre. Where does the stress lie on a particular word and what metrical patterns can we uncover? In counting the metre should we be concerned with syllables, entire words or even sense units? For the purpose of this exercise we will try to make sense of each text as we find it. Thus in this case, though the verb has dropped out, the word for bruise, *chaburati*, clearly is longer than the one above for 'wound', thus the missing syllables from the absent verb are 'made up'. We will see other examples of this kind of 'compensatory lengthening'.

But the second issue is of a quite different kind. Although 'wound' and 'bruise' have similar meanings and so are readily interchangeable, what do we make of the fact that the first half-line refers to a 'man' (*ish*), but the second to a 'lad', Hebrew *yeled*, that commonly means a 'child', from the root meaning 'to give birth'? That is to say that whereas they do have in common their 'maleness', there does seem to be a disjunction between their ages. This problem was already noticed in an early Rabbinic comment:

Rabbi Jacob bar Idi asked Rabbi Yochanan: If a 'man', why a 'child' [in the parallel position]; if a 'child', why a 'man'? He was a 'man' in deeds, but a 'child' in years! (*Genesis Rabbah* 23.4 on Gen. 4.23)

In this particular case there may have been a difficulty for the author in finding an appropriate synonym for 'man'. The options would include *adam*, also a term for a 'man', but since it is the name of the first human being, within the same set of Genesis stories, it could have led to enormous confusion to use that word. The same problem might have arisen with the word *enosh*, also a proper name as well as a term for 'man'. But he might have used *gever*, suggesting a 'strong man', so there is something of a question mark over the use of *yeled*. Which leads us to consider further the issue already raised by our example from Psalm 20 – the parallelism form can also be used to offer a contrast instead of a simple reinforcement of the same idea. 'They' boast of horses, but 'we' boast of God. Thus the verse could be suggesting that Lemach killed both 'a man' and 'a lad'. Now in this particular case, despite the age difference, it does not seem very likely that such a thing is intended. But in many other biblical verses a contrast is clearly intended, and sometimes it is not at all certain which of the two possibilities, a repetition or a contrast, is meant, especially when one or other of the terms is unfamiliar. (We often rely on parallelism to help explain obscure words when they appear in the second half-line in parallel to a word we do know.)

Having said that it is unlikely that 'man' and 'lad' refer to two different people, nevertheless that is precisely how it was understood in a Midrashic comment (from Tanchuma) that is quoted by Rashi, the great medieval Jewish Bible commentator, on Genesis 4.23. The story runs as follows: Lemach was blind, but he used to go hunting with his son, Tubal-Cain, 'the forger of instruments of bronze and iron', who also used to manufacture weapons. Tubal-Cain would spot the target, point his father in the right direction and the latter would shoot his bow and arrow. On one occasion the son saw a horn peeping over the top of a hedge, assumed it was a wild animal, aimed at his father and off went the arrow. Unfortunately, the son did not realize that the figure behind the bush was actually Cain, for, in one Rabbinic view, the 'mark of Cain' (Gen. 4.15) that would protect him was a horn that appeared on his head. When Lemach discovered that he had killed his great-great-great-grandfather Cain, he was so angry that he hit his son – and killed him! Then he had to go back to his wives and explain how this disaster had come about!

Adah and Tzillah	hear	my voice
wives of Lemach	attend	my word,
for a man	I killed	for my wound
and a lad		for my bruise.

By this reading 'for my wound' does not mean 'because someone wounded me' but rather 'because of my wound', namely my blindness. And the 'man' is Cain and the 'lad' his son Tubal-Cain.

There is a certain elegance about this reading when taken in the context of Genesis 4. Cain is ultimately punished for killing his brother – but God's promise to Cain (4.15), 'whoever kills Cain will be requited ''sevenfold'' is also enforced. For Lemach, who kills him, is the ''sixth generation'' and Tubal-Cain, who is responsible for the accident is the ''seventh''.'

Though that may be a somewhat fanciful example and of no great consequence, it is worth noting another case which leads to a very significant interpretation in the Gospel stories. Zechariah 9.9 contains structures of the sort with which we are now familiar:

gili me'od bat tsion
harí'i bat yerushaláyim
hinneh malkeich yávo lach
tzaddik v'nosha hu
ani v'rochev al chamor
v'al áyir ben-atonot

| Rejoice greatly | O daughter Zion |
| be glad | O daughter Jerusalem |

behold your king will come to you
righteous and triumphant is he
humble and riding on an ass
on a colt, the foal of an ass.

The first part is straightforward parallelism: Rejoice/be glad; O daughter Zion/O daughter Jerusalem. The second pair of phrases belong to the more problematic classification we will be examining later, where it is not certain whether we can legitimately speak of 'parallelism'. But the third pair raise precisely the same problem we have seen in Genesis 4. The structure would assume parallelism of the sort:

```
a        b        c
                  c'
```

In this case the space left by the missing words 'humble and riding' is made up by a longer description of the animal – 'on a colt, the foal of an ass'. So will the 'king' come into Jerusalem riding on one animal, described in some poetic detail, or should we read this as two separate animals? Matthew 21.1–7 goes for two different animals:

> The disciples went and did as Jesus had directed them; they brought the ass and the colt, and put their garments on them, and he sat thereon. (Matt. 21.6–7)

John, on the other hand, seems to accept the parallelism for what it is (John 12.14–15):

> And Jesus found a young ass and sat upon it; as it is written,
>   'Fear not, daughter of Zion;
>   behold, your king is coming,
>   sitting on an ass's colt!'

We can now return to Genesis 4 and the last of the three parallel phrases:

ki shivatáyim	*yukam*	*qáyin*
v'lémech		*shiv'im v'shiv'ah*

for sevenfold	was avenged	Cain
but Lemach		seventy-seven times.

Using our usual scheme we would find the following:

```
a        b        c
c'                a'
```

Here, again, the second part is missing the verb, but it can be supplied from the first half. In this case the subject of the verb is different in both cases, Lemach instead of Cain in the second part, so that we have here not a 'synonymous' parallel but a contrast. In line with what we observed in the previous part of Lemach's song, and again in Zechariah, when a significant word has dropped out, there is some kind of compensatory lengthening to make up the number of stresses – here '*shiv'im v'shiv'ah*', 'seventy-seven', easily makes up for the missing word.

But what is new here is that the pattern of the verse has been

reversed in the second half, the element that came at the beginning
now appearing at the end and vice versa. If we look at this schematically, but providing the missing word from the second line, we
have the form:

a   b   c
c'   b'   a'

The same structure can also be shown as follows:

a
    b
            c
            c'
    b'
a'

In this form, there is some progression of ideas towards a central
point and then a return to the start. It can also be expressed by noting
that the first word and the last word are related (a and a'), and
similarly the second word and the penultimate word (b and b') and
so on. This form is known as 'chiastic', 'crossing over' or as 'concentric' and it seems to be one of the key building blocks for Hebrew
writing, both in poetry and in prose. Thus the pattern outlined above
holds good when a, b and c are words within a sentence, or entire
sentences within a poetic or prophetic unit and even whole chapters –
see, for example, the cycle of stories about Abraham (Gen. 12—22)
in my book *Bible Lives*,[4] and the similar work on the Jacob cycle
in Jan Fokkelman's important *Narrative Art in Genesis*.[5]

At this point I have to declare a particular interest in this form,
to the extent that my students sometimes suspect me of being
obsessed by it. In self-defence I must plead that I am very conscious
of the dangers of imposing such a structure on innocent biblical
passages when it is not really present, but that nevertheless it is a
well-recognized feature. Moreover, it often allows us to uncover the
unity of passages where surprising leaps seem to take place between
the individual verses – it is when the overall pattern is clarified that
the integrity of the piece can be seen. We will look at three different
examples of Psalms built on such a concentric pattern in the next
chapter, but it is worth seeing how it operates over a smaller unit.
The following passage from Amos 5.4–6 is a fine example:

dirshúni   vichyu
    v'al-tid'r'shu   bet-el
        v'haggilgal   lo   tavó'u
            uv'ershéva   lo   ta'avóru
        ki   haggilgal   galo   yigleh
    uvet'el   yih'yeh   l'áven
dir'shu   et-adonay   vich'yu

Seek Me and live
    And do not seek Beth El
        and to Gilgal do not go
            and to Beersheba do not pass over
        for Gilgal will surely be exiled
    and Beth El shall become nothing.
Seek the Eternal and live!

Unfortunately the wordplays of the Hebrew do not translate into English. Thus the town Gilgal will literally 'split' into two, *galo yigleh*, because of the play on the name, the verb *galah* meaning 'to uncover' or 'expose' and hence to send into exile. Similarly Beth El, literally the House of God, will become what Hosea has called it elsewhere (Hos. 4.15; 10.5), Beth Aven, the house of 'nothingness'. But the structure itself works on a number of levels. It begins and ends with 'seeking God', and then takes the reader or listener on a geographical journey to the shrines in the Northern Kingdom of Israel, even crossing over the border to another shrine in Beersheba. But all these pilgrimages are in vain, partly because these shrines (inauthentic ones in Amos' view) will disappear, but also because the important thing is not completing the formalities of a pilgrimage and performing endless empty rituals, but the genuine seeking of God and life, in both the literal and figurative sense.

I have already touched on the vexed problem of rhythm and metre. We do not know how Hebrew was originally spoken. The Jewish 'Masoretic' tradition of punctuation and verse subdivision and accentuation of the biblical text is relatively late (completed by the eighth century CE), though based on earlier traditions. But you only have to listen to the different kinds of pronunciation within the Ashkenazi and Sephardi Jewish traditions, to hear the difference in the way that words are stressed. Moreover, the problem of metre becomes additionally complicated the moment we try to impose a regular measure on texts that for one reason or another do not fit our Western modes. Do longer words count as more syllables to be stressed or not? If a half-verse is much shorter than its matching half does this mean that something has dropped out or is the shortness an intentional effect? And anyway, if some of these passages were sung, how far did the music allow one to stretch out words to fit? I remember my first, and till now last, attempt to appear in a theatrical performance when I was a medical student – the 'Manic Depressives'' annual Christmas concert at Middlesex Hospital Medical School. The director used to sing madrigals and was most insistent that whenever we produced a parody text to a popular song the new words must fit the score exactly. He would tolerate no 'lo-ove' or 'you-ou' to make it scan. But oriental musical traditions seem to be more flexible in such matters and who knows what David could accomplish with his harp, let alone the flutes, trumpets, rams' horns, ten-stringed lutes, harps and lyres of the Temple orchestra.

And yet! We do read biblical Hebrew today with a kind of modern Israeli Sephardi intonation and do feel a certain rhythm running through it, even if it may not be what it was in biblical times. So the following passages are simply attempts to indicate a range of poetic 'effects' that seem to emerge from the biblical text. The stress usually lies on the last syllable, so I shall use a French acute accent to indicate when it occurs on a different one.

The first example is from the Song at the Sea, Exodus 15.9–10. It is noticeable that a series of Hebrew words begin with the same letter *alef* (the first of the Hebrew alphabet) which gives an alliterative effect. But what is particularly striking is the rhythm as the boasting enemy pursues the escaping Israelites.

> *amar oyev erdof asig*
> *achaleq shalal timla'éimo nafshi*
> *ariq charbi torishéimo yadi*
> *nasháfta b'ruch'cha kisámo yam* . . .

The enemy said: 'I will chase – overtake!
Divide the spoil!
Devour my fill!
Draw my sword!
My hand destroy them!'
One puff of Your breath and the waters covered them . . .

The staccato repetition of the enemy's boasting words, each with the single accent on the last syllable, conveys the galloping rhythm of the pursuing horses and chariots. But when God intervenes, the rhythm abruptly changes. The words '*nasháfta b'ruch'cha*' not only create a different rhythm (the accent falling on the penultimate accent in the first word and on the final one in the second), but the sound of *nasháfta* is softer, and the word itself means simply 'to breathe out'. God does not even need to blow very hard totally to destroy this vaunted noisy triumphant army. Thus the contrast of rhythm, sound and meaning all reinforce each other.

Even more subtle is Isaiah's description of an enemy army coming to attack Jerusalem (Isa. 5.26). Here the rhythm undergoes a number of changes as the enemy draws ever closer – but this time without God intervening:

> *v'hinneh m'heirah qal yavo*
> *eyn-ayeif v'eyn-kosheil bo*
> *lo yanum v'lo yishan*
> *v'lo niftach eizor chalatsav*
> *v'lo nitaq s'roch n'alav*
> *asher chitsav sh'nunim*
> *v'chol kashtotav d'ruchot*
> *parsot susav katsar nechshávu*
> *v'galgalav kassufah*

> Behold speedily fast he comes.
> None is weary, no one stumbles,
> no one slumbers, no one sleeps;
> no girdle-cloth is opened up,
> no sandal-thong is broken off.
> Their arrowheads are sharp
> and all their bows are drawn.
> Their horses' hooves are sharp as flint,
> like whirling winds their wheels!

I have tried to capture in English the changing rhythm. After the 'starting up' motion of the opening words, '*v'hinneh m'heirah qal yavo*', it settles into a two–two rhythm with the emphasis on the second word of each pair: *ayeif, kosheil, yanum, yishan*. Then it changes into two sentences with three words, with the major stress on the last of them:

asher chitsav sh'nunim
v'chol kashtotav d'ruchot

no girdle-cloth is opened up,
no sandal-thong is broken off.

Once again it changes into a pattern of four words and then a final
two which bring the passage to an abrupt end. This threefold change
of rhythm corresponds nicely to a movement from trot to canter to
gallop. And as the enemy comes close enough for the sparks of the
horses' hooves to be seen we are suddenly overwhelmed as their
wheels literally ride over us and are past.

A similar rhythmic effect is created in the Song of Deborah (Judg.
5.22) where the horses' hooves are described as:

daharot daharot abirav

which is only partly captured by the English 'galloping galloping
on'.

While still in this military context it is worth nothing the following
example of 'sound effects' introduced by Jeremiah (4.5). The passage
tells of warning the people by the blast of the *shofar*, the ram's horn,
about the approaching enemy:

haggidu vihudah uvirushaláyim hashmíyu
v'imru v'tiq'u shofar ba'árets
qir'u mal'u v'imru hei'asfu
v'navó'a el-arei hammivtsar

Tell it in Judah and make it heard in Jerusalem
and say you, and sound you the ram's horn in the land.
'Calling you! Gather you! Inform you! Assemble you!
let us enter the fortified cities!'

Once again the translation cannot capture the fourfold stressed final
syllable 'ooo' which mimics the sound of the *shofar* itself: '*qir'u*
mal'u v'imru hei'asfu'.

Let us examine one more example where rhythm, sound and content combine to dramatic effect. In Psalm 93 there is a description
of God's power:

nas'u n'harot adonay
nas'u n'harot qolam
yis'u n'harot dochyam
miqqólot máyim rabim
adirim
mishb'rei-yam
adir bammarom adonay

The floods may rise, O Eternal,
the floods may rise and roar,
the floods may rise and thunder;
but above the roar of great waves,
mighty ones,
breakers of the sea,
mighty above them is the Eternal.

These two successive sentences convey the tempestuous storming of the sea, but in quite different ways. The first one, with its sibilant '*nas'u, nas'u, yis'u*' and the similar threefold repetition of the key word *n'harot*, conveys the effect of repeated waves rising and crashing down upon each other. Moreover, each of the words that close the two latter phrases, *qolam* and *dochyam*, by placing the stress on the last syllable convey the effect of the wave curling over and falling. The best way to illustrate this might be with the following kind of layout, in which we read 'up' the page, allowing each wave of sound to crash down upon the preceding one:

>   *yis'u n'harot dochyam*
>   *nas'u n'harot qolam*
>   *nas'u n'harot adonay*

But the second sentence creates quite a different effect with its repeated *mem's* and *resh's*, a sort of rumbling, murmuring sound. It emphasizes the power of the sea, the rumbling sounds interspersed with the 'crash', *mishb'rei* of the great 'breakers' (actually a literal translation of the verb *shavar*, which, in the intensive *piel* form, means 'smash'). But having established that these powerful sounds belong to the sea, it ends by ascribing to God the same word for 'might', *adir*, but places God's power *marom*, 'on high', above all this – and to make the point even more clear, places the name of

God at the last, and 'highest', place in the sentence. Again it helps to 'read up' the page:

adonay

bamarom

                                        adir

                         mishb'rei-yam

                    adirim

    miqqolot mayim rabim

Over 30 years ago in Jerusalem I heard a Chasidic explanation of this passage from my teacher, Rav Shmuel Sperber, *zichrono livracha*. The world, he explained, is full of disasters, waves pass over my head, breakers crash down on me, troubles, the world is blowing up about my ears – you need an awful lot of strength to remember God is above these!

Examples of such 'sound effects' and patterns could be multiplied, as, indeed, other such literary games. Perhaps it is sufficient for now to realize that we have to remain open to many such levels of pattern, sound and meaning within the Hebrew text of the Bible and be on the lookout for them as we enter the world of the composers of the Psalms.

3

David Sings the Blues – On Concentric Psalms: Psalms 145 and 92

Having come relatively late to Jewish studies, and particularly to the Hebrew Bible as a focal point for my own exploration, I was very conscious of my 'amateur' status. In the earlier days there were two very obvious elements to this sense of insecurity. The first was my awareness of how little I knew of so much of Jewish tradition, let alone the many scholarly disciplines needed for any 'serious' work on the subject – both the 'tradition' and the 'academy' have ways of de-skilling, or at least unnerving, the 'outsider'. The second problem was that in those early years, for some inexplicable reason, I seemed to see the texts in a different way from most others, certainly from the conventional approaches of the standard biblical commentaries.

Today this sense of 'otherness' has largely changed with the growth of the literary approach to biblical texts. Rather like Molière's *Bourgeois Gentilhomme*'s pleasure at discovering that he had been speaking 'prose' all his life without really knowing it, it was a great joy to learn that I had been pursuing a 'synchronic', as opposed to a 'diachronic', approach to the texts. (It took some considerable time to get the hang of these two terms, but the latter means the attempt to trace the origins of a particular text in history, seeking within it evidence of its sources and editing, while the 'synchronic' approach means treating the final text before us in its wholeness. There is a debate about whether or not these two approaches are mutually exclusive.) I must confess, however, that the more I attempt to keep up with the complexities of the 'new' literary criticism, which is always being superseded by something that is 'post-new', the more I feel at sea once more. That is in no way to decry the attempt to find a theoretical underpinning to the study of texts, and I have gained enormously from these new approaches, though often when filtered through the writings of gifted interpreters. But for me the dialogue with the text itself has always been the starting point, with the layers of classical and modern interpretation then entering to challenge both my assumptions and conclusions.

The above remarks were sparked by remembering the origins of this particular chapter in a lecture I gave to the British Association for Jewish Studies in 1981. By then I had acquired some degree of security in my approach to biblical texts, but here was the testing ground where both those well-rooted in the Jewish tradition, some of whom were my own teachers, and those who functioned in the academic world came together. Discussing 'concentric structures in Psalms' during that period with such an audience felt like a distinct risk and a challenge at the same time. I survived the occasion – though one of my former teachers whose views I greatly respect suggested afterwards, quite casually, that he did not believe a word of it! But I suppose those are the moments we all need to face as we grow up into whatever discipline we wish to master.

PSALM 145

I wrote up my lecture and it was published in the *Heythrop Journal*.[1] The version that follows has been developed with this book in mind, where minor excursions into other than purely academic areas are possible. I have omitted the study of a third Psalm (137) from the original article because I have treated it in *Bible Lives*.[2] However, on rereading my lecture I was happy to notice that I started off with a bit of leg-pulling at the expense of some conventional 'scholarly' opinions, so I cannot have been quite as scared of the occasion as these opening remarks might suggest. In fact I had obviously discovered early in my academic career that you can be quite rude about the views of other scholars as long as you write with apparent scholarly detachment. I quote: 'I would like to begin with Psalm 145, and I cannot resist quoting from a recent article by Walter Brueggemann.[3] In examining Psalms as a reflection of reactions to distressful situations, he notes that some Psalms can be classified as Psalms of Orientation which reflect people who "enjoy a serene location of their lives", with a "sense of the orderliness, goodness and reliability of life" (p. 6). One example is our own Psalm which he describes as follows: "It may be regarded as a not very interesting collection of clichés. But in fact, it affirms God's providential care. The unimaginative style makes the confident claim" (p. 7). Bruegge-

mann is, of course, echoing other similar judgements on the Psalm.
Gunkel called it "mehr eine Kunstelei als ein Kunstwerk", "more
an artefact than a work of art".[4] Perhaps Buttenwieser's remark is
most devastating. "Poetically the hymn is worthless. It appears to
be a product of the time of literary decadence"![5] Though there are
contrasting views that find it a religious and poetic gem, and see in
its artifice "no sign of mechanical construction",[6] one can sympathize with these viewpoints that question its poetic value. Nevertheless,
these judgements seem to have overlooked some stylistic points.'
Let's look at the text:

1. *A Psalm of Praise. David's*
   I will glorify You, my God, the king
   and bless Your name forever and ever.
2. Every day I will bless You
   and praise Your name forever and ever.
3. Great is the Eternal and much praised
   and His greatness is beyond research.
4. One generation shall praise Your deeds to the next
   and tell of Your mighty acts.
5. The splendid glory of Your majesty
   and Your wondrous deeds will be my theme.
6. They will speak of the power of Your awesome acts
   and I will describe Your greatness.
7. The fame of Your great goodness they will proclaim
   and sing aloud of Your righteousness.
8. Gracious and compassionate is the Eternal,
   slow to anger and great in faithful love.
9. Good is the Eternal to all,
   and His compassion is upon all His works.
10. All You have made shall thank You, Eternal
    and Your faithful loving ones shall bless You.
11. They shall tell of the glory of Your kingdom
    and speak of Your power,
12. to let all humanity know His mighty acts
    and the glorious splendour of His kingdom.
13. Your kingdom is an everlasting kingdom
    and Your rule from age to age.
14. The Eternal supports the falling
    and raises all those bent low.

15. The eyes of all look to You
    and You give them their food in its time.
16. You open Your hand
    and satisfy the needs of all that live.
17. The Eternal is righteous in all His ways
    and lovingly faithful in all His deeds.
18. The Eternal is near to all who call to Him,
    to all who call to Him in truth.
19. He fulfils the needs of those who fear Him
    and hears their cry and saves them.
20. The Eternal guards those who love Him
    but all the wicked He destroys.
21. My mouth will speak the praise of the Eternal
    and let all flesh bless His holy name forever and ever!

I must confess that at a first reading it is possible to sympathize with those views that find this Psalm somewhat pedestrian or even complacent. We shall have to see what we can find under the surface.

What is not obvious from the translation is that it is an alphabetic acrostic, each verse beginning with a different letter of the alphabet, except that one verse is missing where we would expect the letter *nun*. This use of the alphabet contributes to the sense of formality of the Psalm, but it also raises the question as to why the author has chosen such an artificial form and whether this concern with structure ends with the opening letters of each verse. The use of the alphabet may have been an *aide-mémoire* for community worship – certainly the Psalm has found its way into a number of locations in the traditional Jewish liturgy, having a very prominent place at the start of the afternoon service. Nevertheless, it is a kind of artistic challenge to accept the constraints of a particular medium and by working within it, or against it, to create something that subverts or transcends its limitations. How has our author worked with this structure and these self-imposed limitations?

In the previous chapter we have seen something of concentric structures and, in particular, the way they can extend over a wide range of verses. When they function within a passage of limited size, for example a Psalm, it becomes relatively easy to spot them. So how does one do so? To some extent it is a matter of trial and error, with the ever-present risk of imposing some sort of artificial structure on the passage in question. But it is always worth looking for words that repeat themselves and seeing where they are located and how far they are in equivalent positions.

The overall effect of such repetitions is to give the listener a sense of pattern and a clue to the development of the structure and content of the Psalm. The analogy that comes to my own mind, as an occasional, but mean, harmonica player, is the 12-bar blues. Over the 12 bars the music moves to a peak and then comes down again. As one improvises against the background chords it becomes clear when one has passed the centre and begun to move towards the closing resolution, before the next 12 bars begin. Hence the old joke among those who improvise together for fun – 'at least we finished together!' (There are more refined musical versions of this pattern but I am not up on music theory.) In the same way, by picking up the repeated words, or some other similar clue, we can follow the inner coherence of thought and structure of the passage as it moves towards its end.

The easiest way to spot repetitions is to work with coloured pencils or marker pens – one of the great adjuncts to biblical scholarship, second only to the computer! For the colours stand out and the pattern of relationship, or its absence, becomes extraordinarily clear. This does not resolve the problem of what repetitions are significant – for that a special judgement has to be made. Moreover, at a later stage of analysis other things, for example the presence of quotations or certain themes, might be the determinative element – we will see a surprising example in a later chapter when we look at Psalm 115.

If we apply the 'colouring' technique to this Psalm certain things emerge at once. The root *halal* 'to praise', appears in verses 2–3 and again in verse 21 as a noun. Similarly the verb *barach* 'to bless', appears in the first two verses and the last. In the identical places comes the closing formula '*l'olam va'ed*', 'forever and ever'. And just to complete the list the noun *shem*, 'name', is also in verses 1, 2 and 21. This is quite an intensive gathering of 'key' words. Granted they all belong to the conventional terminology of 'praising the name of God', but with this arrangement they effectively put a bracket around the entire Psalm, an 'inclusio'.

Our colours will also bring out the appearance of the root *malach* 'to rule', 'be king', in verses 11, 12 and 13, which is the geographical and also thematic centre of the Psalm. Given the opening statement: 'I will glorify You, my God, the king', it becomes clear that this is the metaphor that governs the Psalm. It is also an odd but interesting fact that at the centre of the Hebrew alphabet are the three successive letters, *kaf, lamed* and *mem*, that are those of the root *malach* but in the reverse order. Perhaps this fact led our author to play with the concept of 'king' in this very specific 'alphabetical' way.

We thus have a Psalm neatly divided into two parts by these central verses, so it now becomes important to examine the contents and structure of verses 4–10 and 14–20. At this point we enter a much more subjective part of the analysis, and in a sense have to make up the rules as we discover them. Or at least test out our findings against other instances elsewhere and some sort of law of probability.

It must be admitted that verses 4–10 seem to reflect that 'unimaginative style' which Brueggemann mentions. They appear to be a set of repetitions of standard clichés from other Psalms of praise. Is there nothing that distinguishes one or other of the verses? One thing does emerge on closer scrutiny. Verses 4–7 and 10 are all about the people or groups that will sing God's praises (generation to generation, 'I', the Psalmist, and 'they'). They all refer to God in the second person – they will praise Your deeds, Your power, Your glory, Your wonders, Your awesome acts, Your greatness, Your great goodness and Your righteousness. But in the middle of this 'catalogue' come verses 8 and 9 which are instead *third-person* descriptions of the 'attributes of God'. In fact very specifically, verse 8 is a variant on the list of God's qualities given in Exodus 34.6, those which speak of God's compassion and mercy and faithful love. Now all of these verses can simply be lumped together as a somewhat extravagant but undifferentiated collection, but suppose we accept that verses 8–9 can be treated separately. If so then they are a specific set of 'attributes', coming from a traditional source, sandwiched between the words of praise addressed directly to God.

What happens if we look at the second part of the Psalm, verses 14–20? Again they are a unit of seven verses. It does not seem possible to apply the same second-person/third-person distinction in this case – the mixture seems to be rather random. However, there is a different factor that sets one verse apart from the rest. Whereas all the rest of the verses speak of God in terms of the divine relationship to others, God's generosity to human beings and animals, verse 17 lists attributes of God purely in terms of an inner divine state with no external referent:

17. The Eternal is righteous in all His ways
    and lovingly faithful in all His deeds.

So yet again we have a 'sandwich', this time more symmetrical, with three verses on each side of the central one; statements of God's generous actions to others enclosing one about God's own inner qualities. Though animals are also included by implication (vv. 15–16), we seem to be describing primarily God's generous actions to human beings. Comparing this section with 4–10 we can see that in both of them we have a central statement of the qualities of God (vv. 8–9, 17), surrounded by passages which speak about the divine–human relationship. In the first section the focus is the praise human beings give to God; in the second section it is the nourishment that God gives to human beings. So the two sections correspond to each other and are effectively mirror images of each other. Both speak of how God and humanity are related – but together they speak of the reciprocity of that relationship.

We can show the overall structure schematically as follows:

1–3	I praise God		
4–7		People 'give' to God	
8–9			Attributes of God
10		People 'give' to God	
11–13			God the King
14–16		God gives to people	
17			Attributes of God
18–20		God gives to people	
21	All praise God		

The two sets of divine attributes are linked by a nice wordplay in the Hebrew. Both sets end with the phrase '*kol ma'asav*', which means literally 'all His doings/deeds' or 'all He makes'. But whereas in verse 9 it refers to the compassion God shows to 'all His creations', in verse 17 the identical words have to be translated to indicate that God is 'lovingly faithful in all His deeds'. Actually this switching between the two different senses of the word *ma'aseh*, from the root *asah*, to 'make' or 'do', runs through the Psalm. In verse 4 each generation shall praise 'Your deeds'; towards the centre verses 9 and 10 use the term to mean God's creatures, who receive God's compassion and in turn express their gratitude; before switching back to the meaning 'deeds' in verse 17. Perhaps like the fourfold repetition of *malchut*, 'kingdom', 'rule' or 'sovereignty', in verses 11–13, they help reinforce the sense of God's absolute rule over all creation and all creatures. And yet, the verb *asah* does have one further appearance – in verse 19, where God 'fulfils' the desires or 'answers the needs' of those who fear God. This points to an interesting distinction that is also made in the second half of the Psalm. In verses 14–16 it is emphasized that God responds to the distress and needs of *all* creatures (the word *kol*, all, coming four times within the three verses – *all* who fall, *all* who are bowed down; the eyes of *all* turn to God who satisfies *all* living). But after verse 17, the second set of divine attributes, the categories of people to whom God responds is somewhat qualified – 'all who call to him *in truth*', 'those who "fear" (i.e. are in awe of, worship) God' and those who 'love' God. It points to an inner circle of people who have a very particular relationship. This distinction is already present in verse 10. It points to one of the problems of 'parallelism' we have already noted in the previous chapter. Because two words are in the same place in the separate halves of a parallel statement need they necessarily refer to the same thing?

> 10. All You have made shall thank You, Eternal
>   and Your faithful loving ones shall bless You.

Following the list of divine qualities in the previous verse, where God's goodness and compassion are offered to all, it is fitting for all of creation to 'thank' you (the root *yadah*, meaning to 'confess', 'acknowledge' and hence 'thank'). But within that general class are the *chasidim*, those who belong to the covenant with God which is 'sealed' with *chésed*, faithful loyalty and love. In fact the Psalm plays throughout with this important covenant term. Verse 8 retains the word *chésed* from Exodus 34.6 in its quotation of God's attributes, and God is also described as *chasid* in his actions in verse 17.

I fear that this is getting somewhat complicated, but we need to look at two more textual links before attempting to pull this all together. Moses in Exodus 33 had asked God to show him God's 'ways' (v. 13) and 'glory' (v. 18). In response comes the reply:

> I will make to pass all my 'goodness' (*tov*) before your face and call in the name of the Eternal before you. (Ex. 33.19)

Thus the word *tov*, 'good', is a term for the list of attributes of God ('gracious and merciful', etc.) that are first listed in Exodus 34.6–7 and reproduced in various forms in later sections of the Bible, as here in verses 8–9. (We will be examining this Exodus passage in detail in chapter 5 when we study Psalm 25, so the following is only a brief outline of the topic.) So when our verse 7 states:

> 7. The fame of Your great 'goodness' they will proclaim
>   and sing aloud of Your righteousness

the 'goodness' would appear to mean these attributes that are listed in the following verses 8 and 9, including the word *tov*, 'good', itself in verse 9. This set of attributes, particularly in this version, is universalistic – God's gracious love is available to all of creation. But missing from the original Exodus formulation is one full phrase, namely that God is also great in *chésed ve'emet*, 'faithful love and truth', a combination which signifies reliable, 'trustworthy', loyalty and love – that is to say, the very specific bond that ties God to Israel within the covenant. In Exodus the stress is on the paradox that God's love is overflowing, unbounded and endless on the one hand, but also consciously constrained so as to be contained within a covenant with human beings, where mutual responsibility is required. Here, however, a slightly different distinction is being made. God's unbounded love and 'goodness' are now available to all of God's creatures, but there remain some restrictions that are dependent on human behaviour. That is why the second part of verse 7 talks about 'Your righteousness'. Moreover, whereas God's 'goodness', from the first half of the verse, appears in the first set of divine attributes (vv. 8–9), it is God's 'righteousness' that is featured in the second set of attributes in verse 17:

> 17. The Eternal is righteous in all His ways
>   and lovingly faithful in all His deeds.

Once this element has been introduced, God's love bounded within the commitment to a covenant, where righteous behaviour is expected of the covenant partners, it is no surprise to find that a more restricted group of people are mentioned in the following verses. Moreover, it is only in this section that the threat of punishment is offered to those who behave 'wickedly' (v. 20).

But this distinction between those outside and those within the covenant is not the final word. In verses 1 and 2, it is 'I', the Psalmist who will 'bless', *barach*, God. The words 'bless' and 'praise' (*halal*) are often interchangeable, but here some sort of distinction seems to be maintained. In verse 10 it is clearly the *chasidim*, those within the covenant, who bless God – the group to which the Psalmist presumably belongs as well. But in the very last verse it is not just that 'in-group' that will come to bless God, but 'all flesh'. All will enter into the full covenant with God.

So beneath the apparently calm façade of this Psalm there is some serious theological reworking of the covenant theme. If God is the creator and sovereign of all the universe, what is the relationship between Israel, within the covenant, and those without? By not mentioning Israel by name, the Psalmist is able to introduce categories: those who call to God in truth, who fear and love God. This enables him to extend the covenant to the rest of humanity, if they are willing to take on the conditions it entails. And in this way the solitary praise and blessing of the Psalmist (v. 1) will become a universal one, for all flesh throughout all time (v. 21).

If the Psalm appears at first glance to be conventional and even complacent, it seems to be part of a much larger inner religious debate when we look beneath the surface. Perhaps the formality of the structure, the use of the alphabet and this concentric pattern, is even intended to give it the air of an established religious truth, whereas the question of the extent of God's love to other peoples remained open throughout the biblical period. I recognize that it would be a mistake to push this argument too far – and in some sense try to 'over-sell' the inner tensions within the Psalm so as to counteract those who would undervalue it. Nevertheless the structure is subtle and complex and that has to be taken into account in any serious reading.

Before leaving the Psalm there is one Rabbinic view that is worth noting (*Berachot* 4b). It deals with the missing letter *nun* in the alphabetic acrostic. They located the missing verse in Amos 5.2:

'She has fallen, not to rise again, the virgin Israel'.

The Hebrew starts with the verb *naflah*, 'she has fallen', providing the missing *nun*, but in such a pessimistic verse, in this Rabbinic view, that it was removed from the Psalm. (Actually, even in Amos they re-interpreted the verse by shifting the punctuation to read: 'She has fallen! No! Rise up again, virgin Israel!') They could justify this change by reference to our Psalm itself. For the next letter in the alphabet is *samech*, and does not verse 14 say quite clearly: '*someich adonay l'chol hannoflim*', 'the Eternal supports *all* who fall'!

PSALM 92

My own engagement with concentric structures can be traced directly back to this Psalm. I was familiar with it from its prominent place in the Friday evening *shabbat* service, as indeed the heading indicates: A Psalm. A Song for the Sabbath Day. I had become accustomed to reciting the slightly truncated version that appears in the 1930 edition of the West London Synagogue prayerbook, 'Forms of Prayer'. A liberal sensitivity had cut out the verse suggesting that 'I would see the fate of my enemies'. But something used to irritate me about the Psalm, probably because I had to practise how to read it in public when conducting a youth service in the synagogue. Somehow, just when you thought you had got into a nice rhythm reading the verses, many of which were built on parallelism, there came some odd irregularity with three units to a verse instead of the expected two (v. 8), followed by an extremely short one. None of this either made much sense to me, or mattered very much, as a youth leader. But within a few years I found myself having to translate the Psalm for a new edition of the prayerbook. We had decided on a particular way of laying out the Psalms, and when the first proofs of the Hebrew text appeared, Psalm 92 was suddenly revealed in all its symmetrical splendour, with the awkward short verse 9 sitting in the exact middle and two of the longer verses surrounding it. The next step was to see if the geographical symmetry was matched by the content.

1. *A Psalm. A Song for the Sabbath Day*
2. It is good to give thanks to the Eternal,
   and to sing praises to Your name, O Most High;
3. to tell in the morning of Your faithful love
   and Your trustworthiness every night.
4. With the ten-stringed lute, with the lyre,
   with the gentle sound of the harp.
5. For You made me rejoice in Your deeds, Eternal,
   at the works of Your hand I sing out.
6. How great are Your works, Eternal,
   how deep are your thoughts.
7. A stupid man does not know,
   and a fool does not understand this,
8. when the wicked flourish they are like grass

and when all workers of evil spring up,
  it is to be destroyed forever.
9. But You are exalted forever, Eternal!
10. For, see Your enemies, Eternal,
  for, see Your enemies shall perish,
  scattered shall be all workers of evil.
11. But you exalted my 'horn' like an ox,
  anointed me with fresh oil.
12. My eyes looked upon my foes
  when evil ones rise against me, my ears have heard.
13. The righteous shall flourish like a palm tree,
  grow tall like a cedar in Lebanon.
14. Planted in the house of the Eternal,
  they shall flourish in the courts of our God,
15. bearing new fruit in old age,
  still full of sap and still green,
16. to declare that the Eternal is upright,
  my rock in whom there is no wrong.

Though it is not quite so evident from the translation, the Hebrew text has a clear 'shape' as suggested above: the first and last six verses are relatively short lines; they enclose within them the two longer ones, with the shortest verse in the centre.

The first four verses (2–5) and the last four (13–16) share a key word, *l'haggid* (vv. 3, 16), to tell the praises of God, initially for God's *chésed* and *emunah*, the reliable faithfulness and loyalty we have discussed above as part of the covenant relationship, and at the end for God's 'uprightness', in which there is no fault. The opening verses describe the joy of singing such praises to God with the musical instruments of the Temple; the latter praise the fate of the *tsaddiq*, the righteous person who lives within the courtyards of the Temple. They are thus complementary to each other.

In my original study I was hard-pressed to find a satisfactory link between the next two sections (vv. 6–7 and 11–12). Having explained my reservations I offered the following suggestion:

Verses 6–7 speak of the depth of God's thoughts which are not always comprehensible to man. The particular aspect of God's actions which is implied here is His treatment of the wicked, something a foolish man does not understand. In the equivalent place in the second half (vv. 11–12) we hear of the success of the speaker, one who does understand God's ways, and benefits from his adherence to them: his horn is lifted up and he is safe from the attack of his enemies. Without raising the question of who the speaker may be, the only obvious connection between these two verses is their shared sense of security in the triumphing of God over evil, identified as the enemies of God and of the speaker itself. On another level, the *depths* or profundity of God's thoughts (*m'od am'qu machsh'votécha*) contrast with the heights to which the speaker's horn is raised and the position from which he can look down upon his enemies. But again the point must be made that some sort of connection can always be constructed whether genuine or not.[7]

I was therefore delighted to discover an analysis of this Psalm by Harold Fisch.[8] He also reads it as a concentric structure, and offers a very subtle understanding of the nature imagery it contains:

> What the psalm is saying here is that to 'expound' God's faithful love by means of a poem – this poem in fact – is a good and comely exercise for the inquiring mind. But what is the matter that has to be expounded, the riddle, so to speak, that has to be solved? This begins to come to light in verse 4: 'For thou, Lord, hast made me glad through thy work ... I will sing for joy in the works of thy hands ...' These terms for 'work' and 'the works of thy hands' point forward clearly to the imagery of vegetation shortly to be introduced into the poem ...
>
> It is the wise man's understanding of nature that is here the issue – i.e. what intellectual and moral profit he will derive from the consideration of the grass, the blossoms, the cedar, and the palm tree, and how he will relate them to the life and duty of man. (pp. 128–29)

The 'flourishing' and 'springing up' of the grass also points to its transience. This is linked to the wicked who will thus inevitably perish. But the righteous also perish, and the only way to extend life is to be associated with God who is high and exalted, and who 'exalts' the horn of the Psalmist.

> From the height that he has now achieved with the help of the image of the horns of the wild creature of the hills and with the help of the anointing oil by which he feels his existence to be consecrated, he can now face the enemies who rise against him

(v. 11). But the confrontation with the enemies is not quite so simple as the usual English translations suggest. RSV reads: 'My eye has seen the downfall of my enemies, /mine ears have heard the doom of mine evil assailants.' But there is nothing in the Hebrew text to correspond with 'the downfall of' or 'the doom of' ... There is no guarantee in the verse that the raising of the speaker by means of the image of the horns of the *re'em* has disposed of the threat of the enemies. The outcome of the confrontation remains undetermined. His eye will look at them, his ears will hear them. Thus while God's enemies are sure to be scattered and to perish forever (v. 9), the enemies of the speaker are not so unambiguously defeated, for height and pride are qualities that they too can achieve. (pp. 130–31)

So nature is called upon again with the image of the lofty cedars. Fisch points out (p. 132) that cedars were not planted in the Temple courtyard. Instead he sees the closing imagery as referring to the cedar wood that was used in the very structure of the Temple itself.

We are talking indeed of the organic life of nature, but nature has been raised and sanctified, inserted (literally) into the structure in which God and man meet. The witness of the natural world is part of that meeting, built into the fabric of the building as it is built inseparably into the fabric of the poem. By evoking this as the final triumphant image in this poem, the cunning poet has found a term of resolution; no longer defeated and betrayed by those images and signs of growth and vitality by which man is linked to the organic life of nature, he can now establish the covenantal discourse firmly on the three foundations of man: God: nature. (pp. 132–33)

He sees the concentric structure of the Psalm as follows:

We have a series of four terms or topics in the order of A, B, C, D – they are *declaring* (*l'haggid*, 2), references to the *Temple worship* (2, 3), *blossoming* (*bifroach*, 7), and *height* (*marom*, 8). Then in the second half of the poem we have the same key terms or topics in the reverse order of D, C, B, A, viz., *height* (*vattarem*, 10), *blossoming* (*yifrach, yafrichu*, 12, 13), *the Temple* (*bet YHWH*, 13), and *declaring* (*l'haggid*, 15). (p. 134)

I find Fisch's views very helpful in pulling the various components of the Psalm together. However, there are certain other elements that

I want to look at. When we read in verse 8 'when the wicked spring up like grass', we have an image of grass appearing at great speed and in great quantities – even though, as the end of the verse comforts us, bound for ultimate destruction. But the reappearance of the root *parach* in verses 13 and 14 as describing the fate of the righteous draws the significant contrast – for the righteous is like a palm tree or cedar. Unlike the grass that is multiple, the tree stands unique, alone. Unlike the grass that is transient, the tree endures, renews itself, produces fruit. In fact by using the image of the grass first, so as to show the rapid growth and spread of the wicked, the Psalmist has set up the reader to accept their omnipresence and power – turning the reader himself into the 'foolish man' who does not understand God's ways. For it is only with the verse about the success of the righteous that the contrasting fate, of transience against permanence, is actually spelled out.

But most spectacular in the composition is the location of the middle verse. As we have already noted it is in the exact geographical centre and it makes the statement that God is always supreme. Coming as it does between the two verses about the apparent success and ultimate downfall of 'all workers of iniquity', it is as if we have burst through a circle of evil to emerge on the other side in the presence of God; or, in terms of the foolish man who does not understand, we have broken past this feeling about the freedom of evil to work in the world so that God's presence is temporarily eclipsed, to the encounter with God.

But there is another dimension to be seen once we look again at the nature of concentric structures. They move towards some central point and then reverse themselves back to their starting point. There are thus two effective points of 'climax', the centre where some major point is made and the end where a second 'climax' pulls together all the different elements. So far we have shown such concentric structures using the following 'outline':

a

      b

            c

      b'

a'

but it would be equally possible to represent such a pattern 'vertically', as follows:

If we look at the shape of our Psalm in terms of a mountain peak towards which we are climbing and from which we then descend – Fisch too has emphasized the feeling of 'height' at the centre – then we find ourselves passing the 'workers of iniquity' on our way up and on our way down – but at the summit, as the climactic word of the central sentence, we find YHWH, *adonay*, the name of God. And we have reached it after stepping solemnly over three similarly stressed and accentuated words: '*v'attah marom l'olam adonay*', 'You – on high – forever – Eternal!' It is the geographically 'highest' point in the Psalm, it is the conceptual peak and it closes with the single word, the name of God, towards which the whole direction of the Psalm has been turned.

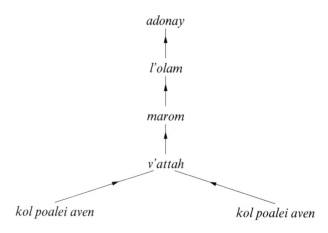

We will see other examples of concentric units within Psalms and entire Psalms built on this pattern in the chapters ahead. Now it is time to introduce a new dimension – the voice of the interpreter.

4

Through Rabbinic Eyes: Psalm 23

Having devoted two chapters to examining some of the 'internal' patterns and structures of the Psalms, it seems appropriate to look at how they were interpreted by later Jewish tradition. Rather than generalize I thought I would study one Psalm in detail through Rabbinic eyes.

Which one to choose? In the end I have settled for Psalm 23 because it is familiar enough for most people to have some view of what it might mean. Moreover, it could well have a special place in their own religious life or personal experience so that looking at different understandings would present a real challenge. Interpretation never exists in a vacuum and it is up to us to decide whether we wish to try to be aware of what we bring to our own reading of a text. By examining the different views, say of the Rabbis, we may get some sort of perspective on our own understanding and a broader sense of what such a Psalm can offer.

A price is paid for this approach because we lose the security of knowing that 'this and only this' is what the Psalm means. But Jewish tradition has always preferred the greater security that comes from knowing that such a Psalm is open to continual rediscovery, that it can speak in ever new ways as our own personal circumstances change. In fact we will see that at least two quite contrasting views of the situation or intention of the author will emerge. But first a somewhat literal translation.

1. *A Psalm of David*
   The Eternal is my shepherd
   I shall not want.
2. In green fields He lets me lie
   by quiet streams He leads me.
3. He restores my soul.

He guides me in paths of righteousness
for His name's sake.
4. Though I walk through the valley of the shadow of death
I fear no evil,
for You are with me,
Your rod and staff
they comfort me.
5. You spread a table before me
in front of my enemies.
You anoint my head with oil;
my cup runs over.
6. Surely goodness and faithful love pursue me
all the days of my life
and I shall dwell in the house of the Eternal forever.

This Psalm is so familiar, particularly for an older generation in the King James or RSV version, that any other kind of translation simply feels 'wrong'. Its very popularity also means that it has been studied more than almost any other Psalm so that there is little new to say about it. So let us examine instead something 'old' – some comments from the early Rabbinic Midrash, from the great medieval Jewish commentators, Rashi, Abraham Ibn Ezra and Rabbi David Kimchi, RaDaK, and a few 'moderns'.

Before beginning I cannot resist addressing the problem of translation and quoting two delightful paraphrases. They stem from the seventeenth and eighteenth centuries and help free us from the more familiar cadences and language. The first was composed in 1696 by Nahum Tate and Nicholas Brady:

The Lord himself, the mighty Lord,
Vouchsafes to be my guide.
The shepherd by whose constant care
My wants are all supplied.

In 1712 Addison, in the *Spectator* No. 441, provided this version of 'He maketh me to lie down in green pastures':

When in the sultry Glebe I faint,
Or on the thirsty Mountain pant;
To fertile Vales and dewy Meads
My weary wand'ring steps he leads;

> Where peaceful rivers, soft and slow,
> Amid the verdant Landskip flow.

Apparently he described it as '. . . a kind of *Pastoral* Hymn, and filled with those Allusions which are usual in that kind of writing'. (Which reminds me of Gertrude Stein's remark: 'A bed is always comfortable if you make it that way.')

Just to add a contemporary touch my friend and colleague Fr Robert Murray sent me, alongside a number of such older translations, the following clipping, which he thinks appeared in the *Daily Telegraph*. In a discussion of the attempts to re-translate the Church of England's *Alternative Service Book*, and thus transform the language of King James's day into something more contemporary, the writer cites the following text. Apparently 'five clever young men at Christ Church, Oxford . . . offered *The Times* a properly updated version . . .' The *Telegraph* writer titles it 'David Lyric Two-Three':

> The Lord and I are in a shepherd/sheep situation, and I am in a position of negative need. He prostrates me in a green belt grazing area; he conducts me directionally parallel to non-torrential aqueous liquid. He returns to original satisfaction levels my psychological make-up; he switches me on to a positive behavioural format for maximal prestige of his identity.
>
> It should indeed be said that notwithstanding the fact that I make ambulatory progress through the umbrageous inter-hill mortality slot, terror-sensations will not be instantiated within me due to para ethical phenomena. Your pastoral walking aid and quadruped pickup unit introduce me into a pleasurific mood-state.
>
> You design and produce a nutriment-bearing furniture-type structure in the context of non-cooperative elements; you act out a head-related folk ritual employing vegetable extract; my beverage utensil experiences a volume crisis.
>
> It is an ongoing deductible fact that your inter-relational empathetical and non-vengeance capabilities will retain me as their target focus for the duration of my non-death period: and I will possess tenant rights in the housing unit of the Lord on a permanently open-ended time basis.

The *Telegraph* writer concludes: 'Having read that, I assume the translators of the Authorized Version have adopted an ongoing burial rotation posture.'

It seems almost a pity to move back to the complex reality of the Psalm itself. And yet with the very opening words we are actually in trouble. The familiar opening, 'The Lord is my Shepherd, I shall not want', already conceals a number of problems in the Hebrew.

adonay ro'ee lo echsar

First there is no actual connection between the first two words – they stand apart: 'The Eternal. My Shepherd.' We provide the 'is' in translation to make a recognizable sentence, though the Hebrew could as easily be translated as: 'O Eternal; O my Shepherd.' That is to say, the juxtaposition of the two suggests that God is 'identified' as a 'shepherd', with all the images that this conjures up – of lonely hillsides, the shepherd as guardian and carer – and indeed the classical picture of David himself, the young shepherd who fought off wild animals to protect his father's flocks. The same image is used elsewhere of God's relationship to Israel as a whole (Ps. 80.2; 74.1; 100.3) and Jacob speaks of God very personally in these terms (Gen. 48.15).

The Masoretic system of sentence divisions allows for a further disjunction before the two remaining words of the sentence, and by any reading they stand alone. Moreover, since they consist of the word 'no' and a verb in the imperfect state, they could be translated as a present state: 'I do not lack', or an anticipated future one: 'I will not lack', or even an assertion that this will be the case: 'I shall not lack!' But the imperfect could equally be translated as 'I should not', 'could not', 'would not', 'might not', etc.

One effect of these disjunctions is to give the opening of the Psalm a quite different 'feel' in Hebrew. The English, 'The Lord is my Shepherd, I shall not want' provides a smoothness, continuity and sense of security, one reinforced by the familiarity of the sentence. In the Hebrew the rhythm is actually more staccato and the effect quite different. It could reflect a moment of surprised or joyous revelation at the juxtaposition of these first two words: The Eternal – *my* shepherd! Or it could be the words of someone almost breathless – climbing a mountain in the wilderness or running from danger – in which case it would be an assertion of trust in God, despite what is going on: so that *lo echsar* is not a statement of confident certainty but a way of reassuring oneself – 'I shall *not* lack anything!', God *will* provide, despite present circumstances.

But what is it that God is to provide? The word *chasar* is the opposite of the Hebrew word *malei*, meaning 'full'. In this sense it suggests that something is 'missing' that would make up the full complement of what is needed or expected. Both of the words, 'full' or 'lacking', can take an object in Hebrew or exist by themselves as 'stative' verbs. Naomi, in describing her bitterness, says: *'ani m'lei'ah haláchti'*, 'I, full, went out – but the Eternal brought me back empty' (Ruth 1.21). So *chasar* can suggest that something quite specific is missing or an inner sense of 'lack' or 'need'. In our sentence the verb has no object – so the reader either has to provide something tangible or understand the Psalmist as describing some kind of inner state. It could refer to material needs – God provides everything to sustain or nourish me. Or it could refer back to God – I need no other 'shepherd', whether a person or 'god'. Or simply, while I have God I need nothing else, my entire life is 'self-contained', I am fulfilled – along the lines of Psalm 73.25, 'Whom else have I in heaven? And having You, I want no one on earth.' Because the Psalm continues the metaphor of the lamb led to green pastures and restful waters all these various readings can continue to be present.

The Targum, the Aramaic translation of the Bible, has an unexpected paraphrase of this sentence, but one that is further developed in the Midrash on Psalms.

> The Eternal has fed His people in the wilderness; they lacked nothing.

That is to say, the 'I' of the speaker becomes the people Israel as a whole. The source of this rather unexpected association seems to be our verb *chasar* once again and its presence in a verse in Deuteronomy that describes how God met the needs of the Israelites throughout their time in the wilderness:

> These forty years the Eternal your God has been with you, you have *lacked* nothing. (Deut. 2.7)
>
> Rabbi Judah said in the name of Rabbi Eleazar: The road does three things: it makes a man's clothes worn, his body lean, and his money scarce. But the Holy One, blessed be He, dealt not thus with Israel. For it was said to Israel, 'Thy raiment waxed not old upon thee (Deut. 8.4); the Eternal thy God hath been with

thee (Deut. 2.7) in thy health of body; and 'thou hast lacked
nothing' (ibid.) for thy spending . . .

Rabbi Judah said: As when a king is in a city, the city lacks
nothing, so 'These forty years the Eternal thy God hath been with
thee, and thou hast lacked nothing'. In the world's use, when a
man receives a wayfarer, the first day he kills a calf for him; the
second day, a lamb; the third day, a chicken; the fourth day, he
serves pulse to him; the fifth day he gives him even less, so that
the last day for the wayfarer is not like the first. Now lest one
think that it was the same with the wayfaring children of Israel,
scripture states, 'These forty years the Eternal thy God hath been
with thee, thou hast lacked nothing', and the last day in the
wilderness for the children of Israel was like the first. (*Midrash
Psalms* 23.2)

According to another reading of the same verse in Deuteronomy
God was very indulgent even when Israel's demands became quite
unreasonable. The last word in the Deuteronomy sentence is *davar*
which can mean a 'word' or 'thing' – hence the first interpretation
'they lacked "no thing" '. But using the other meaning, 'word', the
same closing phrase can be read as follows:

Rabbi Nehemiah said: 'Thou hast lacked but saying a word' means
that God said to Israel: Ye had to say no more than a word. No
more than a word was needed, and it was done. Ye said, 'Let the
manna taste like veal in my mouth'; and it did. Ye said, 'Let the
manna taste like fat capon'; it did . . . (*Midrash Psalms* 23.2)

Which reminds me of a story I heard from Louis Jacobs: how did
the rich people in the wilderness fulfil the *mitzvah*, 'commandment',
to do deeds of loving kindness? Since the manna tasted in any way
you wished, the rich would suggest exotic flavours for the manna to
the poor.

Despite this strong tendency to read the Psalm as a collective
statement about the wilderness period, Rashi prefers to relate it to
David personally and suggest a context in which it was composed.
He paraphrases the opening sentence so that the meaning of these
various disjunctions we have noted is clear:

In this wilderness through which I am passing I am certain that
I shall lack nothing.

Presumably he derives the idea that David is in a wilderness from the idea that God will make the exact opposite available to him: 'In green fields He lets me lie.' Rashi identifies the place, and hence the occasion when David wrote the Psalm, as 'the forest of Cheret' (1 Sam. 22.5). This identification is itself based upon an earlier Rabbinic view. The various possibilities are spelled out by Rabbi David Kimchi, RaDaK:

> David recited this Psalm about himself when he went from a time of trouble to one of ease; or else it was said about Israel, that they would recite it when they departed from exile. Hence this Psalm follows the preceding one (literally: 'leans on'). [RaDaK sees Psalm 22 as referring to Israel at the time of the Book of Esther and Haman's plot against them, so our Psalm is a continuation of the previous, recounting Israel's trust in God when they were saved.] But the Midrash explains it in two ways: 'In green fields He lets me lie' – this refers to David when he was fleeing from Saul. What is written there (1 Sam. 22.5)? 'David went and came to the forest of Cheret'? Why is it called the forest of 'Cheret'? Because it was dry like a 'potsherd', but the Holy One, blessed be He, covered it with blossoms out of the richness of the world-to-come.

RaDaK goes on to quote the Midrash on Psalms that applies the various verses of the Psalm to David's situation:

> 'He restores my soul' – this refers to the kingdom that came to David not because of his own merit but for the sake of God's name.
> 'Though I pass through the valley of the shadow of death' – this refers to the wilderness of Ziph (1 Sam. 23.14–15).
> 'I fear no evil' – Why?
> 'For You are with me'
> 'Your rod' – this refers to the 'chastisements' he received
> 'and Your staff' – this is the Torah.
> 'You set a table before me' – this refers to royalty,
> 'in front of my enemies' – these are Doeg and Ahitophel.
> 'You have anointed my head with oil' – could this be referring to the chastisements? That is why the text specifically continues with the phrase 'surely *goodness* . . .'
> Perhaps this 'goodness' refers only to 'this world'? Hence it

continues, 'surely goodness and mercy will follow me for the length of my days [to include the world-to-come].

'In the House of the Eternal' – this refers to the Temple.

But RaDaK continues by showing how the Rabbis also expounded the Psalm as referring to Israel, for example:

'He makes me lie down in green pastures' – [God says] I myself will be the shepherd of My sheep and I will make them lie down (Ezek. 34.15).

Nevertheless RaDak concludes this introduction by saying he will explain the rest of the Psalm according to the plain meaning. 'David compares himself with a lamb and God with a shepherd. And since God is my shepherd I lack nothing.'

On verse 2 RaDaK becomes quite technical in exploring the image:

The good shepherd leads his flock and pastures them in a place of grass and there he pitches his tent and his 'curtain' in the morning. When the day 'strikes' [with its heat] and at noon he makes the sheep lie down in the shade of his tent, as it says in the Song of Songs (1.7) 'Where will you pasture, where let them lie at noon?' And when he wants to water them, he takes them to 'quiet streams', that is, waters that go slowly and not to fast running water, lest the waters snatch them as they come to drink.

The phrase, verse 2, 'He restores my soul', brings up immediately the echo of Psalm 19.8 and the first description of the qualities of the Torah: 'The Torah of the Eternal is perfect, restoring the soul.' The ideas behind this phrase are very throughly explored by Aubrey Johnson.[1] Hunger or thirst may be described as weakening the power of the *néfesh* ('soul', life, life force). It becomes shrivelled up (Num. 11.6) or empty (Isa. 29.8) or drained away (Lam. 2.12). When such lack of nourishment is met, the vitality of the *néfesh* is restored, it returns (*shuv* – 'to turn, return') to a fuller life.

Whereas the Midrash on Psalms, perhaps inevitably, relates our verse to Psalm 19 and talks of the Torah restoring the soul of Israel. Rashi, perhaps surprisingly, reads the verse more literally:

My soul, which is weakened by troubles and flight, He restores to its former state.

Ibn Ezra and RaDaK, who throughout this Psalm seems to be para-phrasing and slightly expanding on Ibn Ezra's commentary, explains this still in terms of the governing metaphor:

> He mentions that the shepherd does not strike him so as to lead him from pasture to pasture with urgency, but restores his soul through sitting still and resting.

The second part of this verse raises a major translation problem. The phrase '*b'ma'aglei tsédek*' can be translated literally as 'paths of righteousness'. But the word *tsédek*, in its first sense, has a very specific meaning which is best seen in Leviticus 19.36 where the law deals with 'true' weights and measures – '*moznei tsédek avnei-tsédek éifat tsédek v'hin tsédek*', 'true scales, true weights, a true "eiphah" (dry measure) and a true "hin" (liquid measure)'. So it is most likely that in our verse the meaning, rather like the previous images of 'green pastures' and 'still waters', means paths that are 'flat' or 'straight'. Which is how Ibn Ezra takes it:

> He does not lead me over hills and valleys.

On the other hand it is equally possible to see the verse as breaking the metaphor and using the extended sense of the word, 'righteous', 'just'. God, the shepherd, leads the Psalmist in the path of righteous actions or behaviour.

Rashi may be hinting at this latter sense:

> In level paths – so that I do not fall into the hands of my enemies.

The nineteenth-century Rabbi Samson Raphael Hirsch, the founder of modern Orthodoxy, and a great defender of Jewish tradition, clearly goes for the second possible sense. He points out that the word *ma'aglei*, which we have translated as 'paths', is derived from a root which means 'circle'. It is possible that in our Psalm itself the sense would be that the shepherd has a regular route, well worked out and secure, over which he takes his sheep. Hirsch, however, finds here a moral message:

> Those ways of life circumscribed by law, which keep within the bounds of law and order. Anything outside that 'circle' is wrong, transgressing the bounds of righteousness.

Verse 4 offers a more familiar problem with the word *tsalmávet*, 'traditionally' translated as 'the shadow of death'. That is a literal

translation of the Hebrew word in this form, which assumes a com-
pound word made up of *tzel*, 'shade' or 'shadow', and *mávet*, 'death'.
The form is distinctly unusual since Hebrew does not make com-
pound words, and hence the assumption that the original form is
actually *tzalmut*, from a root meaning 'deep darkness'. The change
in pronunciation would allow the introduction of the element of
'death', though this might also be a way of expressing a kind of
emphasis – even unto death. This uncertainty, or deliberate ambiguity, leads to two quite distinct understandings of the Psalm, depending
on whether one thinks the Psalmist is literally in danger of death
(hence the popularity of this Psalm for funerals) or not.

Rashi comes down firmly on the side of 'darkness', and again
assumes David is talking about the Wilderness of Ziph. He ends his
comment by quoting as his source for the meaning 'darkness' Dunash
ben Labrat, a tenth-century Spanish poet and philologist. We tend
to see Rashi in purely 'pious' terms, the great teacher and commentator on the text of the Bible and Talmud. But apart from his own
remarkable intellect, he was clearly closely in touch with mainstream
religious and scientific debates of his time. Today we can take for
granted the existence of a whole range of tools, particularly concord-
ances and grammars, that enable us to have direct access to the
Hebrew text. But in Rashi's time the analysis of Hebrew grammar
was at a relatively early stage, with the bulk of the work taking place
within the Islamic world. If Ibn Ezra is more obviously a philologist,
grammarian and linguist, nevertheless Rashi devotes considerable
space to clarifying grammatical problems. Thus he quotes Dunash
some 20 times in his commentaries, and was presumably aware of
a major controversy in which Dunash was engaged over the first
attempt to create a Hebrew dictionary. Dunash raised 160 objections
to the book, presenting some of them in an extended poem!

In surprising contrast, Ibn Ezra, who is usually quite concise and
restricts himself to linguistic issues or clarifying the 'plain meaning',
becomes suddenly loquacious:

> If there occur one of those decrees of heaven that God has decreed
> from of old that evil should come into the world, and this evil is
> likened to 'the valley of the shadow of death', [nevertheless] 'I
> shall fear no evil', [that is to say] I shall not fear that evil/harm
> will befall me, because Your rod will show me the way until I
> depart from it. And the 'rod and staff' are the things that give

comfort to his heart. And the meaning is that when there comes
a year of evil upon the world, God will make a special arrangement
for those who take refuge in Him, to keep them alive in a famine
and to save their lives from death. And the meaning of 'death'
here is not a natural death but those who die in war or of disease.

Perhaps what is most striking about this verse is the sudden change
of person – God is no longer referred to in the third person but is
addressed directly, 'for *You* are with me'. Such switches between
second and third person and back again are a common feature of
the Psalms and indeed other parts of the Hebrew Bible. They have
been seen as providing evidence of the editing together of a passage
from different sources, but we have become more aware of the
literary implications of such changes. From speaking 'about' God,
the Psalmist, at his moment of fear, speaks 'to' God. The following
comment comes from Ludwig Strauss, the son-in-law of Martin
Buber, a poet who also wrote on the Psalms. This passage was quoted
by Nehama Leibowitz in her little pamphlet on the Psalms.[2]

> When we speak about an object, it is still in the field of objectivity,
> but when we address ourselves *to* the object, it assumes a personal
> image, stands before us face to face, becomes present. The poets
> have made use of this distinction not only once; in order to move
> away from us or bring closer the subject . . . Just in the hour of
> trial in the 'shadow of death' will the closeness of God be felt,
> like as if He withdrew before, beyond sure knowledge; and sud-
> denly He is present, appears before our eyes; suddenly – out of
> the darkness.

With verse 5 comes another image to replace that of the shepherd
and sheep.

> 5. You spread a table before me
>   in front of my enemies.
>   You anoint my head with oil;
>   my cup runs over.

It is a surprising shift, from the pastoral to the domestic, or even the
royal, table. God is a generous host – oil to anoint my head, wine
overflowing, though clearly there are problems with the guest list.
What is emphasized is that God's bounty 'overflows', it more than
satisfies the needs of the Psalmist. Ibn Ezra draws parallels between
this image and the previous one:

'In front of my enemies' corresponds to 'the valley of the shadow of death' . . . the 'table' to the 'green pastures' and 'my cup runs over' is equivalent to the 'quiet streams'.

RaDaK nicely ties this to the opening statement that the Psalmist will lack nothing – here all his material wants are met by God.

The last verse contains another puzzle. The verb *hyird'fúni* means literally 'chase after', 'pursue', and usually has a rather threatening connotation. In the Song at the Sea, it is the boast of the Egyptian enemy galloping after the helpless Israelites stranded on the shore: '*erdof asseeg*', 'I will chase, overtake!' The conventional understanding is that these two gifts of God, '*tov vachésed*', 'goodness and faithful love', will 'chase after' the Psalmist, they will be abundantly available to him. We have to remember that both these terms have powerful associations with the covenant promises of God – as explored in our discussion of Psalm 145, and we will discuss the implications of this at the end.

Rabbi Daniel Jeremy Silver, a leading American Reform Rabbi and scholar, in an article on this Psalm, argues that the Psalmist is not quite as optimistic as these words might suggest at first:

I may be wrong, but I know something of the author. I know him as a deeply disturbed man whose faith does not run on as serenely as these verses seem to indicate. We speak of faith when we need faith. When the sun shines we take faith for granted. He wrote this verse to renew his courage. In the writing his courage was reborn. 'Truly a generous goodness will pursue me all the days of my life and I shall be with God as long as I live.' I have the feeling also that the author felt his faith surge up and become certain, and that he knew his language to be hyperbolic. No one in the shadowed valley believes in endless good fortune. Who of us is really comforted when life knocks us about or when we are forced to take the lonely hike across the dark valley? There is something plaintive in the concluding verse which can be read: 'Would that goodness and mercy might follow me all the days of my life.' The author knew that he must die. He knew that to love is to lose and to live is to be bruised. There is no promise here of endless health, unbroken pleasure and a handsome annuity. There is only the promise that God is near. The House of the Lord is not a sorcerer's cave where base metal is transformed into gold, where illness is healed miraculously, and where men can drink of the fountain of eternal youth. The sanctuary is a place where men and women worship. There is no magic here, only a sense of the nearness of God. In the House of the Lord there is that faith which strengthens, and men of faith have always believed they possessed the most precious of gifts.[3]

That same feeling that Rabbi Silver detected seems to have affected Ibn Ezra. His commentary on these closing verses goes against the obvious meaning, and instead of his customary detachment, he seems to be exposing here something of his own spiritual commitment:

The meaning of this Psalm is about the servants of God who forsake the desires of the world and they rejoice in their portion and believe that bread and water are equal to all the pleasures of choice foods, for their minds and hearts are set on the pleasures of the world-to-come. Therefore they set aside the pleasures of the moment for the sake of eternal pleasure. Hence he says, this is the whole of my thought. And the meaning of 'they pursue me' [in the phrase 'surely goodness and faithful love pursue me all the days of my life'] is, I will so accustom myself to do good and loving deeds, good things for my soul and loving deeds to others, so as to teach and instruct them to serve God, that this will become second nature to me [literally, 'a law'], so that even if I wished to set aside goodness for even a moment, it would pursue after me.

These last two comments have emphasized the serious, or even darker, aspects of the Psalm. We will see how these emerge from the text in our summing up. But as I mentioned at the beginning, two quite contrasting views of the Psalm can be found in the different interpreters and I was charmed to come across the following estimation of the Psalm that emphasizes its 'sunnier' aspect. It was written by Henry Ward Beecher in *Life Thoughts*, and I found it quoted by the American Bible Scholar Moses Buttenwieser who taught generations of Reform Rabbis at the Hebrew Union College in Cincinnati.[4] It stands in fairly stark contrast to the evaluation of Daniel Jeremy Silver.

The twenty-third Psalm is the nightingale of the Psalms. It is small, of a homely feather, singing shyly out of obscurity; but oh! it has filled the air of the whole world with melodious joy, greater than the heart can conceive. Blessed be the day on which

that Psalm was born! What would you say of a pilgrim com-
missioned of God to travel up and down the earth singing a strange
melody, which when one heard, caused him to forget whatever
sorrow he had? And so the singing angel goes on his way through
all lands, singing in the language of every nation, driving away
trouble by the pulses of the air which his tongue moves with
divine power. Behold just such a one! This pilgrim God has sent
to speak in every language on the globe. It has charmed more
griefs to rest than all the philosophy of the world . . . Nor is its
work done. It will go singing to your children and my children,
and to their children, through all the generations of time.

Having looked at such a variety of interpretations of the Psalm I
would like to add a few observations of my own.

First, the sense of peace and calm that pervades the Psalm is
underpinned by the choice of vocabulary and a number of wordplays.
Two verbal roots which often play upon each other in the Bible
appear in a variety of forms. *núach*, to rest, and *nacham*, to be
'comforted' (in one of its meanings) appear together in the play on
the name of Noah (*nóach*) in Genesis 5.29, 'this one (*noach*)
y'nachaméinu, will comfort us . . .' In our Psalm the 'quiet streams'
are '*mei menuchot*', literally 'waters of rest', which plays on both
verbs. The word '*yanchéni*', 'He guides me' (v. 3), is from the root
nachah, 'to lead', but the wordplay on *noach* is inescapable. 'Your
rod and staff *y'nachamúni*, comfort me'.

In line with Ibn Ezra's recognition that there is a correspondence
between the two images in the Psalm, the shepherd/sheep and
host/guest, there may even be an intentional wordplay between the
'green pastures', '*n'ot déshe*' and 'you anointed with oil', '*dishánta
vashémen*'.

Of a different order are the two little adverbs, *gam* ('even', 'also')
(v. 4) and *ach* ('surely', 'nevertheless', 'but') (v. 6), that make quite
a striking intrusion into the otherwise smooth flow of ideas. Having
established the security of lush pastures, still waters and straight
paths, the sudden descent into the valley of gloom and darkness is
prefaced by *gam*. Yes, the shepherd will try to ensure that the
environment is calm, peaceful and secure, but nevertheless reality
must include dangerous moments and risky paths, when 'Your rod
and staff', to goad me on and protect me at the same time, are needed
to give comfort. The equivalent image of dining in the presence of

enemies is a reminder both of the reality of physical danger (David on his road to kingship; Israel surrounded by enemy nations, whether at home or in exile; any individual in turbulent times) and the support and providence of God. The 'darkness' is there, but God, the shepherd and host, will provide all that is needed.

This unease within the images of 'ease' is also hinted at with the *ach* of verse 6. It reminds us of its startling appearance as the very first word of another Psalm, 73, which we will study in a later chapter:

> *ach tov l'yisrael elohim l'varei leivav*
> But surely God is good to Israel! to those who are pure in heart!

That dramatic 'surely!' opens a Psalm that is anything but certain about God's providence and justice, in the face of the prosperity of the wicked. The *ach* in Psalm 73 is a very strong 'but' or 'nevertheless'; despite appearances to the contrary, this is the case. Its very assertiveness implies the doubts that lie behind it. Perhaps here too in our Psalm the 'surely!' expresses both certainty and a need for reassurance, and indeed 'comfort', at the same time.

This might explain why it is the language of the covenant promises that enters here, God's '*tov vachésed*', God's goodness and faithful love. Perhaps also the 'dwelling in the House of the Lord' is not meant only literally, indicating the Levitical origins of the Psalm. It suggests the security that comes from an existence within the covenant with God, the only certainty for the Psalmist in an uncertain world.

It is precisely this evocation of the covenant that allows for both the individual and collective reading of the Psalm. God is likened to a shepherd to Israel in a number of passages, as we noted above. The Psalmist applies God's promised relationship to the people as a whole to himself alone. As we noted at the very beginning, the seemingly calm 'the Eternal is my shepherd' could equally be a startled recognition of a hitherto unrecognized truth: 'the Eternal is *my* shepherd!'

This way of expressing both security and danger within the same composition may explain the secret power of this Psalm – that it can comfort without being dishonest to disquieting realities. It reflects our human quest for some sort of inner security in the turmoil and suffering of the world. It is at one and the same time affirmation, consolation and a prayer.

5

Rewriting Tradition: Psalm 25

As a child I was an obsessive reader, graduating from comics like *Rover* and *Adventure* (which had proper full-length stories and serials and not merely cartoons!) to Biggles to The Saint to Edgar Wallace. I collected them and devoured them. I suspect my large biblical library derives as much from the same lust for completeness as it does from any academic interest. But once I got to Edgar Wallace and detective story-cum-thrillers, a whole host of interests were set in train. I graduated through Agatha Christie to a range of 'English' detectives, and was deeply impressed by Dorothy L. Sayers' introduction to an anthology of them in which she showed how Edgar Allan Poe had already established certain basic rules of the genre: where do you hide something? in the most obvious place – a letter in a letter rack (*The Purloined Letter*); when everything else has been eliminated then whatever remains, however unlikely, must be the answer (*The Murders in the Rue Morgue* – a murdering monkey).

But once I discovered Raymond Chandler, the gentility of the English genre was no longer appealing. I wanted it hard-boiled and racy, the lone hero walking mean streets. When in doubt, have someone come through the door shooting a gun! I suppose my preference for a series of novels built around a particular hero reflected a need for a kind of security. Whatever was happening, however dangerous it looked, sooner or later the hero would escape and solve everything – so that he could appear in the next episode. The demise of Sherlock Holmes was clearly unacceptable – luckily he had long been resurrected before I discovered him.

But Holmes and Poirot and all the great detectives who solved mysteries by the clever observation of things that others overlooked sparked my imagination. In a way they, or at least their authors, had set the reader a challenge. Could we read with sufficient skill to beat the detective/author at his/her own game? In time Agatha Christie's villains became a bit obvious, and the marvellous Father Brown was also fathomable once you got used to Chesterton's love of paradox. And then along came Ellery Queen.

Some way through the early Queen books, which were in themselves quite a hefty read, came a separate page with the 'Challenge to the Reader'. All the relevant information has now been given – can you beat Ellery Queen to it and guess whodunit?!

I rarely did – perhaps I didn't take it quite that seriously. But I acquired a taste for riddle-solving – and eventually for trying to crack the puzzles that lay behind the biblical passages I was studying. Here the puzzle was less a whodunit and more a question of 'what in heaven's name is going on?' I was intrigued from early days by all the things that have become the bread and butter of a whole generation of biblical scholars concerned with a literary approach to the Hebrew Bible – the problem of the 'gaps' left by the author that the reader has to fill, the apparent duplications or redundancies that the historical critical approach could remove but not actually resolve, etc.

So I tend to approach a new piece of Bible with the enthusiasm of a *Times* crossword puzzle solver. Long before I start seeking the 'religious meaning' or otherwise of the piece I am asking questions about structure and form: what is the author trying to say, and how is he or she saying it?

This particular approach lends itself to the Psalms since they are all independent pieces and in a way represent 150 different 'riddles' to be solved.

Now this may not always be an appropriate way of starting, and some Psalms resist such a headlong assault. But some do invite such an approach, usually because of some striking feature that demands explanation within the total context of the Psalm. A good example is Psalm 25 for the simple reason that, like Psalms 9/10, 34, 37, 119 and 145, it is an alphabetic acrostic. Now anyone who bothers to compose a Psalm using the sequence of letters of the Hebrew alphabet to start each line has already established a kind of formality of composition that demands analysis. There may be other questions later about how far such a structure aids or hinders the emotional experience behind the author's words – a question that has to be raised about the whole Book of Lamentations which is similarly alphabetically built. But for the time being the formality of the structure demands a search for some inner pattern of the sentences themselves.

In the case of Psalm 25 there seems to be one, but before I offer my own reading, you may like to try to find it out for yourself. So in the time-honoured tradition of Ellery Queen let me simply point out that certain words, by their repetition, establish relationships between different sections of the Psalm. Moreover, the way the Psalmist switches between talking about himself and talking about others allows for a further series of subdivisions. Most of these points can be obtained from a good English translation though, as usual, some word connections may be lost. With that information let me offer a

Challenge to the Reader.

You now have enough clues to break the Psalm up into 'sense units' which at least help understand the argument that lies beneath it. Read no further for the time being if you want to try to figure it out for yourself!

THE TEXT

1. *David's*
   On You, O Eternal, my life depends.
2. My God, In You I trust,
   let me not be put to shame,
   do not let my enemies triumph over me.
3. No, let none who hope in You be put to shame,
   ashamed are those who betray without cause . . .

4. Eternal, let me know Your ways,
   teach me Your paths.
5. Guide me in Your truth and teach me,
   for You are the God of my salvation,
   for You have I hoped all day long.
6. Remember Your compassion, Eternal, and Your faithful love
   for they have existed since ages past.
7. The sins of my youth and my wrongdoing do not remember,
   but in Your faithful love remember me
   for the sake of Your goodness, Eternal.

8. Good and upright is the Eternal,
   therefore He shows the way to sinners.

9. He guides the humble in justice,
   and teaches the humble the way.
10. All the paths of the Eternal are faithful love and truth
    for those who keep His covenant and His testimonies.
11. Eternal, for the sake of Your name,
    forgive my guilt for it is great.

12. Whoever the person who fears the Eternal
    He will show him the way he should choose.
13. His soul shall live in goodness
    and his seed inherit the earth.
14. The counsel of the Eternal is for those who fear Him,
    His covenant to give them knowledge.

15. My eyes are ever on the Eternal
    for it is He who releases my foot from the snare.
16. Turn to me and be gracious to me
    for I am lonely and poor.
17. The sorrows of my heart have increased,
    bring me out from my distress.
18. See my poverty and my suffering
    and take away all my sins.

19. See my enemies, how many they are,
    and how violently they hate me.
20. Guard my soul and deliver me;
    I fear no shame for I shelter in You.
21. Innocence and integrity shall preserve me
    for I have hoped in You.

22. God, redeem Israel from all his troubles!

A CONCENTRIC STRUCTURE

Let's compare notes. First, a word on the use of the alphabet itself. As can be seen from the Hebrew, the second letter of the alphabet, *bet*, is actually the second word of the second sentence, a minor bit of cheating, but from then on every sentence begins with the normal alphabetical sequence except in two places. In verse 6 we would expect to find the sixth letter of the alphabet, the *vav*, and it is simply left out. In verse 18 where we would expect the letter *quf*, the author uses instead the next letter in the alphabet, the *resh*, which is also used in verse 19. We are thus one letter short to make up the whole alphabet of 22 letters, though the gap is made up by the concluding verse which clearly steps out of the pattern of the entire Psalm and generalizes the personal 'story' to cover all of Israel. It is worth noting that in Psalm 34 the *vav* is also missing and a concluding verse, no longer in the alphabetical sequence, is also added to make up the number 22 (if we exclude the long title verse from consideration). In fact all of the alphabetic Psalms have such minor irregularities, except the incredible Psalm 119 which manages to find words beginning with the same letter for eight successive verses before moving on to the next one in the alphabet.

In terms of the structure of the Psalm, certain things are quite striking – remember we are doing a fairly mechanical task at the moment of identifying words that repeat or sections that have a similar content. First, there are four words that occur quite prominently in verses 1–3 and reappear again in verses 19–21. They are the word *nafshi*, 'my soul' (vv. 1 and 20), the word *oivay*, 'my enemies' (vv. 2 and 19), the root *bush* (to be ashamed, shamed or disappointed) which appears in various forms in vv. 2, 3 and 20), and the verb *qavah*, to wait for, to hope, which appears in verses 3 and 21 (as well as v. 5). Verses 1–3 stand together as a kind of affirmation of the Psalmist's faith in God – having trusted in God he knows that he will not be 'shamed/disappointed' nor will all those who similarly hope in God. It is a kind of heading to the Psalm the implication of which will be explored in the rest of the Psalm.

If we isolate these three verses in this way, then the next 'sense unit' is verses 4–7 which are a series of direct addresses and pleas to God by the Psalmist on his own behalf. In contrast verses 8–9 are more general statements about God's qualities and the way God deals with others. Similarly verses 12–14 speak about God's dealings in general with people who fear God. With verses 15–18 the Psalmist returns to describing his/her own personal situation, external dangers and internal torment, and asks for God's concern and forgiveness. Finally verses 19–21 pick up the terms used in verses 1–3, but use them to put further emphasis on the need for God to intervene.

You will have noticed that I skipped over verse 11 which stands out amidst the verses (8–10 and 12–14) where the Psalmist speaks about God's dealings with others since it is again a highly personal statement, asking God to forgive his/her sins. It is thus effectively isolated at the very centre of the Psalm which gives it great weight. The structure can therefore be shown schematically as follows – the form is 'concentric':

```
1–3    A
          4–7   B
                  8–10 C
                          11 D
                  12–14 C'
          15–18 B'
19–21  A'
22
```

At this point, however, disaster strikes! Having got so far in my own analysis I decided to have a look at the latest scholarship on the subject and discovered that back in 1932 in the distinguished journal the *Zeitschrift für Alttestamentliches Wissenschaft* (mercifully abbreviated to *ZAW*) one Möller had already discovered such a structure (also known as 'chiastic'), a view confirmed by a scholar called Ruppert. Well it would have been nice to have been completely original, but such confirmation is also comforting. However, so the more recent commentary I was reading continued, though this construction is attractive and accounts for the constant duplication of certain words, *it is not entirely convincing* (my italics) because there is no detailed equivalence of ideas in the part which match up – so Ridderbos. This accords with the view of the commentary itself, by Peter Craigie in the Word Biblical Commentary series,[1] because the 'acrostic pattern imposes certain limitations on the poet, and as a consequence there is not a clearly developed internal sequence of thought within the psalm'.

We could give up at this moment with our dignity intact, admit we were wrong and gain a certain reward for honesty. Alternatively, we could 'regroup', take a look at another aspect of the Psalm and return to this issue a little later. Bearing in mind that we are still using a rather mechanical approach to the text, looking at repetitions of words and structures, we do indeed need to look more closely at the content, so a brief retreat would be quite in order. '*Reculer pour mieux avancer*' is a bit more dignified than 'He who fights and runs away lives to fight another day', but the sentiment is the same.

THE LANGUAGE OF THE COVENANT

Since we have been examining the repetition of certain words, we will have been struck by a certain vocabulary that belongs to a particular element of the Bible, namely the 'covenant'. In fact this has caused rather a problem for the 'form critical' approach to the Psalms. It seems that whereas some of the terminology belongs to the covenant (words like *berit* (covenant) and *chésed* (the faithful love or loyalty that binds partners in a covenant)), other terms (like *derech*) belong to Wisdom literature, so it is hard to know precisely where to place this Psalm.

I am not altogether sure how far we are entitled to make such watertight categories of thought. More recent literary studies recognize that all writing borrows from its surrounding environment in a highly eclectic way. The conscious or even unconscious quoting of materials to hand is a way of evoking them and at the same time moving them on, 'rereading' them for a new purpose. Surely the Psalmist was no less free to 'borrow' material from the many genres that were available in making a fresh composition. And it may even be that the tension between the various elements that are so 'borrowed' reflects part of the writer's own purpose. For the moment, however, I want to concentrate on the 'covenant' language as I think it points to a very specific location elsewhere in the Bible.

After the creation of the Golden Calf and Moses has smashed the tablets containing the Ten Commandments, he tries to obtain God's forgiveness for the people. He finds himself facing two urgent needs – to bring God back into the midst of the camp of the Children of Israel, and not merely have an angel to accompany them as God has offered, and at the same time to acquire for himself the strength and knowledge to lead this 'stiff-necked' people. The episode is recorded in Exodus 33 and 34 and elements of it take on great significance in later Jewish tradition. There is a conversation between Moses and God that has a kind of tragicomic dimension because we can hear Moses' frustration and exasperation behind his argument:

> Moses said to the Eternal: Look! You say to me, 'Take up this people (on their journey)!' but you do not let me know (*hoda' táni*) whom you will send with me! You have also said. 'I know you (*yada'tícha*) by name' and also 'you have found favour in My eyes'. Very well! if I have 'found favour in Your eyes', please

let me know (*hodi'éni*) Your way (*dérech*). Then I will know You (*v'eda'acha*) so that I may (continue to) find favour in Your sight. And look – this nation is *Your* people! (Ex. 33.12–13)

First, it is worth noting that four times we have the use of the root *yada*, 'to know', a very complex verb implying the most intimate knowledge of someone – from sexual awareness (Adam *knew* Eve his wife and she conceived – Gen. 4.1) to choosing someone for a purpose ('for I have chosen him (Abraham) so that he might command his sons and his household . . .' – Gen. 18.19). Here in Exodus Moses uses it in a variety of senses. He asserts that God has said, 'I know you by name' – probably here with the same implication of 'choosing', a choice made out of intimate knowledge. But he also asks for 'knowledge' of God's ways so that he can continue to act in an appropriate way. The phrase '*hodi'éni na et-d'rachécha*', 'please let me know Your way', appears in our Psalm in verse 4: '*d'rachéicha adonay hodi'éni*', 'Your ways, O Eternal, make me know'. Indeed the word *dérech*, 'way', appears six times in our Psalm, as a noun and a verb (vv. 4, 5, 8, 9, 12).

Back in Exodus Moses now puts in a plea for God to return to the camp of Israel and remain with them, for in this way will the people be distinguished, and God agrees (Ex. 33.15–17). Moses now presses for a greater knowledge of God.

> He said: Please show me Your 'glory'. (The word translated as 'glory', *kavod*, has, as its primary meaning, 'weight' – that which gives someone 'weight' in the eyes of another. By a further development it can mean 'self' or 'presence' – so that with reference to God it can mean how God is manifested, present, in the world, God's immanence.) Then (God) said: I will make to pass before you all my goodness (*tovi*), and I will call out in the name (*v'shem*) of the Eternal before you. And I will be gracious (*v'chanoti*) to whom I will be gracious (*achon*) and I will show mercy/love (*v'richamti*) to whom I will show mercy/love (*arachem*).

This last statement requires some analysis. God offers to show Moses his *tov*, his goodness, and in the same sentence talks of calling out in his 'name' (*shem*). Since someone's name in biblical thought encapsulates their qualities and identity, these two elements are effectively related in our sentence – God's 'goodness' and 'name' are about to be shown. But they will come together also in our Psalm in quite a powerful way. In verse 7 the Psalmist pleads that God will overlook the sins of his youth and remember him instead with *chésed* (a word to which we will have to return), '*l'má'an tuv'cha adonay*', 'for the sake of Your goodness, O Eternal'. But in verse 11 he uses the same construction when pleading with God to forgive his more recent sins: '*l'má'an shim'cha adonay*', 'for the sake of Your name, O Eternal'.

What the implications of these two words (goodness, name) are will be spelled out shortly in our Exodus passage, but already we can see how far there seems to be a conscious borrowing from this passage in the composition of our Psalm. Just as Moses asked to 'know' God's 'way', to understand God's 'name' and 'goodness', so the Psalmist seeks the same knowledge and relies on those same qualities of God in his own situation. (We have also been introduced to two other verbs, *chanan*, 'to be gracious', and *richam*, 'to be merciful/loving', which will reappear shortly and be examined then.)

God tells Moses that he will pass his *kavod*, 'glory', before him, though Moses will not be able to see God's face directly (Ex. 33.19–23). Moses must prepare two new tablets to replace those he had shattered and go up Mount Sinai again.

> The Eternal descended in a cloud and stood with him there and called, *b'shem*, in the name of the Eternal. Then the Eternal passed before him and called: The Eternal, the Eternal, a God who is loving and gracious (*rachum v'chanun*), slow to anger and great in faithful love and truth (*chésed ve'emet*). Keeping this faithful love (*chésed*) for a thousand generations, lifting away (*nosei*) (forgiving) 'wrongdoing', (*avon*), 'rebellion' (*pésha*) and 'failure' (*chet*) but not treating someone as guiltless (who has done wrong), visiting the 'wrongdoing' (*avon*) of the fathers upon the children and the children's children to the third and fourth generation. (Ex. 34.5–7)

There is a lot of material to 'unpack' in this dense but extremely important and sophisticated passage. The list of qualities that God describes came into Jewish tradition as the 'Thirteen Attributes of God' – to get 13 you have to treat the repeated 'The Eternal' at the beginning as two separate qualities (God is merciful before someone sins and merciful after they have sinned). The two terms '*rachum v'chanun*', 'loving and gracious', are the same words God has used above in speaking to Moses. The word *rachum* is related to the

Hebrew term for the 'womb' and implies a deep love, perhaps as felt by a mother for the child in her womb, while *chanun* comes from a root meaning to be gracious, that is, to overflow with generosity, to give without expecting any return. The combination of these two terms, which share the same grammatical form and vowels so that they really sound like a pair, is to create a kind of 'hendiadys', a combination where the two parts interact to create something greater than either of the parts alone. Thus together they mean something like 'overflowing, boundless, unconditional love'.

That is one aspect of God's love, but the same sentence contains another pair of terms that interact, '*chésed ve'emet*'. As we have already noted, *chésed* is the love and loyalty that are to be found between the partners of a covenant. This is a more conscious, formal and bounded sense of responsibility to another. The second word in the combination, *emet* (truth), is derived from the word *amen*, which means that something is 'firm', 'fixed', 'reliable' – hence when we say 'Amen', we 'affirm' what the speaker has said. Thus 'truth', in this Hebrew sense, is that upon which one can rely, and the same root yields the word *emunah*, which means 'faith' or 'belief', again those things which one can trust and rely upon. (The same sort of relationship exists in English between the words 'trust' and 'truth'.) The sense of this combination, another 'hendiadys', is a faithful, loyal love, one that is mutual and which is bounded by a shared sense of responsibility between the two partners – it is thus bounded and in a sense carries sanctions.

The combination of these two sets of terms is to describe the paradox that is God's love – something that is limitless, unconditional, freeflowing, altruistic (*rachum v'chanun*), but at the same time, because human beings are limited, a love that can be contained within a covenant of loyalty, mutual obligations and concern (*chésed ve'emet*). This twofold nature of God's love remains at the heart of Israelite thought and indeed allows for God's love to continue for the people even when the covenant itself is broken by the people's betrayal of their own responsibilities. As God has already remarked to Moses, his love cannot ultimately be pinned down, categorized and 'controlled' – 'and I will be gracious (*v'chanoti*) to whom I will be gracious (*achon*) and I will show mercy/love (*v'richamti*) to whom I will show mercy/love (*arachem*)'.

Just to clear it out of the way, it is worth nothing that the problematic statement about visiting the 'sins of the fathers upon the children down to the third and fourth generation' is probably to be understood in the way that Martin Buber interpreted it. That is to say, four generations are the number of generations that may be alive at any one point in time – great-grandfather, grandfather, father and son. Therefore this is a warning to the 'patriarch' of a family, who is also the direct partner in the covenant, that what he does wrong has consequences for his entire family *alive at that time*, since he bears responsibility for them.

The Exodus text lists three words for 'sin' and the effect of such a combination is to assert that God is willing to forgive any kind of transgression – provided proper repentance, actions as well as feelings, is made. But each of the three terms has a slightly different nuance, and all three of them appear in our Psalm! The word *avon*, from a root *avah*, 'to be crooked', seems to suggest 'habitual wrongdoing'; *pésha*, the strongest of the three terms, is used elsewhere of a vassal state rebelling against its master – thus it means deliberate flaunting of God's will; *chet*, the word most commonly translated as 'sin', is the weakest of the terms and is derived from the idea of 'missing the target', 'failing'. Yet God forgives, literally *nasa*, 'lifts up' or 'lifts away', all of them, and it is on this tradition that the Psalmist relies when he asks God (v. 18): '*v'sa* (from the verb *nasa*) *et chatatai*', 'and lift away my failures'.

There is yet one more term that is common to Exodus and our Psalm. The verb *natsar*, 'to keep or guard', has a prominent place in Exodus 34.7 – '*keeping* this faithful love . . .' It is particularly emphasized in the Hebrew text because the first letter, *nun*, is written extra large in the traditional text, though the original reasons for this practice are not known. In our Psalm it appears twice: in verse 10 where it speaks of those who are '*notsrei v'rito*', 'keeping His covenant'; and verse 21, 'integrity and uprightness shall *preserve* me'.

If we now look again at our Psalm with this background in mind, we are quite overwhelmed by the number of elements that appear in it. Of this 'covenant' terminology *emet* appears in verses 5 and 10 – indeed the latter contains the combination '*chésed ve'emet*' (all of the paths of the Eternal are faithful love and truth); *chésed* is to be found in verse 6 (in conjunction with *rachum*), verse 7 and 10; the verb *chanan*, 'be gracious to me', in verse 16. The Psalmist refers explicitly to the *berit*, the covenant, in verses 10 and 14. As we have already noted, he appeals to God's 'goodness' (*tov*) which is the collective term for all these qualities of God ('I will pass all my 'goodness' before you – Exodus 33.19) – verses 7, 8, 13. Finally the three terms for 'sin' appear: *chet* in verses 7, 8 (in the form 'sinners') and 18; *avon* in verse 11; *pésha* in verse 7.

It would seem from this that on some level the Psalm is a kind of meditation on this covenant language, and more particularly a reflection on the episode in Exodus 33—34 where Moses, struggling on behalf of his people and his own difficult situation, extracts from God an understanding of God's qualities and the values that are to be found in the covenant relationship. On another occasion after Israel has made a disastrous mistake (despairing of ever entering the land because of the bad report of the spies – Num. 14), Moses tries various arguments to stop God destroying the people out of hand. The final one is to quote some of these attributes back at God – You Yourself have said You were 'long-suffering, full of covenant love and forgiving sin' (Num. 14.17–18), now you have to display those qualities! And indeed variations of the Exodus formula appear in a number of other places in the Hebrew Bible (Joel 2.13–14; Jonah 4.2; Ps. 86.15; 103.8–13; Nahum 1.3) so that it seems to have been the source of much interpretation within the biblical period itself.

Perhaps what is unique in this instance is the application of the formulation to an individual and not just to the people as a whole. What do such qualities of God, such promises, mean when applied directly to my own life? Perhaps that question provides for some sense of continuity in the inner development of the Psalm.

If we ask that question then it is noteworthy that the majority of these terms are concentrated in the first half of the Psalm – in verses 4–7, where the Psalmist talks about his own experience, past sins that he wishes God to forgive and the 'way of the Eternal' that he wishes to follow; and in verses 8–10, where he affirms that God's way is open to all who keep the covenant. The terminology is still there in the second set of affirmations in verses 12–14 – whoever fears God will prosper, experiencing God's *tov*, 'good'. But in the next section of the Psalmist's personal plea, the only term that appears is *chanan*, the plea for God's grace, the unbounded love that transcends the covenant conditions. In fact there is quite a change in emphasis between the two personal sections. Verses 4–7 are almost a 'textbook' set of statements – the formal affirmation of God's qualities and the request that God overlook the Psalmist's past sins because of them. In verses 15–18 such formalities disappear and the personal anguish emerges – for I am alone and afflicted – the sorrows of my heart have increased – release me from my distress – see my affliction and my trouble – and take away all my sins.

It may be that the formality of the structure, alphabetic and concentric, and of the covenant language, actually conceals a deep emotional and religious crisis. To affirm that prosperity will accompany the righteous person who fears God and keeps to the covenant is one thing – but human experience challenges that every day, and indeed this is a classic source of tension within much of biblical writing. But what of the person consumed with a sense of guilt, whether on objective grounds because of past behaviour or because of their own psychological state? The pivotal verse in the concentric structure is 11: 'for the sake of Your name, O Eternal, forgive my wrongdoing because it is great'. And as well as the external enemies he fears, it is the 'sorrows of my heart' on which he dwells. Has he somehow forfeited the forgiveness that the covenant promises would suggest? Is he outside the class of the 'humble' and 'those who fear God' who can rely on these traditional expectations for the restoration of their security and peace of mind? Perhaps that is why the verb *bush* is so prominent at the beginning and end of the Psalm, with its double sense of 'shame', being 'ashamed', and that shame deriving from 'disappointment', that the expected help from God has not come.

Even as I write this I am aware that my thinking may be coloured by studying this Psalm years ago in Jerusalem with my teacher Rav Shmuel Sperber. When reading Psalms like this he would identify it very closely with David and his history and we felt through his teaching the struggles that must have gone on within that powerful but enigmatic figure – poet and politician, passionate and ambitious on the one hand, yet deeply spiritual on the other. One of my notes picks up the emphasis in verses 6–7 on the verb *zachor*, 'remember':

> *Remember* Your compassion, O Eternal,
> and Your faithful love, for they are forever.
> The failures of my youth and my rebellions,
> do *not remember* (6–7).

As Rav Sperber expressed it:

> God, if You must remember, remember Your eternal qualities of mercy and compassion. But with so much to remember, at least You can forget the sins of my youth!

In the same direction a number of traditional sources emphasize David's subtle pleading with God for forgiveness. They focus on verse 11 and the closing statement, 'forgive my wrongdoing, *ki rav hu*, for it is great'. We will see at the end of the next chapter, on Psalm 19, how a passage in Leviticus Rabbah 5.8 reads the opening of Psalm 19 as a kind of flattery of God so that David can make his private request at the end. The same passage is picked up by Rashi in his comment on this verse: It is fitting for a *great* person to forgive a great sin! Since God is described in the list of attributes as '*rav chésed*', 'great in faithful love', the Rabbis can measure this greatness, *rav*, against the greatness, *rav*, of David's sin. (Within the verse itself the word 'great' may refer to the 'wrongdoing', but it could equally refer back to the beginning of the sentence – it is God's *name* that is great, so God is capable of forgiving this wrongdoing.) Though at first glance the Rabbinic reading of David's argument looks like a kind of arrogant 'special pleading' on his part, it is taken to have a deeper significance. Because if God can forgive David's sin (the seduction of Bathsheba and the killing of Uriah), then no one should feel that their sin is so great that they cannot find their way back to God; the doors of repentance are always open.

How we understand and experience this Psalm must inevitably depend on our own mood at the time of reading it, for we can find within it expressions of affirmation or of anxiety, trust or a cautious kind of hope. Indeed all of these possibilities are bound up in the opening words which we have not yet examined.

The Hebrew reads literally: 'To You, O Eternal, my soul I raise (I lift up my soul). But *néfesh* has a variety of meanings – 'soul', 'self', 'person', 'life'. Moreover, the verb *nasa*, though it literally means 'to lift up', carries a number of nuances, as we have seen above in our discussion of Exodus 34.7, God 'lifts up', i.e. 'lifts away', 'forgives', sins. But *nasa* is used in conjunction with *néfesh* elsewhere. The most poignant case is in Deuteronomy 24.15 where you are instructed to pay the wages to your hired worker on that same day before the sun sets: 'because he is poor (*'ani*) and upon it (his wage) he "lifts up his soul"', that is to say, he is totally dependent upon it for his existence. So the opening of the Psalm may carry that implication: 'upon You, O Eternal, my life is utterly dependent' – not only in the obvious sense that all life derives from God, but in my present state of guilt, I can only depend upon Your grace to save me since I am beyond the conventional provisions of the covenant promises. Is it a coincidence that the Psalmist refers to himself in the latter part of the Psalm as *'ani*, 'poor/afflicted', as an echo of the worker in Deuteronomy? Even if it was not the writer's intention, the echo works for the reader, and that is how it was understood in one Rabbinic interpretation.

> *Of David. To You, O Eternal, I lift up my soul.* These words are to be considered in the light of the verse 'In the same day you shall pay him his wage, neither shall the sun go down upon it; for he is poor, and he lifts his soul to him (Deut. 24.15). The Holy One, who is blessed, asked David: 'Why do you lift up your soul to Me?' David replied: 'Because upon Your earth I am a hired labourer before you, ''a servant that longs for the shadow and a hired worker who hopes for the payment for his work''' (Job 7.2). It is written of a hired worker in the Torah of Moses, 'in the same day you shall pay him his wage'. And so, 'to You, O Eternal, I lift up my soul.' Because in normal life the hired worker who completes his work for the owner asks the owner for the wage of this work, and the owner gives it to him. So shall it not be the same with the Holy One, who is blessed? Now if it is said of the hired labourer who asks the wage which the owner owes him, 'he lifts up his soul to him', how much more should the same be said about us whose lives depend on You! (*Midrash Psalms* 25.1)

The same Rabbinic collection brings this comment on the last verse which makes a fitting end to this exploration.

> *Let innocence and integrity preserve me; for I wait for You.* The sages said of this verse: When someone prays and receives no answer, let them pray again, and wait again on the Holy One, who is blessed, because He will not shame those who wait for Him. As it says, Wait for the Eternal; be of good courage, and God will strengthen your heart. Wait for the Eternal (Ps. 27.14).

6

A Stairway to Paradise: On Psalm 19

So far the Psalms we have examined have had an obvious unity, integrity and structure. But since the advent of modern critical scholarship there has been a major quest to get behind the final form before us to discover the components or 'sources' from which a particular passage was composed. It is at this point that 'classical' and 'modern' kinds of Bible study have clashed. Both approaches have their inner logic and inevitably lead to different conclusions. Today the pendulum has swung back and there is a growing trend to set aside the questions of 'origins' and examine instead the final form of the text that lies before us. Nevertheless we cannot ignore the prehistory of the text, and it will be part of the background material we bring with us to each analysis. In some cases the Psalm seems to be so clearly made up of disparate material that it becomes a real challenge to find how the various parts hold together, to find an inner logic to their construction.

One such example is Psalm 19 which seems to evoke quite different responses among scholars. So it offers us the opportunity to explore how these different views operate and make our own attempt to discover its inner coherence and integrity.

1. *For the Choirmaster. A Psalm of David*
2. The heavens declare the glory of God,
   and the sky tells the works of His hands.
3. Each day pours out speech to the other
   and night to night passes on the knowledge.
4. No speech at all! There are no words!
   Their sound cannot be heard!
5. And yet their scope extends through all the earth
   and their words to the end of the world.
   In them He set a tent for the sun;

6. which is like a bridegroom coming from his bridal chamber,
   like a champion who rejoices in running a race.
7. At one end of the heavens it comes out
   and its course is to the other end;
   and nothing is hidden from its heat.

8. The teaching of the Eternal is perfect,
        restoring the soul.
   The testimony of the Eternal is reliable
        making wise the simple.
9. The duties of the Eternal are right,
        rejoicing the heart.
   The command of the Eternal is clear,
        enlightening the eyes.
10. The fear of the Eternal is pure,
        standing forever.
   The judgements of the Eternal are true,
        all of them together are righteous.

11. They are more to be desired than gold,
    even the finest gold.
    They are even sweeter than honey
    as it drips from the honeycomb.
12. Through them Your servant is warned,
    in keeping them much follows.
13. Who can understand one's own failings,
    from hidden [faults] make me innocent.
14. Preserve Your servant from 'the arrogant',
    let them not rule over me
    then I shall be blameless,
    innocent of grave rebellion.
15. May the words of my mouth and the meditation of my heart
    be acceptable to You,
    O Eternal, my rock and my redeemer.

Here is Artur Weiser:

Psalm 19 consists of two independent songs which in subject matter, mood, language and metre differ from each other so much that they cannot be composed by the same author. 1–6 – a nature psalm arising from a poet's profound vision and expressed in forceful language. v. 7–14 comprise a psalm whose theme is the Law and whose thoughts and language are characterized by a homely simplicity. Why these dissimilar poems were united in one single psalm cannot any longer be established with any degree of certainty.[1]

Mitchell Dahood[2] is a little more encouraging on the possibility of linking the two parts of the Psalm.

> The psalm clearly divides into two distinct but related parts. The first 7 verses are probably an adaptation to Yahwistic purposes of an ancient Canaanite hymn to the sun. vv. 8–15 are a dialectic poem describing the excellence of the law, often in terms which properly describe the sun.

A traditional Jewish approach is presented in the series of commentaries published by the Soncino Press. The volume on Psalms written by Revd Dr A. Cohen is particularly impressive. In view of the 'fundamentalist' tendency of more recent 'Jewish' Bible commentaries, it is ironic that Cohen expresses the inner unity by quoting from Kant![3]

> There are two things that fill my soul with holy reverence and ever-growing wonder – the spectacle of the starry sky that virtually annihilates us as physical beings, and the moral law which raises us to infinite dignity as intelligent agents.

When we have examined the Psalm ourselves in more detail we may be able to make some sort of judgement on its integrity. But it is worth noting that these are not the only questions that one may wish to address to such a composition.

Rabbinic tradition works on the assumption that the majority of the Psalms were composed by David, unless the heading explicitly names another author. In this case the Psalm is ascribed to David which led them to make the following observation:

> There are four Psalms which one would have expected Adam to compose but which David composed:
> *Psalm 24* 'The earth is the Eternal's and the fullness thereof.' Why Adam? Because the earth and its fullness were created for him.
> *Psalm 19* 'The heavens declare the glory of God'. Why Adam? Because he was the first to behold the heavens.

Psalm 92 'A Psalm for the Sabbath Day.' Why Adam? Because the Sabbath saved him from immediate destruction.

Psalm 15 'For the Leader. Upon the *nehilot* (inheritances).' Why Adam? Because he was the first inheritor of the world. (*Midrash Psalms* 5.3)

This Rabbinic view reminds us of the power of the opening statement of our Psalm. It is precisely the dazzling array of stars in the sky at night that evokes wonder in the writer. How overwhelming that must have been to the first man, as indeed it is for us whenever we see it in its full splendour. This accords with a Rabbinic view that each day the soul returns to us and we are reborn – so must thank God 'for Your wonders that are daily with us' and never allow our vision or experience to grow stale.

Whatever the vision that inspired the writer, in composing the Psalm he is transmuting that experience into the dimension of words, so we must pay close attention to how he sets about this. The opening sentence of our Psalm has a chiastic structure which is lost in the usual English word order (v. 2):

2. The heavens declare the glory of God,
   and the sky tells the works of His hands.

If we follow the Hebrew word order in our translation we will see how this works:

The heavens	declare	the glory of God
The works of His hands	tells	the sky.

If we write it out in the following way the 'crossing over', 'chiasmus', can be seen more readily:

The heavens
> declare
>> the glory of God
>> the works of His hands
> tells
the sky.

The opening and closing words, 'heavens' and 'sky', are almost interchangeable synonyms, as are the two verbs, 'declare' and 'tell' – they could be swapped around without making any difference to the sense of the sentence. But that leaves us with two phrases that are likewise equated even though they are not, in any literal sense, identical. So we are asked to make the equation ourselves.

The 'glory of God' seems to make direct sense – the blazing lights in the sky at night are the splendour and glory that surround a king, here writ large. Though we have to remember that the word translated as 'glory', *kavod*, has the sense of 'weight', emphasizing God's almost physical presence or 'immanence'. It is also important to note that the verb 'declare', as well as suggesting that the glorious night sky 'shows' us 'God's glory', also hints at what will come next, that something is also 'told', some sort of language is actually being invoked. But, to link our phrase with its parallel, how is the 'glory of God' actually manifested? Through the 'works of His hands' – the whole of the physical creation is evidence of God's glorious activity.

On one level this asserts most strongly that behind all the wondrous manifestations of nature is the directing creative hand of God, a very firm statement against the deifying of any aspect of nature – which is why the sun, for all its magnificence, will be described also as God's creation, set in its tent by night and running a pre-ordained path by day. But conversely it also reminds us that in every aspect of creation we are to see evidence of the work of God. The whole universe becomes a hymn to God's creative actions.

But having established that certainty, the writer suddenly introduces a riddle with which we must grapple (3–5).

3. Each day pours out speech to the other
   and night to night passes on the knowledge.
4. No speech at all! There are no words!
   Their sound cannot be heard!
5. And yet their scope extends through all the earth
   and their words to the end of the world.

It is worth making the technical point that the Hebrew which is literally translated as 'day to day pours out speech', could also be read as 'day *by* day', or 'each day', rather than having the day pass on a message to the next day. But that does not address the central contradiction of 'speech' going forth, but there is no 'speech' or 'words' or sound to be heard.

There are ways of resolving the problem. The most radical is to translate the Hebrew in such a way that it renders the opposite meaning. Most translations assume that we are dealing here with three parallel statements: 'No speech at all! There are no words! Their sound cannot be heard!' However, the last phrase is introduced by the word *b'lee*, 'without', and we could read the passage instead as: 'There is no speech, there are no words, without their sound being heard.' That is to say, that this heavenly voice is to be heard within all speech and words that are uttered. The Targum, the Aramaic translation, follows this interpretation:

> There is no expression of excitement, nor any words of confusion, in which their voice is not heard.

But if we follow the more conventional translation, some assume that the wondrous spectacle of the heavens, the daily appearance of the sun, causes the whole of the rest of creation to utter songs of praise. Abraham Ibn Ezra, who, as well as being a grammarian and philosopher, was an astronomer, suggests that the one who studies the movement of the spheres, the cycles of the heavenly bodies, will understand the meaning of this hidden speech.

But there is another approach entirely to the problem by the Jewish scholar Harry Torczyner (who changed his name to Tur Sinai on immigrating to Palestine).[4] He sees in these verses a riddle, and a second one in verse 7. Both riddles are based on the idea of things which 'are' and at the same time 'are not'. Thus here we have 'speech' whose voice is nevertheless not heard. How do we resolve this puzzle? The answer lies in the word we translated above as 'scope'. The more conventional translation is 'line', and the Hebrew word *qav* is used of a measuring line. Since the meaning of the word is not altogether clear, some scholars wish to amend it, by adding a single letter, to read not *qavam*, their 'line', but *qolam*, 'their voice' – which makes a lot more sense and is attested by the Septuagint, the earliest Greek version of the Bible.

Nevertheless I prefer to try to work with the Hebrew, and Tur Sinai reminds us that in Isaiah 28.11 the word *qav* also stands for an actual letter of the Hebrew alphabet. The prophet is playing with the image of teaching newly weaned children how to read, letter by letter – and he takes two successive letters of the Hebrew alphabet, those we call today *tzáde* and *quf*.

ki tzav l'tzav tzav l'tzav qav l'qav qav l'qav z'eir sham z'eir sham

The Hebrew actually works on two levels since it is possible to read this purely in terms of teaching the letters of the alphabet:

'For *tzáde* by *tzáde, tzáde* by *tzáde, quf* by *quf, quf* by *quf*, here a little, there a little . . .'

Or, since *tzav* can be related to the verb to 'command':

'For precept upon precept, precept upon precept, line upon line, line upon line, here a little, there a little . . .'

So in Tur Sinai's view the solution to the riddle is 'writing' – which is how speech can be communicated without a sound being heard. In Accadian, he points out, the spread of the stars in the heavens is called 'the writing of the heavens'. So what would God have written in the heavens? Clearly the Torah! Which provides both an answer to the riddle of what was this silent language and an opening to the middle section of the Psalm which is a hymn to the Torah.

If the blazing stars in the sky represent the glory of God and communicate this knowledge 'night by night', then the sun is the single magnificent evidence of this 'day by day'. Its power is conveyed by two telling images, the bridegroom emerging, presumably strutting, from the bridal chamber, and the warrior proudly rejoicing as he begins a race. From one end of those heavens, with which we began the Psalm, to the other, the sun makes its way. But unlike the stars which retain their distant majesty, the heat of the sun can be felt everywhere on earth, 'and nothing is hidden from its heat'. This image is literally true, but the use of the word *nistar*, 'hidden', will return with a quite different sense in verse 13, when the Psalmist uses the same word in the form *nistarot*, to mean 'hidden things inside us' – failures hidden even from ourselves, but all too visible to God.

At the geographical, and ideological, centre of the Psalm is a series of six statements praising the qualities of the Torah, the teaching that comes from God. The sentence division sets them in pairs, but to understand their symmetry, it is best to lay each statement out separately.

torat	*adonay*	*temimah*	*m'shívat*	*náfesh*
eidut	*adonay*	*ne'emanah*	*machkímat*	*péti*
pikudei	*adonay*	*y'sharim*	*m'samchei*	*lev*
mitzvat	*adonay*	*barah*	*m'eerat*	*eináyim*
yirat	*adonay*	*t'horah*	*omédet*	*la'ad*
mishp'tei	*adonay*	*emet*	*tzadku*	*yachdav*

  8. The teaching of the Eternal is perfect,
          restoring the soul.
     The testimony of the Eternal is reliable
          making wise the simple.
  9. The duties of the Eternal are right,
          rejoicing the heart.
     The command of the Eternal is clear,
          enlightening the eyes.
  10. The fear of the Eternal is pure,
          standing forever.
     The judgements of the Eternal are true,
          all of them together are righteous.

It is the most perfect example of 'parallelism' in the Hebrew Bible – six identically structured sentences, with the same rhythm, and with the name of God, *adonay*, located at the exact same place in each. They are effectively illustrating what the first line is actually saying – that the Torah of God is 'perfect' – and how better to show this than with such a 'perfect' structure!

Of course the symmetry is not complete. The first four use the word 'Torah' itself and three synonyms – testimony, statutes, commandment. In all four instances the verse indicates its effect upon those who come under its influence – Torah restores the soul, makes the simple wise, makes the heart rejoice and enlightens the eyes. The last two focus on the Torah 'itself'. The first does so indirectly: 'the fear/awe of the Eternal is pure, standing forever'. Here there may be an intentional play on the opening statement: in place of '*torat adonay*' we have '*yirat adonay*' – not the Torah that comes from God but the awe we have of God. There is a sound play between *torat* and *yirat*, but the root of the word for *torah* is *yarah*, meaning 'to shoot arrows at a target', and only one silent letter separates the word from the root *yarei*, 'to fear'.

The last line sums up the whole idea – 'the judgements of the Eternal are true, all of them together are righteous'.

After the irregular sentences of the opening verses of the Psalm, describing the wonders of the heavens and the journey of the sun, this formal, structured listing of the qualities of the Torah, with its regular stately rhythm, comes as a shock – as if the very phrases themselves suggest the order that Torah imposes upon an otherwise seemingly anarchic universe. It is therefore no surprise to realize that the final section of the Psalm is likewise made up of irregular sentences as it describes our inner life. The two patterns at the beginning and end of the Psalm complement each other, isolating this perfect structure in the centre. We will return to note another possible understanding of this set of six verses once we have examined the closing section.

The transition from the image of the sun to that of Torah is not completely clear. Ibn Ezra follows the views of Saadia Gaon in suggesting that there is a word missing which would make the sun 'say' the following words about the Torah. Another suggestion makes the analogy between the sun and the Torah itself. We have noted the phrase that 'nothing is hidden from its *heat*'. The Hebrew word for heat, *chamah*, is also used as a term for the sun itself. Amos Chacham, the author and editor of a number of traditionally oriented commentaries on the Bible, draws our attention to a verse in the Song of Songs (6.10) which speaks of the beloved woman in the Song as 'beautiful as the moon and "pure" as the sun (*chamah*)'. He suggests that this makes a link between the heat of the sun and the 'purity' of Torah.[5] But, as Rashi points out, it is also clear that the sun brings light to the earth as well as heat, just as the Torah 'brings light to the eyes'. So again the image of the sun slides into that of Torah, both of them filling the world with warmth and light, making visible even the darkest corners.

The last section of the Psalm picks up these hints in a variety of ways. Torah is 'more precious than gold', even much fine gold, and sweeter than honey and the flowing of the honeycomb. These two images work on a number of levels – most obviously that Torah is to be valued above all else and is sweet to the taste. David Clines[6] has drawn attention to the way these images and those in the 'hymn to Torah' above echo words that appear in the story of the tree of the knowledge of good and evil in the Garden of Eden, which was 'good to eat, attractive to the eyes and "desirable" for understanding'. Here the Torah is even more 'desirable'.

But I wonder if there is also another level on which this image works – as a play on the golden light of the sun, the colour of gold itself and of honey, all of which are somehow precious reflections of each other. Their effect on human beings is described with the word *nizhar*, which is usually translated as 'warned' – 'moreover your servant is warned by them'. But the root, *zahar*, also means to shine – hence the title of the famous mystical work the Zohar, the

Book of Splendour. So it is possible to understand that through the Torah one is 'enlightened', or even that one comes to 'shine' oneself.

The last part of the Psalm dramatizes the effect of Torah upon us, in that it makes us conscious of our own imperfections – those of which we are aware and those that are 'hidden within us'.

13. Who can understand one's own failings,
     from hidden [faults] make me innocent.
14. Preserve Your servant from 'the arrogant',
     let them not rule over me,
     then I shall be blameless,
     innocent of grave rebellion.

This is a rare instance of an attempt by the Hebrew Bible to describe our inner life, our 'psychology'. The word 'hidden' stands by itself, and only the context suggests that it refers to other 'faults' or 'sins'. On hearing the word we remember again the sun, from whose heat nothing is 'hidden'. The sun, and by analogy God, can indeed see that which is hidden within us, so that the opening and closing parts of the Psalm are linked together.

What are 'the arrogant'? The plural form *zeidim* is more commonly used of others, 'arrogant people', who threaten the existence of the good. But here it would seem to be internalized: it is the pride and arrogance of the Psalmist that is being described, another element in his psychology.

But there is another remarkable word play here. Because if 'the arrogant' are not able to rule over him, he will be *tam*, probably derived from the verb *tamam*, meaning 'whole', 'perfect', 'innocent' – one of the first words used above in the description of the Torah: 'the Torah of the Eternal is *temimah*, perfect'.

We have a paradox here. The contemplation of the perfection of the Torah, which is such a source of wonder, wisdom, joy and enlightenment, has the effect of giving the Psalmist a sense of his own inadequacy, failure, arrogance and rebelliousness. Only if God helps him can he begin to approach the 'perfection' that is Torah.

The closing verse sums up the lesson the Psalmist derives from this understanding, but it also links us once again with the opening image of the Psalm. There is, once again, a verbal link through the word *amar*, to speak, hence 'speech' or 'word'. Having described the communication that goes on in heaven from day to day and night to night, verse 4 suddenly tells us that 'there is no speech, *ómer*'. Now the Psalmist prays that the 'speech' of my lips and the thoughts within my heart/mind may be acceptable to God. That is to say that there be an integrity between his inner and outer world – the silent, unfathomable worlds within him and their external expression. So that just as the heavens in their outer manifestation proclaim the glory of God, but the means of that communication is inaudible and mysterious, so too the Psalmist is aware of the inner and outer realities of his own human existence. If he too is to 'proclaim the glory of God', he must seek his own wholeness, where his own inner and outer worlds meet.

Whatever the origins of the various components of the Psalm, in its finished form it has a completeness – well characterized by the words of Kant. But there is perhaps another dimension that makes for a unity, one that can only be seen by looking at the Hebrew text as it is laid out in the Appendix. For this exercise we can ignore the words entirely and simply look at the shape. The irregular lengths of the sentences at the beginning and end stand in stark contrast to the central hymn to Torah. But what is the form of that central passage? When asking my students at various times they tend to see it as a 'square', I suppose because we notice the outer form. But actually it consists of six parallel symmetric lines and if we see them simply in this form they are actually like the rungs of a ladder. Is it possible that the writer had such a conceit in mind? For the Torah would thus be the ladder that links the cosmos to the microcosm that is the individual human being. Such an image is available in the story of Jacob's ladder, with the angels ascending and descending, and in the steps that led up to the Temple, which may have been the basic idea behind the 'Psalms of Ascent', to be recited on going up to the Temple.

One need not press the image too far – though it is worth noting that there are other examples where the 'shape' of a composition is as important as the content (for example, the list of female ornaments listed by Isaiah (3.18–23)). Nevertheless it is a reminder of the subtlety and complexity of these compositions with the long tradition of poetry in the Ancient Near East behind them. A tradition so ancient that the Psalmist could comfortably integrate the elements of a hymn to the sun, a praise of Torah and an attempt at exploring human psychology into a new composition.

I would like to end with a totally different view of our Psalm, a delightfully unexpected one. It comes from the Midrash collection Leviticus Rabbah 5.8. In the view of Gordon M. Freeman[7] beneath its mixture of practical wisdom and implicit humour is a serious exploration of strategies for addressing authority.

Rabbi Shimon said: What skilled craftsmen are the Israelites that they know how to appease and win the favour of the Creator! Rabbi Yudan said: Like those Cutheans who are clever at begging. One of them came to a woman and said to her, have you an onion? Give it to me. When she gave it to him, he said: Can one eat an onion without bread? When she gave it to him he said: Can one eat without drinking? So he got food and drink.

Rabbi Aha said: Some women are clever at asking, some are not. A woman who is clever at asking comes to her neighbour. The door is open but she knocks and says: Peace be with you, neighbour. How are you, how is your husband, how are your children? May I come in? The other answers: Come in, what do you want? She replies: Do you have such and such a thing, will you give it to me? She answered: Yes. The woman who is not clever at asking comes to her neighbour. The door is shut. She opens it and says: Have you such and such an article? The answer is no.

Rabbi Haninah said: Some tenant farmers are clever at asking, some are not. The clever one observes that he is going downhill on his farm. He plucks up heart of grace. He combs his hair, he whitens his clothes, and with a bright countenance and with the stick in hand and rings on his fingers, he goes to his landlord who says: How is the land, will you be able to eat of its fruits with joy? How are the oxen, will you be able to enjoy their fat? How are the goats, will you set yourself with the kids? What do you want? The farmer says: Have you ten dinari? Will you give them to me? If you want twenty, take them.

He who does not know how to ask goes with unkempt hair, dirty clothes and with a miserable face to his landlord, who says to him: How is the land? He replied: Oh that it produced what we have put into it. How are the oxen? They are weak. What do you want? Can you give me ten dinari? He replied: Bring me first what you owe me.

Rabbi Onias said: David was one of the clever farmers. He

first sang God's praises and said: 'The heavens declare the glory of God' (Ps. 19.2). God said: Perhaps he wants something: He said, 'and the sky tells the works of His hands.' God said: Perhaps he wants something. He said: 'Day by day utters speech'. Then the Blessed Holy One said: 'What do you require?' David replied: 'Who can understand his errors? Pardon the errors that I have done before You.' God said: They are dismissed and forgiven. Then David said: 'Cleanse me from secret faults, from the hidden sins that I have committed before you.' God replied: These, too, are dismissed and forgiven. Then he said: 'From the presumptuous sins keep back Your servant; the premeditated sins. Let them not have dominion over me, then shall I be innocent.' These are the big iniquities – 'and pure of transgression.' For David said to God: Master of the world, for You are a great God and my sins are great. It befits the great God to pardon the great sins, as it is written: 'For the sake of my name, pardon my iniquity, for it is great' (Ps. 25.11).

7

Why Have You Forsaken Me? Psalm 22

1. *To the Choirmaster. According to 'The Hind of the Dawn'.*
   A Psalm of David.
2. My God, my God, why have You forsaken me,
   far from rescuing me,
   from the words of my roaring?
3. My God, I cry by day and You do not answer,
   by night, and find no rest.

4. Yet You are holy, enthroned on the praises of Israel.
5. In You trusted our fathers
   trusted, and You delivered them,
6. to You they cried and were rescued,
   in You they trusted and were not 'ashamed'.

7. But as for me, I am a worm and no man,
   a reproach of men and despised of people.
8. All that see me, mock me,
   they open their mouths and shake their heads:
9. 'Let him turn to the Eternal,
   let Him deliver him!
   Let Him save him, since He delights in him!'

10. For You are the one who took me from the belly,
    You taught me trust on my mother's breasts.
11. Upon You have I been cast from the womb,
    from the belly of my mother, my God are You!
12. Be not far from me, for trouble is near
    and there is none to aid.

13. Many bulls surround me,
    strong bulls of Bashan encircle me.
14. They open wide their mouths at me.
    like a devouring and roaring lion.

15. I am poured out like water,
    and all my bones are pulled apart;
    my heart is become like wax
    melting away within me.
16. My strength is dried up like a potsherd
    and my tongue sticks to my jaws –
    You lay me in the dust of death.

17. For dogs surround me,
    a company of evildoers has enclosed me,
    like a lion, at my hands and feet.
18. I can count all my bones
    – they look and gloat over me.
19. They divide up my garments amongst them
    casting lots for my clothes.

20. But You, O Eternal, be not far,
    my strength, hurry to my aid.
21. Save my life from the sword,
    my very self from the power of the dog.
22. Rescue me from the mouth of the lion,
    You have answered me from the horns of the wild oxen.

23. I will tell Your name to my brothers.
    In the midst of the assembly I will praise You.
24. 'You who fear the Eternal praise Him,
    all the seed of Jacob, honour Him,
    and stand in awe before Him, all the seed of Israel!
25. For He has not despised or scorned the affliction of the afflicted
    nor hid His face from him,
    and when he cried to Him, He heard.'

26. From You comes my praise in the great assembly,
    my vows I will pay before those who fear Him.
27. Then the poor will eat and be satisfied,

those who seek Him will praise the Eternal!
May your hearts live forever!

28. All the ends of the earth will remember
    and turn to the Eternal,
    all the families of nations will bow before You.
29. For dominion belongs to the Eternal,
    and He rules over the nations.

30. All the fat ones of the earth shall eat and bow down,
    before Him shall bow all who go down to the dust,
    even he who cannot keep his soul alive.

31. A seed shall serve Him.
    It shall be told of the Eternal to the next generation.
32. They shall come and tell of His righteousness,
    to a people yet to be born, that He has done it.

There is something foolhardy about tackling this Psalm. It is long, complex and puzzling, particularly in the sudden switch in mood that occurs in the last section. It is customarily divided into two parts (vv. 2–22, 23–32) but the inner development suggests that verses 2–12 have a particular unity, as do 13–22. Let us tackle it a section at a time and see how far we get.

The first section (vv. 2–12 – excluding the title) seems to define itself quite clearly – largely because of the theme, but also because of the repetition of certain words and elements that suggest a concentric pattern. In fact it is quite densely packed with poetic structures.

The first word to note is the verb *rachaq* – to be far, distant. The Psalmist complains in verse 2 that God is 'far' from his 'help', 'rescue', despite the words of his cry. The same verb reappears in verse 12 with the plea, 'do not be far from me', thus linking these two verses. But it also reappears in the similarly worded plea in verse 20 – and so we will have to see how these uses also link together.

We should also consider the word 'roaring' in verse 2 (Hebrew *sha'ag*). Many translations prefer 'cry' or 'moaning', but the word is the one conventionally used for the roaring sound of a lion, and is even used metaphorically of God (Amos 3.4, 8). In fact it will crop up in verse 14, 'like a lion tearing (its prey) and *roaring*'. Since it seems inappropriate here some prefer a different text to be found in the Septuagint instead or suggest emendations, presumably because 'roaring' seems psychologically out of place in someone praying to God. Perhaps we are also conditioned by the Christian associations of this verse quoted by Jesus on the cross. It has become part of our general culture. But if we step back from that image to the Psalm itself and its own language and inner logic, perhaps the 'roar' is also appropriate. Perhaps the Psalmist should not be seen as simply a weak and helpless victim begging for aid from God but as a person of power and importance in his own right who finds himself in a totally unexpected situation of helplessness – it is, after all, ascribed to King David. Here would be a man of extraordinary power and passion, self-confident and assured, suddenly experiencing his weakness, helplessness and dependency, beset by self-doubts. From such a mouth might come a roar of anger and bewilderment such as would shake the very heavens, before it might turn into a moan or whimper. The whole Psalm has something of this grandiose dimension – the powerful animals that attack him, the call to all the nations to celebrate God's power. There is a world of belief at stake here.

A couple of other words repeat themselves in localized verses that suggests their interaction with each other. The most obvious is the root *batach*, to trust, which occurs four times, in a tight relationship in verses 5–6, and once again in verse 10. In fact it points to a neat little 'chiastic' structure in verses 5–6:

b'cha batchu avotéinu	*batchu vat'faltéimo*
eilécha za'aku v'nimlátu	*b'cha vatchu v'lo vóshu*

In You *trusted* our fathers
    trusted, and You delivered them,
      to You they cried and were rescued,
in You they *trusted* and were not 'ashamed'.

It is a very powerful construction: three times comes the insistent 'in *You*', 'to *You*', 'in *You*' – You were there to be addressed and You delivered! Three times the verb 'trust' – they knew You were to be relied on, why is *my* trust unanswered? Three times comes a statement of rescue – twice using verbs, *palat* (deliver) and *malat* (rescue) with similar sounds, and once expressed in the negative – they were not 'ashamed/disappointed'. The two inner half-verses stress how they were 'rescued'. The two outer ones begin with

the trust in God experienced by the fathers, models for the correct
relationship with God and end 'and were *not* disappointed' – hinting
strongly at the 'disappointment' being experienced by the Psalmist.

The second chiastic structure straddles verses 10–11 and relates
to synonyms for 'womb':

ki attah gochi mibbáten   *mavtichi al-sh'dei immi*
alécha hoshláchti meiráchem   *mibbéten immi eili áttah.*

For You are the one who took me from the *belly*,
     You taught me trust on my mother's breasts.
     Upon You have I been cast from the womb,
from the *belly* of my mother, my God are You!

Here the word *béten*, 'belly', and hence also 'womb', forms the outer
ring: from before I was even born You were with me, my God. The
inner part reinforces again the word 'trust' (*batach*), 'You taught me
trust . . .' A more literal translation might be 'you kept me safe/
secure on my mother's breasts', but I wanted to keep the echo of
the same root that recurred in verses 5–6. I would also argue that
since the central issue here is the Psalmist's trust in God that he
feels has been betrayed, his earliest experience of this 'trust' is
precisely the point he is making. 'I learnt trust from the experience
of drinking at the breast of my mother.' Since the baby is utterly
dependent upon others for its survival, the Psalmist can see the
provision of milk as evidence of being 'cast' upon God for support
from the moment he left the womb.

But we must also notice that the closing phrase in Hebrew, *'eili
áttah'*, 'my God – You [are]', uses the same word for God as in the
opening cry of pain – *'eili eili lama azavtáni'*, 'My God, my God,
why have You forsaken me?' Other words for God appear elsewhere
in the Psalm, but here, where his relationship with God is inextricably
intertwined with feeding at the breasts of his mother, *eili*, 'my God',
becomes his most intimate term of closeness and endearment. So
the initial cry comes back with extra force – where is that God of
childhood on whom he could utterly rely? Why is he so utterly
forsaken?

These two sets of chiastic structures, both describing 'trust' in
God, surround the central three verses, 4–7, in which the Psalmist
talks of his humiliation. He sees himself as being taunted by others
telling him to turn to God. Again it is conventional to accept this at

its face value – within the circle of those who know him he is subject to taunts – or, by a broader reading, Israel is taunted by the nations; but if we stay with the first reading, we have to recall how he will be restored to his place in the community at the end without any apparent resentment on his part of those who had formerly scorned him. Perhaps, remembering Job's experience, it might be that their advice is actually well-intentioned – that he should turn to God for help – but in his present situation the Psalmist can only experience this as a mocking of his suffering, a kind of insensitive piety on their part.

> Let him 'roll' to the Eternal, let Him deliver Him.
> Let Him rescue him, for He delights in him.

The word for 'deliver' repeats the term used in verse 5, so perhaps these 'mockers' are indeed speaking out of the same tradition of trust in God that the Psalmist is relying on. But that must seem doubly bitter for the one who is suffering. Even more ambiguous, however, is the closing phrase, '*ki cháfetz bo*', 'for he delights in him', since it is not at all clear who is the subject and who the object of the verb. It can equally mean that God 'delights' in the Psalmist – pointing again to some favoured and powerful position that he holds – or that the Psalmist 'delights' in, feels a special relationship to God. If it is the latter, the speakers ask or taunt him to make use of it.

We can now see that the whole of this section has a concentric structure:

> 2–3 (4): I cry to You in vain, you are *far* from me
>   5–6: Our fathers *trusted* in You
>   and were not disappointed.
>   7–9: They mock me – 'let him turn to God!'
>   10–11: I have *trusted* in You from the womb
> 12: My plea – do not be *far* from me.

As we have noted in our discussions of biblical poetry, the concentric structure has two 'climaxes' – it moves towards a central verse where the first one is to be found, and then a second climax occurs at the end, linking up with the beginning and rounding off the composition. Before looking at our section in these terms, there is one more verse to examine which we have overlooked, verse 4. 'But You are holy, dwelling in the praises of Israel.'

It has a certain familiarity to Jewish readers because of its presence in the liturgy – in a section of petitionary prayers towards the end of the morning service. Because it stands there introducing the verse from Isaiah 6, 'Holy, holy, holy . . .', it feels as if it steps out quite naturally from our Psalm. So it is conceivable that it belonged to some liturgical context even in biblical times. It would then be cited here by the Psalmist to contrast this liturgical view of God's presence in the midst of Israel's prayers with his own personal experience of God's distance at a time of need, theology clashing with a powerful reality. But whether quoted or created by the author, it forms a kind of bridge to the next section: 'But You are holy, dwelling in the praises of Israel, our fathers trusted in You . . .' However, over against the emphatic '*v'attah*', 'but You', comes the equally emphatic '*va'anochi*', 'but as for *me* – I am but a worm . . .' In contrast to the heights of praise upon which God sits (the word *kadosh*, 'holy', contains the sense of separateness, apartness, distance), the Psalmist feels himself so low that God cannot hear him, a mere worm, not even human. And this low point comes at the centre of our structure.

Yet, despite his ambivalent feelings about the advice/mockery of others telling him to turn to God, that is precisely what he does – not as the God of the fathers and out of the tradition of praise, but as the God of his own experience from the very womb, as close to him as his mother's breast, and on whom he relied for his survival as much as he relied on his mother's milk. How can that God, who was so close, really be far – unless God himself wills it? Hence the concluding plea of this section, 'do not keep Yourself far from me'.

The next section, verses 13–22, contains a dramatic shift of emphasis focusing on the enemies without, characterized as wild animals, and on his inner dissolution.

The enemies are described as powerful bulls and as a lion, threatening to tear him apart. But the same verb, *s'vavúni* (they 'surround' me) that introduces the bulls (v. 13), also introduces the 'dogs' that likewise 'surround' him (v. 17). If the former are those who seek to destroy him, the latter are scavengers, feeding off the remains. At this point the images switch from animals to a 'company of evildoers' picking over his very clothing, explaining the animal metaphor but raising further questions about what is going on. Who are these enemies and scavengers? It is possible to read them as enemy nations surrounding Israel, so that the entire Psalm can be understood as referring to the people as a whole. But it could also mean powerful opponents of the Psalmist, himself a leader of the people. Though the image of dividing up his clothing could be taken literally, it is important to remember that 'clothing' also symbolizes rank and authority in Israel – think of the play made in the Book of Samuel on the cloak of the prophet Samuel and how the tearing of the cloak symbolized the tearing of the kingdom from King Saul. Here, too, it would be consistent to consider the 'scavengers' as dividing up among themselves the various bits of power from the dead leader.

The continuity with the previous section is found in a few elements. In verse 8, those who mock him have 'opened up their mouths' to express their feelings against him; now the wild animals open up their jaws, but to devour him. In both sections he asks for help (*éizer*) (vv. 12, 20); and to their mocking, 'let Him *save* him' (the root *natsal*) (v. 9) comes his own plea to God, '*save, hatsílah,* my life from the sword' (v. 21). But an even stronger link is the plea to God in both sections: 'be not far from me' (vv. 12, 20).

One textual problem in verse 17 should also be considered. Verse 17 (16 in the RSV) is translated in some versions as 'they have pierced my hands and feet', following the Septuagint. The Hebrew text can literally be translated as: 'Like a lion my hands and feet' and is certainly rather strange, so it is understandable that a variety of amendments has been proposed. Nevertheless, it is important to note that there are a number of other verses in this Psalm that may be understood as having a similar 'elliptical' structure, as pointed out already by Rabbi Abraham Ibn Ezra in the twelfth century. That is to say, some word may be missing in the second part of a sentence that the reader has to supply from the first part. Thus verse 2 reads literally:

> My God, my God, why have You forsaken me,
> far from rescuing me,
> the words of my roaring?

In this case the 'why' of the first part of the sentence continues to operate in the rest of it – why are you far from rescuing me ... Likewise the 'from' of the second part belongs also with the third phrase:

> My God, my God, why have You forsaken me,
> *why* are You far from rescuing me,
> *from* the words of my roaring?

Similarly in verse 15:

> my heart is become like wax
> (*my heart is*) melting away within me.

Also verse 29:

> For dominion belongs to the Eternal,
> and (*the Eternal*) rules over the nations.

Given such a consistent technique, the Hebrew text of verse 17 may simply conform with that pattern:

> a company of evildoers has enclosed me,
> (*they have enclosed*) like a lion my hands and feet.

Within this animal imagery, that emphasizes his external danger, comes a striking series of descriptions of his inner state – images of liquids, of melting away, and then of dryness, as the fluids within him are poured out leaving him dried up within, returning to the dust of the earth from which he was created. He is so weakened that his bones seem to separate out, he can even count them.

Again, as with the animal imagery, the metaphors allow for a multitude of interpretations – from real physical situations of illness and wasting, to a psychological state of fear or anxiety, dread or paranoia. We can read it as a continuation of our previous interpretation of the desperation of someone used to a measure of power, utterly shattered by the sudden loss of control over events and even his own physical self. The outer enemies may be real or not real – and indeed some are to be despised as they pick over his remains now that he is helpless – but it is his inner dissolution that seems the greatest burden, and his fear of impending death.

Just as this second section began with bulls and a lion and then dogs, so does it end by reversing the sequence – the dog reappearing in verse 21, followed by the lion and a wild ox (v. 22).

In his Hebrew commentary to the Psalms, Amos Chacham,[1] a remarkable Bible scholar who works within a traditional Jewish framework, has a very fine sense of the repetition of key words and their interaction. Thus he, too, divides this Psalm into two parts (vv. 2–22 and 23–32), but particularly on the basis of two words. At the beginning of the Psalm the author complains that he cried to God, '*v'lo ta'aneh*', 'and You do not answer'. In verse 22 comes the reversal, in the (grammatical) perfect form, '*anitani*', literally, 'You have answered me'. This word appears so abruptly at this point that it is hard to reconcile it with what has gone before. The RSV follows the Septuagint and Syriac versions and reads the similar word meaning to 'oppress', hence 'my afflicted (soul)'. Chacham argues that after a series of imperatives, the perfect here concludes his requests and expresses his trust that his prayers will indeed be answered – much as the 'prophetic perfect' allows the prophets to speak of future events as if they had already come to pass or were certain to happen. Despite the abruptness, this effectively forms a bridge to the third part of the Psalm which is a hymn of praise to God.

Some such transition is clearly needed, though the change in mood and content in the last section remains puzzling. Hence the suggestions that the Psalm is part of some cultic process whereby a priest or prophet would intervene at this point with the announcement of a divine oracle, that God has indeed heard the petition and all will be well. Another common approach is to recognize in the Psalmist a powerful religious awareness – the very complaint to God, in all its depth and hurt, reassures him that there is a God to be addressed, an idea reinforced by his reference to the trust of his forefathers and his own experience. Thus the transition comes from within himself, the sense of an answer that leads him into the hymn of praise. A variant of that suggests that the closing section is actually the content of a vow he makes, the things he will say and do, if God does indeed answer him.

Despite the abruptness of the change there are again a number of linkages with earlier parts of the Psalm. Though he was 'despised by people' (*bazui am*) in verse 7, God does not 'despise' (*bazah*) the poverty of the poor. Though he had been placed in the 'dust of death' (*aphar mávet*) (v. 16), he knows that all who 'go down to the dust' (*yordei aphar*) will bow down before God. There is even a strange play on two (related) meanings of the root *saphar*, to 'count' or 'recount' – the same play works in English with the two meanings of the word 'tell'. In verse 18 he 'counted' his bones, in verse 23 he will 'recount' God's name, i.e. praise God, and this will happen in future generations as well (v. 31), 'it will be told' (*y'suppar*). (Amos Chacham sees this repetition of the root at the start and end of this section as the key word that helps define it.) Most obviously the root *halal*, 'to praise', that was raised in verse 4 as a kind of protest – where is the God who 'is enthroned on the *praises* of Israel'? – now reappears no less than four times (vv. 23, 24, 26, 27).

Again, at the risk of appearing obsessive about word repetitions (!), the various verses in this section are linked together. In verses 23 and 24 we read that he will 'praise' God in the 'assembly', so that those who 'fear God' will also praise. All three of these words or phrases will reappear in verses 26 and 27 where he talks about fulfilling his vow in the great 'assembly', before those who 'fear' God so that all will come to utter 'praise'. This linking of verses places emphasis on the reason for this great hymn of praise that is located between them in verse 25: because God does not despise the poor and answers them. Perhaps this is to be understood as a lesson that the Psalmist has been able to learn now from his own experience of helplessness, material and physical.

But the Psalmist's canvas is broader than simply Israel and his own generation – he moves beyond them to see all the ends of the earth, all the families of nations, and all peoples, rich and poor alike, those who are 'fat' and those who can barely keep themselves alive, worshipping God. (It is suggested that verse 28 and perhaps some parts of the following ones are actually liturgical statements to be uttered by the congregation that is assembled to join him in celebrating his recovery, sharing in the festive meal with him.)

Finally, in contrast to the images of death that have so dominated the Psalm, he talks of future generations, linking verse 24 that speaks of the 'seed' (*zéra*) of Jacob and the 'seed' of Israel with the 'seed' (v. 31) of a people yet to be born.

How do we pull together the various elements and dimensions of this Psalm, even assuming that a single 'interpretation' would suffice? We can approach it 'scientifically' and try to classify it – a Psalm of personal lament that moves into a 'thanksgiving' Psalm at the end. We could note the sudden transition from despair to thanksgiving and postulate a ritual context in which the priest responds to the author's cries and says that God has heard his plea. The ritual is then followed by a festive meal to which the poor are invited. Though such an approach is helpful, in suggesting a public context for the use of the Psalm, its very vagueness of detail allowing it to be used in many situations of recovery from trouble or distress, such a view also tends to rob the Psalm of its uniqueness. It is as if we are saying, now that we have been able to classify it we have no further responsibility to explore what it means.

Because it is so much a part of our common culture, it is impossible, even for a Jewish reader, to separate the opening of the Psalm from the way it features in the Gospel story and the suffering of Jesus on the cross, calling out to God – 'why have you forsaken me?!' As most commentaries indicate, a number of other verses have been blended into the Gospel story, the dividing up of the clothing, the piercing of the hands. When I referred to this as a 'Christian tradition', I was reminded by a Christian Professor of Systematic Theology in Germany that it was more accurate to speak instead of a text deeply embedded in the contemporary Jewish world out of which the Gospels emerged – that is to say, the possibility of such an interpretation was there within various different Jewish modes of understanding of biblical texts. The Psalm seems to have had an important place in the popular consciousness, which is borne out by the fact that there is also a well-developed Rabbinic tradition, to be found in the Midrash on Psalms, of reading the Psalm as a reflection of the experience of Queen Esther! She is likened to the 'Hind of the dawn', the mysterious term *'ayyélet hasháchar'* of the title. It remains an open question whether such a reading derives from purely internal Jewish concerns or is in part created precisely to counter the Christian use of the Psalm – to assert a Jewish 'alternative' reading.

In the following quotations from the 'Midrash on Psalms', the collection of Rabbinic comments on the Psalms which contains materials ranging from the first to the ninth century CE, I am indebted to the translation of the late Rabbi Dr William G. Braude, as I am for previous quotations from that source.[2] He was one of those rare figures who managed to combine his tasks as Rabbi of a large congregation, in Providence, Rhode Island, with a dedication to Jewish scholarship, producing a series of important translations of Rabbinic texts. I was privileged to study with him in Jerusalem and invite him to teach at Leo Baeck College in London. It is possible to hear his voice as he attempts to put these difficult texts, that depend on a number of different interpretations, some seemingly artificial, of the same biblical words, into a coherent and stately English.

Why is Esther likened to the dawn? When the dawn awakes the stars set, and so in the court of Ahasuerus, as Esther awakened, the stars of Haman and his sons set.

In another comment, Rabbi Benjamin bar Japhet taught in the

name of Rabbi Eleazar: 'As the dawn ends the night, so all the miracles ended with Esther.' (*Midrash Psalms* 22.10)

The details of the Psalm also find their place in such a Midrashic reading:

> You will find no days as fearsome as those days of the time of Haman, for then the children of Israel were in deep darkness, living in gloom and anguish. This was when Haman said to Ahasuerus: 'There is a certain people scattered abroad ... their laws are diverse ... neither keep they the king's laws' (Esther 3.8). Esther being told of this, immediately said to Mordecai: 'Go, gather together all the Jews that are present in Shushan, and fast ye for me ... I also and my maidens will fast in like manner' (Esther 4.16). And as she was saying 'And so I will go in unto the king, which is not according to the law' (Esther 4.16), the people of the palace began to say: 'Now the king will be angry at Esther, and death will be decreed for her.' And every one said: 'I shall take Esther's apparel', this one saying 'Me, I shall take her ornaments'; and that one saying 'Me, I shall take her earrings,' as is known from Esther's statement: They part my garments among them, and cast lots upon my vesture (Ps. 22.19). Now because Esther perceived and understood what was going on, she prayed and said: 'Be not Thou far from me, O Lord; O my Strength, haste Thee to help me' (Ps. 22.20). (*Midrash Psalms* 22.7)

Likewise the following:

> 'My God, my God, why hast Thou forsaken me?' (Ps. 22.2). Esther said, ' "My God", Thou wert at the Red Sea; "my God", Thou wert at Sinai, "Why hast Thou forsaken me?" ' Why should the order of things, even the story of the Matriarchs turn out different for me? Our mother Sarah was taken for only a single night unto Pharaoh, and he and all the people of his house were smitten with great plagues, as is said "The Lord plagued Pharaoh and his house with great plagues because of Sarai, Abram's wife" (Gen. 12.17); but I who have been forced all these years to endure the embrace of such a wicked person – for me Thou workest no miracles.' (*Midrash Psalms* 22.16)

There is even a legitimate biblical peg upon which to hang references to Esther since she was an orphan:

'Thou keptest me in safety, when I was upon my mother's breast'
(Ps. 22.10) means that Esther said: 'After my mother conceived
me, my father died; and my mother died while giving birth to
me. But Thou keptest me safe, for Thou gavest me breasts in place
of my mother's breasts.' 'Mordecai . . . brought up Hadassah, that
is Esther' (Esther 2.7), that is to say that Mordecai's wife gave
suck to Esther, and that Mordecai brought her up. (*Midrash
Psalms* 22.23)

By other readings, in conjunction with biblical verses that speak of
'light', the 'I' of the Psalms stands for the people of Israel, and 'the
dawn', of the Psalm heading, comes to symbolize the light that will
arise for Israel despite the enemies that surround them. But the
following picks up another familiar biblical theme:

'But I am a worm, and no man' (Ps. 22.7). Like a worm whose
only resource is its mouth, so the children of Israel have no
resource other than the prayers of their mouths. Like a worm
which roots out a tree with its mouth, so the children of Israel
with the prayers of their mouths root out the evil decrees which
[hostile] nations of the earth devise against them. Of this it is
written 'Fear not, thou worm Jacob, and ye few men in Israel; I
will help thee, saith the Lord' (Isa. 41.14); and the passage goes on
to say, 'Behold, I will make thee a new sharp threshing instrument
having mouths; thou shalt thresh the mountains, and beat them
small' (Isa. 41.15). (*Midrash Psalms* 20.20)

That such a variety of readings can come from this Psalm is hardly
surprising. It is full of allusive language that leaves us with any
number of questions. Why is he in such a desperate situation in the
first place – how has his world so fallen apart that men despise him
and God seems to have forsaken him? Has he committed some crime
or other unacceptable action, or has he suffered a loss of power or
status through events beyond his control so that he now finds himself
spurned by those he formerly thought of as his friends? Is he experiencing a grave illness, so that the images of his life force being
poured out and nothing but dry bones remaining is an accurate
description of his physical state – or are these metaphors for inner
fears and hopelessness? Who are these wild beasts that surround
him? Are they real or imagined, personal enemies or other nations

threatening his people? How far is he in control of objective reality and how far caught in some kind of paranoid nightmare? Or, to repeat the uncomfortable line: Just because you're paranoid doesn't mean that they aren't out to get you! And again that puzzling matter of the sudden transition from distress to thanksgiving, the awareness of being answered, with no external reference to help explain the change. Whether it comes from a priestly oracle or a sudden psychological change of perception, it remains another riddle.

These uncertainties allow for a multiple use of the Psalm, the various metaphors permitting us to fill in our own fears or distress. This would indeed make it ideal for some liturgical role in the Temple – the worshipper, while still in distress, or after recovery, bringing his offering and reciting this as part of a formal act of worship. In which case the power of the opening words and the extremes of emotion the Psalmist describes will give whoever uses the Psalm in such a situation a feeling of their own significance, and even heroism, in confronting and transcending such terrifying experiences.

In attempting to read the Psalm as a whole, having looked at the individual parts and sections, I find myself struck by a few elements. First, the time span within which it operates. In asking why God has abandoned him he cites the experience of his ancestors – they called on You in the past and You always answered them. That is a given of his own religious life, a truth that has been handed down to him by word of mouth. It is therefore appropriate that the Psalm should end by asserting that the story of God's righteousness will be told to generations yet unborn. The chain of tradition will continue through his own experience. He has been answered so he can legitimately pass on that tradition – but the Psalm reminds us also that the help from God is neither to be taken for granted nor certain. His own experience of abandonment and helplessness was known by his ancestors as well – the simple formula that 'they cried to God and were answered' now has a tougher and deeper dimension because of the experience the Psalmist brings. Precisely because he is in direct line with that tradition he cannot leave it unchallenged, or else the next generation will be undefended against the pain of reality. He can offer the joy and comfort of the presence of God only because he has known God's absence.

It is interesting to note in this connection how far the imagery of birth and breast-feeding introduce the 'mother' into what otherwise seems to be a 'father'-oriented story. The stories handed down by the fathers may reinforce his sense of God's presence, but it is something he learned in the first place by direct experience at his mother's breast. And that experience, of intimacy and of life created and nourished, provides the energy for his struggle against death, drained of the fluids that support life.

This recognition in turn draws our attention, unexpectedly, to the role that 'eating' has in the Psalm. There are animals around him seeking to devour him – though as mere skin and bones, unable to take in nourishment himself, he provides little for the scavenging dogs to enjoy. But in the closing section, as well as praising God, the community, particularly the poor, are invited to tuck into a major festive meal. That that was part of the Temple ritual is evident, but the importance of food for the survival of life itself is very strongly emphasized in these closing verses. Its importance is indicated in the puzzlement some commentators have expressed about verse 30, 'all the fat ones of the earth' who will eat and worship. Since the rest of the verse speaks of 'those who go down to the dust' and those who cannot 'keep their souls alive', it is felt that a parallel term is required at the beginning – hence the suggestion that in place of '*dishnei*', 'well-fed', should be '*y'sheinei*', 'those who sleep – in the earth', borrowing the phrase from Daniel 12.2 – though it should be pointed out that in Daniel it is in the '*admat aphar*', the 'ground – dust', that they sleep (the latter term appearing also in our Psalm) and not in the '*árets*', the 'earth'. But the versions do not justify such an emendation, and perhaps the contrast is intended. In fact the Psalm makes much of the difference between being well-fed and hungry, being rich and poor – God does not scorn the 'affliction' or 'poverty' of the poor (v. 25). This suggests that part of the drama of the story is indeed a change of fortune for the Psalmist, from wealth to poverty and back. The writer knows both states, for only out of such an experience is it possible to speak with any honesty or credibility about the poor praising God, even those unable to keep themselves alive. Surrounded as we are by images of famine victims and those starving to death in civil wars, it is no simple matter to speak of God's love and concern: to be a legitimate witness the Psalmist must have experienced such extremes and still feel able to bow down and sing God's praise. Once again the Psalmist becomes a transmitter of religious truth only through personal experience and a willingness to acknowledge the darker side of human reality.

The above examples help to remind us that the Psalms have played a role in the lives of communities and individuals for thousands of years. Whoever comes to such a Psalm may find in it either a personal or collective meaning. It is only in our 'post-enlightenment' world that we are able to stand back from the text itself and analyse it in quite such a detached manner, and recognize the different ways in which it has been seen by others. And the more such a Psalm seems to have a formal context the harder it is to imagine the original emotion that drove the writer to create it – 'imagine' because we can never really 'discover' it. Perhaps our distance also makes it difficult to identify with it ourselves. It takes another sort of imagination, or act of will, to enter the Psalmist's world and make his (why not her?) feelings our own. And yet, in this case, the cry, '*eili eili lamah azavtáni*', 'My God, my God, why have You forsaken me?', with its despair and anger, its intimacy and sense of loss, speaks to our own sense of ultimate loneliness. We are alone, however much we are supported by the love and companionship of others, and never more so than when facing crises that undermine our sense of security and self-worth, or when confronting the inevitability of our own death. From the Psalmist we know that God 'answers', but how or what is not revealed – for that is what each of us has to discover for ourselves.

8

Did My Mother Conceive Me in Sin?
Psalm 51

What leads us to pay special attention to one of the Psalms? It may arise out of the need of the moment, or the accident of certain words resonating in particular circumstances. Yet neither was the case with Psalm 51. In fact it was one that I had studied many years before and sort of given up on. In my student years I had come upon the phrase 'in sin did my mother conceive me . . .' and a kind of defensive Jewish reaction took over. This was clearly used as a proof text for a particular Christian belief, and 'Jews don't do original sin'! Since this was the only verse in the Hebrew Bible that might be used as a proof text for such a concept, it clearly had to be understood or interpreted in a different way.

Having revisited the Psalm many years later for reasons I shall mention below, I looked up a number of Christian commentaries just to see whether my impression was in fact correct. Most of the recent commentaries seemed to be less interested in following that broader theological line of tradition, focusing instead on the experience of the Psalmist himself and the rhetorical way he was using the phrase. But Artur Weiser goes some way down that anticipated route:

It is the tragedy of man that he is born into a world full of sin. The environment in which a child grows up is already saturated with sin and temptation; and when the child learns to distinguish between good and evil he discovers already in himself a natural tendency of his will that is at variance with the will of God . . . No longer does he see only particular transgressions; rather, all particular sins point back to that demoniac disposition of self-willed humanity addicted to self-glorification which is naturally ingrained in its own nature and threatens to lead it at any time into temptation. The poet realizes that these profound relations between sin and human nature operate in his own life.[1]

If that dark vision of life came pretty close to what I was looking for, in order to counter it, the following comment from the Jerusalem Bible was reassuringly clear on the subject – 'reassuring' in the sense that I could comfortably refute it 'from a Jewish perspective'.

> Man is born in a state of impurity, Jb 14:4 +, cf. Pr 20:9, which is an implicit recognition of his tendency to evil, Gn 8:21. This basic impurity is here pleaded as a mitigating circumstance, cf. I K 8:46, which God should take into account. The doctrine of original sin will be proposed explicitly, Rm 5:12–21, in connection with the revelation of redemption by Jesus Christ.[2]

Of course there are any number of ways in which Christians approach this subject, from fully embracing it to challenging or rejecting it, but to explore that subject is beyond the scope of this book. Nevertheless we will examine the verse itself in its biblical context in more detail later.

My reason for returning to the Psalm at all has been my ongoing work on Jewish liturgy and the need to study commentaries to accompany this. The Psalm itself as a whole does not feature in the Jewish liturgical calendar except when read by those who regularly recite the complete Book of Psalms as part of their own religious practice. But one verse does feature quite prominently in the Jewish prayerbook. The central prayer in the Jewish liturgy – indeed it is known, among other names, as *hatefillah, the* prayer – is the Amidah, or 'standing prayer'. It is also known as the '18 benedictions', though, perhaps inevitably, given the complex development of Jewish liturgy, it actually contains 19 of them! The prayer is addressed to God by the congregation, and throughout, those who are praying recite a text expressed in the first-person plural: 'grace *us* with knowledge', 'bring *us* back to You', 'forgive *us*, our Father, for we have sinned' – yes, Jews sin as well, but differently! However, there is a Psalm verse recited before the Amidah begins, and one at the end as part of a brief meditation after the formal conclusion. The former is a quotation from our Psalm, 'Lord, open my lips and my mouth shall declare Your praise' (Ps. 51.17); the latter comes from Psalm 1915: 'May the words of my mouth and the meditation of my heart be acceptable to You, O Lord, my Rock and my Redeemer.'

I became curious about the choice of these two psalm quotations that bracket the formal prayer, and traditionally are recited quietly to oneself, though often sung in 'Reform' Jewish services. Why were they chosen? Since both are expressed in the first-person singular, I assume that they offer the reader a personal way into the collective prayer that is about to be recited, a kind of private commitment to the words that follow, and then a private moment of reflection at the end. But why these particular verses? What thought did they bring with them? The study of Rabbinic texts sensitizes us to the frequent use of quotations and the fact that the quoted verse often brings along with it the fuller context from which it was taken and not just the verse alone. Indeed to understand its meaning fully in this new location that background may be enormously important. So I looked up these two quotations and, for the first one, found myself back in Psalm 51, but with a new question: What is the function of this particular verse within the Psalm?

We have studied Psalm 19 in chapter 6, and might already note at this point that both the latter part of Psalm 19 and the whole of Psalm 51 include an acknowledgement of the sins, potential or actual, committed by an individual, and point to how reconciliation with God might be achieved. In the immediate context of the Amidah they complement one another, reflecting the intimacy of our relationship with God. Before reciting the Amidah we invite God to open our lips and give us the appropriate words to recite; after the Amidah we ask that our own words and inner thoughts be acceptable to God. It is as if we have become so shaped by the will of God through the prayer that our spontaneous words align themselves with God's wishes.

Having decided to examine Psalm 51, the usual process of repeated reading, of using my trusted multi-coloured highlighters to help pinpoint repetitions of key words, of trying to find some kind of structure, swung into operation, with the results we will now examine.

But first we need the text of the Psalm as a whole:

1. *For the Choirmaster*
2. A Psalm of David when Nathan the prophet came to him after he had been with Bathsheba.
3. Show me grace, God, in Your mercy,
   in your great compassion blot out my transgressions.
4. Wash me free from my guilt,
   and purify me from my sin.
5. For my transgressions I know too well
   and my sin is always before me.

6. Against You, You only, have I sinned,
   and done what is evil in Your sight.
   Therefore, You are right in Your sentence,
   and pure in Your judgement.

7. Even if I was born in guilt,
   and my mother conceived me in sin,

8. behold! the truth is what You desire within me
   and in my innermost place You show me wisdom.

9. Purge me with hyssop, and I shall be pure,
   wash me, and I shall be whiter than snow.

10. Let me hear joy and gladness,
    so that the bones You crushed dance again.

11. Turn Your gaze away from my sins
    and blot out my guilt.

12. Create a pure heart for me, God,
    and put a firm and steadfast spirit in me.

13. Do not cast me away from Your presence,
    or take Your holy spirit from me.

14. Give me back the joy of Your salvation
    and let a willing spirit uphold me.

15. Then I will teach transgressors Your ways
    so that sinners may return to You.

16. Keep me from bloodshed, O God.
    You are the God who saves me.
    My tongue shall ring out Your justice.

17. Lord, open my lips
    and my mouth shall declare Your praise.

18. For You desire no sacrifice, or I would give it,
    burnt offerings You do not want.

19. God's sacrifices are a humbled spirit,
    a broken and a contrite heart You will not despise.

20. Do good to Zion in Your good favour,
    rebuild the walls of Jerusalem.

21. Then You will desire right sacrifices,
    in burnt offerings and whole burnt offerings,
    then bulls will be offered on Your altar.

The overall structure of the Psalm seems fairly clear. There is the superscription linking it to David's affair with Bathsheba. The story, told in 2 Samuel 11–12, tells how David tried to cover up the affair and Bathsheba's pregnancy by encouraging her husband, Uriah the Hittite, to return from the war and sleep with his wife. When Uriah refused, either out of simple loyalty to his fellow troops on the battlefield or because he knew the truth, David arranged for him to be killed in battle. Nathan the prophet subsequently confronted David, who acknowledged his guilt and accepted punishment. In a real sense the story does not end there, because David's family life was subsequently to be haunted by similar tragic betrayals and deaths. Although these Psalm superscriptions are generally deemed to be later editorial additions, this is one of the few that fits directly into the narratives about David.

The body of the text that follows, from verse 3 (according to the Hebrew numbering) to 19 is an extended confession of sin and guilt, followed by the hope for a purification and renewal of his relationship with God.

At the end come two final verses that seem to most commentators to be wildly out of place. From the language of a penitent individual, who suggests that private prayers are an adequate replacement for sacrifices, the verses talk about the physical rebuilding of Jerusalem and the restoration of sacrifices in the Temple, as if in conscious contradiction of the sentiments expressed immediately before (v. 19).

SIN, TRANSGRESSION AND GUILT

There does seem to be a major turning point in the centre of the Psalm at verse 12. Before it the reader is conscious of the overwhelming concern about sin, after it the emphasis switches to a new heart and spirit. This general impression is borne out by examining the language in more detail, and indeed the distribution of certain key words within the section. Thus within verses 3–11, the root made up of the three letters *chet, tet, alef* (*chata*) occurs six times. The root itself means something like 'missing the target', 'failing', but it becomes one of the commonest, and perhaps weakest, words for 'sin'. It is also invisibly present, at least in the translation, in verse 9, in the word 'purge', which is another grammatical form of the same verb – literally, 'de-sin me'. (It sometimes happens that a Hebrew word has a particular meaning but in another grammatical form the exact opposite. Three times we find the word *avon*, derived from the root *ayyin, vav* and *heh*, which means 'to be crooked', that comes to mean habitual wrongdoing, but also by extension the guilt that may be attached to it, hence the translation 'guilt' above. Twice we find the root *peh*, *shin* and *ayyin*, the verb *pasha*, which, in its 'secular usage' means rebellion against a sovereign power. It is probably the strongest of the terms for sin, and means doing something precisely because you know it is wrong. Here it is translated as 'transgressions'.)

The use of these three verbs, and nouns derived from them, reminds us forcibly of Exodus 34.7, the text we considered in some detail in chapter 5. God reveals to Moses the divine attributes, including the forgiving of *avon vafesha v'hatta'ah*, 'guilt, transgression and sin'. The same passage also speaks of God as being 'gracious', 'full of mercy' and 'compassionate' (Ex. 34.6), all three of which terms are evoked in verse 3. It is as if David, in his distress, summons up these merciful and forgiving elements in God's covenant as a means of defence and rescue from the consequences of his actions. Or, to put it another way, the author of the Psalm used the opportunity to write a meditation on these 'attributes', which are similarly explored creatively in Psalm 103.7–10, Jonah 4.2 and in a number of other places.

But even this small section can be seen to have its own structure. Verses 3–6 are direct pleas for purification from his sin, as are verses 9–11. Between them lies the verse that was our starting point, verse 7, and its companion verse 8, which are often better understood as a kind of self-justification. Both sentences begin with the same short Hebrew word *hen*, which may not be noticeable in translations, but is striking in the Hebrew text. It is understood by some to be a variation on the demonstrative particle *hinnei*, usually translated as 'behold!', 'see!', which has the effect of putting the reader into the direct perspective of the writer or character – see what is happening before our eyes! Others see it as simply emphasizing what follows. But suppose we take seriously the fact that both sentences have the same opening word. At the very least it would suggest that the repetition is a way of connecting them, but how?

Here I must confess to committing a scholarly sin, that of wanting to find a particular result from my research before I even began. However, the hunt proved disappointing, at least in the first instance. There are a few other cases where successive verses begin with *hen*, though no obvious causal relationship seems to exist between them. But there is a second meaning of *hen* which is well documented in the 'bible' of my generation of biblical scholars: *Gesenius' Hebrew*

Grammar as Edited and Enlarged by the late E. Kautzsch, Second English Edition, Oxford, 1910. This formidable book of 598 pages is a treasury of information on every aspect of Hebrew grammar. It is so detailed in its collection of examples and proofs that it is unreadable for any length of time – but, like Fowler's *Modern English Usage*, it is a great book to dip into for enlightenment and enjoyable bewilderment. Gesenius attests to the meaning 'if' for the word *hen*, 'always with a *waw* apodosis following'. (To translate: It opens an 'if that is the case . . . then this follows' kind of statement; *waw*, pronounced *vav*, being the Hebrew letter often translated as 'and' that introduces the second part of the sentence.) I got particularly excited to discover two sets of adjacent sentences in the Book of Job each beginning with *hen*, which Gesenius indicated were such 'if . . . then' cases. The RSV translation does not seem to recognize this, treating both cases as 'behold' in the first example:

> Lo, he passes by me, and I see him not;
> he moves on, but I do not perceive him.
> Behold he snatches away, who can hinder him?
> Who will say to him, 'What doest thou?' (Job 9.11–12)

Other translations are similar, but the Jerusalem Bible, without using 'if', follows Gesenius' lead:

> Were he to pass me, I should not see him,
> Nor detect his stealthy movement.
> Were he to snatch a prize, who could prevent him
> Or dare to say, 'What are you doing?'

However, the RSV recognizes *hen* as 'if' in the second occurrence in Job 12.14–15.

> If he tears down, none can rebuild;
> if he shuts a man in, none can open.
> If he withholds the waters, they dry up;
> if he sends them out, they overwhelm the land.

Now this gives me 50 per cent of the solution I am looking for, as verse 7 would now read:

> If I was born in guilt,
> and my mother conceived me in sin . . .

Such a statement becomes a kind of *reductio ad absurdum* of his degree of wickedness – not only am I bad, I was even bad before I was born! But that still leaves us with no 'then . . .' part of the sentence, unless the following sentence, with its introduction through the same word *hen*, could provide it. This time the word *hen* would have to be closer to the meaning of 'behold!' So the complete sentence would read, as translated above, something like:

> Even if I was born in guilt,
> and my mother conceived me in sin,
> behold!, the truth is what You desire within me
> and in my inmost heart You show me wisdom.

That is to say, he cannot call upon some past sin involved in his birth to provide an excuse for his present lapse. However, to translate the second *hen* differently from the first, just to make the point, is questionable! But it may be that this kind of repetition of *hen* was a way of establishing such a sentence, the 'if' part being introduced by the first one, the 'then' part by the second. Certainly such a construction helps to integrate verse 8 that otherwise stands alone, isolated from the surrounding verses. This combination underscores the Psalmist's recognition that no excuse or evasion is acceptable to God, who wants an acknowledgement of the truth if forgiveness is to be possible.

If such a grammatical construct seems a bit forced, though I think it deserves consideration, nevertheless a similar interpretation of the intention of the verse as a form of exaggeration, on different textual grounds, is given by Meir Weiss in his study of classical interpretations.

> We have here neither self-justification nor excuse, neither pretext nor argument nor explanation. No attempt to minimize the seriousness of the sin, but, on the contrary, emphasis on the greatness of the sin is expressed in this verse – not a blurring of personal responsibility but rather the accentuation of it . . . The Psalmist does not intend to give a theoretical lecture on man's corrupt nature, but rather to pour out his heart in a personal confession, a confession of his own sin, which weighs so unbearably on his soul; he feels so deeply the greatness of his iniquity, the weight of his sin, that it seems to him that not only from birth but from his very conception, when he was but a seed, his sin was already

with him. The poetically exaggerated character of this verse –
from which nothing can be learned for dogmatic or theological
purposes – was perceived by Meiri [1249–1316]: 'All my days
from the time I was born, I have done only wicked deeds, since
my very creation and conception. [The Psalmist] said this by way
of exaggeration, as in the verse "and you were called a trans-
gressor from the womb" (Isaiah 48.8)'.[3]

Before looking at the second half of the Psalm, another one of the
author's devices is worth noting. Throughout we find language which
echoes the Temple cult, most obviously with the word 'sacrifice' in
verses 18, 19 and 21. But three other terms dominate the first half,
all of which belong to the language of ritual purification. In verse 3
comes *machah*, 'blot out', in verse 4 *kabas*, 'wash', and *taher*,
'purify'. By now it should be no surprise to learn that when the three
words reappear later in the Psalm it is in the reverse order: verse 9,
'purify', followed by 'wash', so that the last word that actually
completes the process of removing the sin, transgression and guilt,
is 'blot out' at the end of verse 11.

3.	blot out	
4.	wash	
		purify
9.		purify
		wash
11.	blot out	

It is as if two 'systems' are being evoked that would help the Psalmist
regain his relationship with God – the cultic forms of ritual purification and the appeal to God's love and mercy. The two systems
mesh with one another through yet another term, *chafatz*, 'to wish'
or 'desire', which actually draws together the first and second sections and the concluding verses. Thus in verse 8 the Psalmist recognizes that God 'desires' the truth. It is precisely the Psalmist's
willingness to admit his guilt that opens up the door for God's mercy
to be evoked. This builds on our reading of verses 7 and 8. No
excuse or justification based on his birth is acceptable. What God
desires is honesty and integrity. This explains the apparent rejection
of sacrifices in the second part of the Psalm.

> 18. For You *desire* no sacrifice, or I would give it,
>   burnt offerings You do not want.

19. God's sacrifices are a humbled spirit,
    a broken and a contrite heart You will not despise.

On this reading it is not sacrifices that are desired by God but a
significant internal change, one symbolized by a broken and contrite
heart. That would seem to abolish the sacrificial system entirely, or
at least in relation to purification from sin. But the closing verses,
which remain puzzling additions, do repeat for the third time the
theme of what it is exactly that God 'desires'.

21. Then You will *desire* right sacrifices,
    in burnt offerings and whole burnt offerings;
    then bulls will be offered on Your altar.

'Right sacrifices' might simply mean sacrifices that have been carried
out according to proper procedures. However, the word translated
as 'right' is the term *tzedek* which is more commonly used in the
sense of 'justice' and 'righteousness'. Which takes us back to verse
6, where the Psalmist acknowledges that any punishment that comes
upon him is 'right' or 'just', precisely because he has sinned.

6. Against You, You only, have I sinned,
   and done what is evil in Your sight.
   Therefore, You are *right* in Your sentence,
   and pure in Your judgement.

The mechanical act of sacrifice alone is not what is desired by God,
but if the sinner acknowledges his wrongdoing and is truly 'broken
in spirit', then the physical and the spiritual sacrifices together are
what God desires and will accept.

A PURE HEART AND A STEADFAST SPIRIT

The second half of the Psalm takes this idea of fulfilling what God
desires to an even deeper level. Two of our words for sinning from
the first half, *pasha* and *chata*, reappear, but this time referring to
others whom the Psalmist will teach God's ways.

15. Then I will teach transgressors Your ways
    so that sinners may return to You.

The seemingly neutral phrase 'Your ways' may also be intended in
quite a precise sense. When God revealed the divine 'attributes' of

mercy and compassion mentioned above, it was in response to Moses' request to show him 'Your ways' (Ex. 33.13). Since this phrase also features in other places where the attributes are explored (Psalm 103.7), this may well be an intentional echo.

Nevertheless it is a different set of terms that dominate this section. Three times in successive verses comes the word *ruach*, which means 'wind', but also 'breath', and hence becomes internalized as 'spirit' or 'life force'. The word that accompanies it is *lev*, 'heart', which means the intellect or mind, including emotions. At this transitional point the Psalmist asks for a heart that is 'pure', following up the cultic language he has used in verses 4 and 9. But this heart has to be 'created', *bara*, the word used at the creation of the universe in the first verse of the Bible. Alongside the truth that God desires to exist 'within' the Psalmist, together with wisdom in his 'innermost place' (v. 8), now a 'steadfast spirit' will be in him (v. 12). The *ruach*, precisely because it expresses the invisible force of the wind, can be both within and without an individual, reflecting at times our 'mood'. Thus a spirit of prophecy can descend upon someone, or a spirit of jealousy, or even madness. The Psalmist will request that the spirit of God's holiness no more depart from him, and that a willing spirit sustain him.

As in the first section, these two 'key words', 'spirit' and 'heart', reappear in the latter part of the section, forming a bracket around some central verses. As we have already noted, verse 19 describes the kind of spirit and heart that will be acceptable to God:

> 19. God's sacrifices are a humbled spirit,
>   a broken and a contrite heart You will not despise.

The verses in between finally bring us back to our starting point and the meaning of verse 17. In its context it seems to be the logical, if daring, conclusion of a series of thoughts. In verse 15, this newly reborn sinner seems to take on the missionary zeal that is not unfamiliar to converts to any cause – he wishes to teach other sinners the truth that he has experienced about God's merciful ways. If only God will rescue him from the guilt associated with shedding blood, then his tongue will sing out about God's righteousness. From tongue we move in the next verse to mouth and lips, as the former sinner now becomes transformed into someone who speaks for God. But the move is even more daring, because it is God who will open his lips so that the words that come out are literally those of God.

That must be the reason for another radical change that occurs in this verse. Until now, and indeed subsequently, the name used for God is *elohim* (vv. 3, 12, 16, 19), a general term for God that appears frequently in the Psalms. Yet at this crucial point the Psalmist addresses God with a different name, *adonai*. Here a careful distinction must be made. The four-letter name of God, YHWH, the term used to depict Israel's intimate relationship with God, was not to be pronounced. Instead Rabbinic tradition from the earliest period has substituted a word, also made up of four consonants, based upon the word *adon*, meaning 'lord'. Hence the usual reading in Jewish circles of *adonai* whenever YHWH appears. In this particular case, however, it is the actual letters *alef*, *dalet*, *nun* and *yod* that are used and not the substitute for YHWH. Apart from anything else, this is a reminder of the complexity of the use of the different divine names and titles and the fact that the choice of name in any given context requires us to seek out the particular meaning. Clearly a contrast is intended with *elohim* at this crucial point.

The likeliest explanation is that precisely here, where the Psalmist evokes the most intimate possible relationship with God, he turns to a word that can be seen to express the possibility of this intimacy, of the immanence of God within his own individual life. (A similar switching between the use of YHWH and *adonai* similarly occurs in Isaiah 6, where the former reflects God's transcendence and 'otherness', while the latter is the term used when the prophet claims to 'see' (v. 1) and 'hear' (v. 8) and address God directly (v. 11).) So perhaps it is the very unexpectedness of this switch, the extraordinary intimacy of God speaking through the Psalmist, that led to its choice as the meditation before the Amidah.

Yet there is another dimension that may also have played a role. We have seen throughout the Psalm how it plays with the theme of sacrifice and the possibility that honest confession and a change in personality and behaviour could be an appropriate substitute for them. The Amidah prayer itself actually addresses that issue, for it was the central part of the daily liturgy instituted by the Rabbis as a temporary replacement for the Temple sacrifice for as long as the Temple was not rebuilt. Indeed the times of recital, including the additional occasions on Sabbath and Festivals, coincided with the times of the sacrifices in the Temple. Moreover, the 18 benedictions contained expressions of hope for the restoration of the Temple. If the Psalm verse indeed carries with it its entire context in this new location, then the issue of outer sacrifices or inner change are carried over into the daily prayers of the Jewish people.

There remains another inner language connection that is worth noting. Verse 19 speaks of a heart that is 'broken and contrite'. The literal translation of the last word is 'crushed' from a root *dakah*. The same word was actually used earlier in verse 10, which speaks of the bones that God has 'crushed', that will now dance in praise of God. This repetition, that brings the two verses together, emphasizes the difference between the outer, the physical body, and the inner, the spirit and heart.

THE CLOSING VERSES

What do we make of the closing two verses? We have already noted that they bring together the problematic relationship between sacrifices and righteous behaviour. A crude suggestion is simply that someone deeply committed to the Temple and its cult was so horrified by verse 19, which seemed to set the ritual totally aside, that he added a plea for its restoration so that the sacrifices in their fullness could be restored, even at the cost of seemingly undermining the powerful ending in verse 19. The medieval Jewish commentators, reading it as the words of David, saw it as his plea for the future building of the Temple by his son Solomon. But Abraham Ibn Ezra, who combined the developed rationalism of Islamic Spain with a genuine, if somewhat questioning, piety, was a bit more ambiguous in his commentary.

> One of the Spanish sages said that these last two verses were added by one of the pious ones in Babel, who fell down before God and prayed this Psalm – and he had to say this because it was not known that Zion would be the chosen location [for the building of the Temple] till David's old age. But it is also correct that it was said through the 'holy spirit' [i.e. David could write about the Temple being in Zion through divine inspiration].

I began with the problem of the verse, 'In sin did my mother conceive me . . .' and it is appropriate to return to it at the end. I have already indicated that the superscription ascribing the Psalm to David, following the denunciation by the prophet Nathan of his affair with Bathsheba, may well be a later addition, but that the Psalm fits in well with the narrative about the event. Perhaps it fits even better, for it is hard to resist a Freudian touch. When David points to the very act of intercourse as sinful and speaks of his own birth, it is a small step to read this as a projection onto his origins of his own guilt about intercourse with Bathsheba.

A child resulted from that union, one that was doomed to die. Famously David's behaviour was seen as most peculiar by his courtiers. 'When the child was alive you fasted and wept, but when the child died you arose and ate bread!' To which David replied, 'While the child still lived I fasted and wept, for I thought, perhaps the Lord will be gracious and the child will live. But now he is dead, why should I fast? Can I restore him again? I will go to him, he will not return to me' (2 Sam. 12.21–23). If David is the metaphorical child of that event, then he too was doomed to die had God not created a new heart and spirit within him. Reason enough to acknowledge that if God would open his lips, his mouth would tell God's praise.

9

'The Musical!': Psalm 118

Some Psalms lose their power and unique quality because of over-familiarity. Or better said, their frequent use may dull or even distort our awareness of their content. I suspect that this is the fate of Psalm 118 in Jewish circles. It is sung regularly during religious festivals as a part of the Hallel Psalms (see the introduction to Psalm 115 on page 148f.). As a result it is subsumed within this broader context and its individuality is effectively lost in the liturgical unit. Moreover, the way that it is divided up in this context, different parts being read, chanted, repeated or sung, depending on the choral arrangement, affects any apparent inner logic it may contain. The individual passages or verses that need to be stressed within the liturgy serve that particular function within the Hallel as a whole, but the integrity of the Psalm itself risks becoming a secondary concern. Needless to say, my own reading is also subject to a similar critique – the reader finds what he or she wishes to find depending on the method employed, the assumptions made and the skills brought to bear.

The Psalm itself is fascinating because of the light it appears to throw on ritual practices in the Jerusalem Temple. Within it can be found repeated phrases that seem to reflect antiphonal singing by a song leader and choir (vv. 1–4, 10–12, 25). There are phrases that suggest a formal request on the part of an individual or group to enter the Temple, with equally formal responses (vv. 19, 20, 26). There are even apparently stage directions for the procession 'up to the horns of the altar' (v. 27) that appear to have slipped into the text from the notes of the officiating priest. The overall context appears to be an occasion when an individual offers thanksgiving to God. The precise reason is not clear. Some view it as being the result of a military victory, or part of the celebration of a pilgrimage to Jerusalem, the Festival of Tabernacles (Sukkot) being singled out as the particular event because of the reference to boughs of trees being carried in procession. Certainly the inclusion of this Psalm as the last of the Hallel Psalms would reinforce the idea that one of the Festivals was its original context.

In the following translation the tetragrammaton, the four-letter name of God, YHWH, is translated as 'Lord' in the conventional way. We will see later how other divine names are translated.

1. Give thanks to the Lord who is good,
   whose love is everlasting.
2. Let Israel now say:
   'whose love is everlasting'.
3. Let the house of Aaron now say:
   'whose love is everlasting'.
4. Let all who fear God now say:
   'whose love is everlasting'.

5. Out of the straits I called on the Almighty.
   The Almighty answered me with great enlargement.
6. The Lord is for me, I shall not fear.
   What can people do to me?
7. The Lord is for me, amongst my helpers,
   so I confront those who hate me!

8. It is better to trust in the Lord than to rely on people.
9. It is better to trust in the Lord than to rely on leaders.

10. All nations surrounded me –
    by the name of the Lord I cut them down.
11. They swarmed and surrounded me –
    by the name of the Lord I cut them down.
12. They swarmed around me like bees,
    they were quenched like a fire among thorns –
    by the name of the Lord I cut them down.

13. You pressed me so that I nearly fell,
    but the Lord helped me.
14. The Almighty is my strength and song,
    always there to save me.
15. Shouts of joy and salvation
    are in the tents of the just:
    'The Lord's right hand works mightily!

16. The Lord's right hand is raised!
    The Lord's right hand works mightily!'
17. I shall not die, but live
    and declare the acts of the Almighty.

18. The Almighty has taught me sharply
    but has not surrendered me to death.
19. Open the gates of justice for me,
    I shall enter them and thank the Almighty.
20. This is the gate of the Lord,
    the just may enter in.

21. I thank You, for You answered me,
    it was You who saved me.
22. A stone the builders rejected
    has become the corner-stone itself.
23. Through the Lord this came about,
    this wonder to our eyes.
24. This is the day the Lord has made,
    let us be glad and rejoice on it.
25. Lord, we beseech You, save us now!
    Lord, we beseech You, let us prosper now!

26. Blessed is the one who comes in the name of the Lord,
    we bless you from the house of the Lord.

27. God is the Lord who gives us light.
    (Form the procession with the branches
    up to the horns of the altar.)

28. You are my God and I thank You.
    My God, I praise you!
29. Give thanks to the Lord who is good,
    'whose love is everlasting'.

The first thing that struck me on trying to get to grips with this
Psalm is the multiplicity of different voices it contains. Unravelling
these seemed to offer a way into the internal world of the Psalm
itself. Some voices, as we have already indicated, seem easier to
distinguish than others. There is clearly a chorus that repeats certain

key phrases: 'whose love is everlasting', 'by the name of the Lord
I cut them down', 'The Lord's right hand works mightily!'

It would seem likely that a few other cases of repetitions could
also be ascribed to them, such as verses 8–9:

> 8. It is better to trust in the Lord than to rely on people.
> 9. It is better to trust in the Lord than to rely on leaders.

Or verse 25:

> 25. Lord, we beseech You, save us now!
>   Lord, we beseech You, let us prosper now!

There would also appear to be a 'choir-leader' who invites these
responses in some cases, though it is not clear whether to distinguish
this figure, who may play a relatively minor role, from another voice
that would appear to be that of the officiating priest.

Thus the person who opens the Psalm, 'Give thanks to the Lord
who is good', seems directly related to the choir, but is it the same
one who speaks at the dramatic point where the Temple doors are
opened and the individual or procession is ushered in?

> 26. Blessed is the one who comes in the name of the Lord,
>   we bless you from the house of the Lord.

In the same vein, some of the 'running commentary' on the events
(such as vv. 22–24) could equally be choral or the words of an
officiating figure:

> 22. A stone the builders rejected
>   has become the corner-stone itself.
> 23. Through the Lord this came about,
>   this wonder to our eyes.
> 24. This is the day the Lord has made,
>   let us be glad and rejoice on it.

However we might differentiate the particular roles, all of these
passages clearly belong to the liturgical apparatus of the Temple.
They either comment on events, or evoke a response, or respond
collectively, presumably with full musical accompaniment.

There is, however, another voice, equally distinctive in most cases,
that of the person who seems to be the subject of all this choral
attention. In fact the continual switching between the individual
speaker and the choral apparatus is quite theatrical, even operatic.

When I have taught this Psalm I have usually allotted different voices to the different parts, and even at this rather basic level of performance the effect is powerful. It is a reminder that this is one aspect of the Bible, its own inner aesthetic sensibility and rhetorical, even theatrical, power, that is often neglected.

By isolating the verses that speak in the first-person singular, a distinctive voice and coherent story emerges:

5. Out of the straits I called on the Almighty.
    The Almighty answered me with great enlargement.
6. The Lord is for me, I shall not fear.
    What can people do to me?
7. The Lord is for me, amongst my helpers,
    so I confront those who hate me!
10a. All nations surrounded me –
11a. They swarmed and surrounded me –
12ab. They swarmed around me like bees,
        they were quenched like a fire among thorns –
13. You pressed me so that I nearly fell,
    but the Lord helped me.
14. The Almighty is my strength and song,
    always there to save me.
17. I shall not die, but live
    and declare the acts of the Almighty.
18. The Almighty has taught me sharply
    but has not surrendered me to death.
19. Open the gates of justice for me,
    I shall enter them and thank the Almighty.
21. I thank You, for You answered me,
    it was You who saved me.
28. You are my God and I thank You.
    My God, I praise you!

I have my doubts about whether 10a, 11a or 12ab belong to the voice of the individual, since they are embedded in a choral response. But in fact they point to the artifice of this Psalm as a finished piece of composition. The 'I' voice we have isolated offers a coherent account of an individual experience: of danger met by trust in God which was vindicated by rescue and hence the desire to express gratitude. The text we have isolated could stand alone as an effective prayer or, indeed, Psalm. However, the incorporation of this individual voice within the apparatus of the Temple changes the nature of the experience from an individual one to a collective one, and transforms the individual speaker, telling of his own experience, into a performer in this ritualized event. Moreover, what could be a private experience of danger, in verses 10–12, precisely because of the added choral voice becomes instead a collective statement, presumably about a national deliverance. The 'I' of the individual becomes the 'I' of the nation.

This tension in verses 10–12 leads to the possibility that the 'I' in question is in fact a representative figure of the nation as a whole, namely the king. Since Israel's kings, with the exception of David and Solomon, are rarely credited with literary skills, this would suggest that even this voice has been artificially created, or that a genuine individual prayer has been seconded to this new context. But whatever the origins, the performance aspect now seems to dominate in terms of the Psalm as a whole. Nevertheless there are elements in the 'individual voice' that deserve further examination.

What is often a common starting point for me in analysing a Psalm is the use of the names of God, and there is a striking example at the heart of this one which I have tried to preserve in the translation. In fact if we had started by addressing the names of God, we would have isolated many of the verses belonging to the individual voice on these grounds alone. Verse 5 introduces us to the name *yah*, translated throughout as 'Almighty'. It is a divine name that tends to appear in early poetic texts (e.g. Ex. 15.2; 17.6), depending on how one dates such passages, and in other poetic texts (e.g. S. of Sol. 8.6). It is most familiar, of course, as the closing name of God in 'Hallelujah', 'Praise God!', and indeed can be found in a number of Psalms, associated with the verb *hallal*, 'to praise'. Its origins are debated – is it, for example, a shortened form of the four-letter name YHWH or an original name, perhaps a kind of shout? What is significant for our Psalm is its location in verses 5 (twice), 14, 17, 18 and 19, all of which belong to the individual speaker. However, the individual voice also uses the name YHWH ('The Lord' in our translation) as does the 'choir' throughout. At two other points at the end different divine names are introduced. Verse 27 begins with the divine name '*el*', here translated as 'God', placed beside the name YHWH, though their relationship here is not clear. Similarly in the last 'individual' voice, verse 28, the speaker talks of God as '*eli*', 'my God', and then as '*elohai*', also translated here as 'my

God'. Both the term *el* and *elohim* are general terms for God – and the Psalmist may have had to use them in part because it is not possible to attach 'my' to the name *yah*.

Why this use of the name *yah*? Perhaps it offers a clue to the early origins of this part of the Psalm, or a conscious attempt to give it an ancient resonance. But what may have inspired the use, however, is that one of the sentences reproduces a verse that appears in two other locations in the Hebrew Bible. It is always difficult to explain such cases. If something appears in two places, is there a causal connection? If so, does A quote B, or B quote A, or do both borrow from a common source, or has an editor inserted the same passage twice? Most of such positions can be argued and justified. My own feeling in this particular case is that the Psalmist has borrowed his verse from elsewhere, indeed has consciously built the words of the 'individual' on this original source. The passage in question comes at the beginning of the 'Song at the Sea', Exodus 15, the triumphant song sung by Moses and the children of Israel, and subsequently by Miriam, after the crossing of the Sea of Reeds and delivery from Pharaoh and his army.

> The Almighty is my strength and song,
> always there to save me. (Ex. 15.2)

(The other occasion, slightly modified by adding the name YHWH, occurs in Isaiah 12.2 where it is introduced by *kee*, meaning 'because', which suggests that it is consciously introduced as a quotation. The context is a hymn of praise to God, a doxology, which closes that section of the Book of Isaiah.)

Were this the only echo of Exodus 15 in our Psalm we could note it but pay little more attention to it. However, a second near-quotation from the same source occurs at the end of the Psalm in the 'individual' closing statement of gratitude.

> 28. You are my God (*eli*) and I thank You.
>   My God (*elohai*), I praise you!

Compare this with the second part of our verse from Exodus 15:

> This is my God (*eli*) and I glorify Him,
> The God (*elohei*) of my father, and I praise him.

In both cases the word translated as 'praise' is from the root *room*, literally to 'elevate'.

For a further linkage between the two texts is the imagery of God's 'right hand', raised in defence of his people, compare verses 15–16 in our Psalm:

> 15c. 'The Lord's right hand works mightily!
> 16. The Lord's right hand is raised!
> The Lord's right hand works mightily!'

with Exodus 15.6:

> Your right hand, O Lord, is full of power!
> Your right hand, O Lord, destroys the enemy.

One could easily imagine a poet composing this individual song of thanksgiving as a meditation on this verse in Exodus, associating his (or his nation's) rescue from another military danger with that legendary event, celebrated in the Exodus passage. Thus the Psalmist inserts his own text within the two halves of Exodus 15.2.

Whether this gives us an insight into the actual composition of this part of the Psalm or not, the echo of the 'Song at the Sea' is clearly present. It may be that a second stage was the 'arrangement' and orchestration of this individual thanksgiving prayer within the liturgical framework of the Temple. If so, the 'choruses' could be responses to particular elements within the 'individual' passage. On the wish of the individual to thank God (vv. 19, 21, 28) are built the choral 'thanksgiving' verses at the beginning and end (vv. 1, 29). In response to the rhetorical question 'If God is with me what can people (literally *adam*, man) do to me?' (v. 6), the choir responds 'It is better to trust in God than in people' (*adam*) (vv. 8, 9). In verse 5 the individual 'called on the Almighty' by name and the chorus sings of defeating the enemy 'in the name of God' (vv. 10–12). In verse 19 the individual asks that the 'gates of justice' be opened for him, and, presumably, the gatekeeper responds in the next verse: 'This is the gate of the Lord, the just may enter in.'

As a finished text the Psalm works as a marvellous choral offering that holds together well. However, there is a kind of tension between the 'individual voice' and the chorus, if only because of the inter- actions between them at various points – particularly with the request to enter through the 'gates of justice'. But my attention was drawn to a different kind of tension within the Psalm through a particular encounter. Very briefly, since I have recorded the story in detail elsewhere,[1] at an interfaith discussion in Germany I was partnered with a Lutheran minister from Bethlehem, Dr Mitri Raheb. Our subject was this Psalm and I had offered as an introduction this distinction between the individual voice and the chorus. Dr Raheb focused on the opening words of the individual voice:

> 5. Out of the straits I called on the Almighty.
> The Almighty answered me with great enlargement.

The Hebrew reads literally 'out of the *meitzar*', a word that means a narrow, restricted place, whether confined by enemies or circumstances. God answers the Psalmist with '*merchav*', literally 'a broad space'. Dr Raheb talked of his situation as a Palestinian of being closed in, restricted in his movements. But while he could identify very closely with the situation of the 'individual' in the Psalm, he had problems with the 'choir'.

> It is military language – the enemy will be cut off in the name of God. How much violence is conducted in the name of God, not only in the Middle East. How many use the name of God. Verses 15–16 speak of the right hand of God acting mightily. The Hebrew word is *hayil*, a term used for the Israeli army! In other parts of the Psalm, where the enemy surrounds us, it is clear where God stands – God is mine . . . The individual voice cries to God – this speaks to us. But when placed as a national religious ideology it becomes a problem – worse still, it is anchored in liturgy. Man is also narrow in this Psalm . . . The greatest challenge to us: can we as Jews, Christians and Muslims give God space to take us out of our nationalistic ideologies. It is not only the enemy that makes us narrow.

I found his remarks very challenging, partly because of current political issues, but also because they provided a deep insight into one aspect of the nature of the Psalm. The language that I had taken for granted as part of the familiar rhetoric of the Psalm now took on a different dimension. Indeed, some of the sentences that simply work as a choral celebration of God's power may well have had their origins in a wartime situation. We know of the shouts that were employed by armies in the biblical period both to encourage your own troops and frighten the enemy. Two of the passages would fit such a situation extremely well: 'by the name of the Lord I cut them down' and 'The Lord's right hand works mightily!'

Thus the choral use of these phrases now takes on a powerful overtone and is a forcible reminder of the reality of war and armed conflict as a background to biblical history. To some extent, relocating such phrases within a liturgical context of thanksgiving blunts their militaristic overtones. Indeed, unless one's attention is drawn to these elements, they are almost lost in the way that the Psalm is used in the synagogue today. They become poetic metaphors for trust in God in difficult times. Nevertheless the reality that lies behind them remains, and can re-emerge quite forcibly as in this example.

This unexpected dimension led me to enquire how Rabbinic tradition had viewed this Psalm, or rather what values or lessons have been derived from it. As is usually the case, there is no coherent view of the Psalm as a whole, beyond attempting to relate the story of the 'individual' to various biblical figures, including the patriarchs, King David and Israel as a nation in exile. Instead, individual verses have been extracted and commented upon.

The beginning of the Psalm lists three categories of people: 'Israel', the 'house of Aaron' and 'those who fear/revere the Lord'. This last category, as we will note briefly regarding the same groups in Psalm 115 (page 154), seems to move beyond Israel as a nation or religious community to include a more universal category of people who turn to Israel's God. This 'universal' theme is explored by the Rabbis through the use of the word *tzedek*, 'justice', which appears in various forms within the Psalm (vv. 15, 19, 20). Thus the Midrash (Rabbinic commentary) collection Sifra, on the Book of Leviticus, comments on the verse: 'You should keep My statutes and laws through which by doing them, a man shall live' (Lev. 18.5). It notes that the verse speaks about a 'man' and not a priest or Israelite. It then adds:

> Likewise it does not say: 'Open the gates so that Priests, Levites and Israel may enter', but instead 'so that the righteous may enter'. And similarly: 'This is the gate of the Lord.' It does not say Priests, Levites and Israelites may enter, but that the righteous may enter.

On the question as to who such a righteous man might be, the collection Midrash Psalms (118.17) responds:

> When a person is asked in the world to come: 'What was your work?' and answers: 'I fed the hungry', it will be said: 'This is the gate of the Lord, enter into it, O you who fed the hungry.' If the

person answers: 'I gave drink to the thirsty', it will be said: 'This is the gate of the Lord, enter into it, O you who gave drink to the thirsty.' This will also be said to those who clothed the naked, brought up the fatherless, gave alms or performed deeds of loving kindness. King David said: 'I have done all these things. Therefore let the gates be opened for me.' Hence it is said: 'Open to me the gates of justice. I will enter into them. I will give thanks to the Lord.'

The Rabbis were also conscious of the ceremonial aspect of this Psalm and the antiphonal nature of some verses, so introduced their own version of the choreography that might have accompanied it:

From inside the walls of Jerusalem the men of Jerusalem will say: 'Lord, we beseech You, save us now!' and from outside the men of Judah will say: 'Lord, we beseech You, let us prosper now!'

From inside the men of Jerusalem will say: 'Blessed is the one who comes in the name of the Lord', and from outside the men of Judah will say: 'We bless you from the house of the Lord'.

From inside, the men of Jerusalem will say: 'God is the Lord who gives us light.' And from outside the men of Judah will say: 'Form the procession with the branches up to the horns of the altar'.

From inside the men of Jerusalem will say: 'You are my God and I thank You.' And from outside the men of Judah will say: 'My God, I praise You!'

Then the men of Jerusalem and the men of Judah, together opening their mouths in praise of the Blessed Holy One will say: 'Give thanks to the Lord who is good, whose love is everlasting.' (Midrash Psalms 118.22)

Having tried in various ways to 'orchestrate' this Psalm, it makes sense to offer a version that seeks to identify the different voices, though a variety of options is possible. Perhaps it will encourage someone to provide a musical setting that brings out the perspectives and tensions of the many voices it contains.

1. **Choirmaster:** Give thanks to the Lord who is good,
   Choir: whose love is everlasting.
2. **Choirmaster:** Let Israel now say:
   Choir: 'whose love is everlasting'.
3. **Choirmaster:** Let the house of Aaron now say:
   Choir: 'whose love is everlasting'.

4. **Choirmaster:**   Let all who fear God now say:
   Choir: 'whose love is everlasting'.
5. **Individual:**   Out of the straits I called on the Almighty.
                       The Almighty answered me with great
                          enlargement.
6.   The Lord is for me, I shall not fear.
                       What can people do to me?
7.   The Lord is for me, amongst my helpers,
                       so I confront those who hate me!
8. **Choir:**   It is better to trust in the Lord than to rely on
                          people.
9.   It is better to trust in the Lord than to rely on
                          leaders.
10. **Individual:**   All nations surrounded me –
    Choir: by the name of the Lord I cut them down.
11. **Individual:**   They swarmed and surrounded me –
    Choir: by the name of the Lord I cut them down.
12 **Individual:**   They swarmed around me like bees,
                       they were quenched like a fire among thorns –
    Choir: by the name of the Lord I cut them down.
13. **Individual:**   You pressed me so that I nearly fell,
                       but the Lord helped me.
14.   The Almighty is my strength and song,
                       always there to save me.
15. **Choirmaster:**   Shouts of joy and salvation
                       are in the tents of the just:
    Choir: 'The Lord's right hand works mightily!
16.   The Lord's right hand is raised!
                       The Lord's right hand works mightily!'
17. **Individual:**   I shall not die, but live
                       and declare the acts of the Almighty.
18.   The Almighty has taught me sharply
                       but has not surrendered me to death.
19.   Open the gates of justice for me,
                       I shall enter them and thank the Almighty.
20. **Priest:**   This is the gate of the Lord,
                       the just may enter in.
21. **Individual:**   I thank You, for You answered me,
                       it was You who saved me.
22. **Priest:**   A stone the builders rejected

		has become the corner-stone itself.
23.		Through the Lord this came about,
		this wonder to our eyes.
24.		This is the day the Lord has made,
		let us be glad and rejoice on it.
25.	**Choir:**	Lord, we beseech You, save us now!
		Lord, we beseech You, let us prosper now!
26.	**Priest:**	Blessed is the one who comes in the name of the Lord,
		we bless you from the house of the Lord.
27.		God is the Lord who gives us light.
	Levite:	(Form the procession with the branches
		up to the horns of the altar.)
28.	**Individual:**	You are my God and I thank You.
		My God, I praise you!
29.	**Choirmaster:**	Give thanks to the Lord who is good,
	Choir:	'whose love is everlasting'.

10

Maker of Heaven and Earth – A Text in Context: Psalms 115, 121, 124, 134, 146

This chapter is based on a study I did some years ago for a Festschrift for Rabbi Dr William Braude whose translation of the Midrash on the Psalms I have mentioned and quoted on a number of occasions. Because of the length of time it took for the book to appear, what was meant to be a celebration of his seventieth birthday became, sadly, a memorial volume.

Since his field was the Midrash, the earliest Rabbinic interpretation of the Bible, I wanted to look at some aspect of interpretation. I remembered that a particular phrase describing God as 'Maker of heaven and earth' kept cropping up in different Psalms. The more I looked at the different appearances, the more I realized that though the words were identical in each case, the particular context of each Psalm gave the phrase a quite different meaning every time. So I thought I would look at each example and try to see how the meaning, or at least some aspect of it, changed.

The 'context' for the actual work on the topic was also slightly different from my favourite 'café, coffee and cake' environment. In fact I studied the passages during the filming of the movie 'King David' on which I was the technical adviser. (I have 'celebrated' that experience in chapter 6 of my book, *A Rabbi Reads the Bible*. I received a number of favourable comments on that particular chapter, the best being a letter from a clergyman in the North of England. He wrote that he had visited the Christian spiritual centre of Taizé with some of his students and had taken my book along with him. They had a two-hour period for silent meditation on the Bible, and he used the opportunity to read chapter 6 – 'My Part in the Downfall of "King David"'. Unfortunately reading it gave him the giggles so much that he could not control himself and got thrown out for disturbing the meditation! He seemed quite happy with the experience, so I suppose it simply confirms that the Bible is ultimately a very subversive book – or at least encourages subversive commentaries.)

During the making of the film, on mountain-tops in Sardinia and in a fibreglass, two-thirds life-size replica of Jerusalem in Matera in Southern Italy, with nothing much to do for hours at a time, I sat down with my Bible and studied the particular Psalms where this phrase appeared – 115.15; 121.2; 124.8; 134.3; 146.6.

It is important to make the point from the beginning that there is nothing very surprising about this observation that words mean different things in different contexts. It is always difficult to think of good examples when you need them, but the following makes the point, if somewhat crudely:

> You are right to assert your right to challenge the right, but having left, and being left alone, you may get little support from the left.

Many puns and jokes depend on such vagaries of language. There is a famous comedy routine of Bud Abbot and Lou Costello called 'Who's on first?' that depends on the fact that the baseball player at the first base has the name 'Hoo'. So the question 'Who's on first?' keeps getting the response, 'That's right, Hoo's on first!' After playing on this for some time the exasperated questioner tries a different tack: 'What's the name of the player on first?' But that only leads to the inevitable 'No! *Hoo's* on first! *Wat's* on second!'

In a way they are cheating, since 'Hoo' and 'Wat' are hardly common surnames, but the point is quite clear – the word has a certain meaning for the speaker and a different meaning for the listener.

Most of the time we hardly even notice the problem of different meanings of the same word. It is only when we meet with people who do not share our set of suppositions, particularly when some real act of translation is needed, that we begin to notice the problem of communication. A good example is the problem of religious language – a shared vocabulary between people of different faiths can nevertheless mean something quite different to each of them. Even common words can have religious significance to one but seem mysterious or jargon to another. The following story illustrates the problem nicely. It was told to me by a Rabbi who had heard it from a Bishop.

An elderly Jewish man was knocked down by a bus. A passing priest seeing him lying there and fearing that he was near death and might be in need of absolution bent down and asked him urgently: 'Do you believe in the Father, the Son and the Holy Ghost?' The elderly Jew opened one eye, looked up and complained: 'I'm dying, and he asks me riddles!'

To return to our Psalms, rather than follow the precise order in which they appear in the Hebrew Bible, I will start with those where the distinctive meaning of the phrase is clearest.

PSALM 121

1. *A Pilgrim Song.*
   I will lift up my eyes to the mountains,
   whence will come my help?
2. My help is from the Eternal,
   Maker of heaven and earth.

3. He will not allow your foot to slip,
   your guardian does not slumber.
4. See, He neither slumbers nor sleeps,
   the guardian of Israel.

5. The Eternal is your guardian.
   The Eternal is your shade at your right hand.
6. By day the sun will not strike you,
   nor the moon by night.

7. The Eternal will guard you from all evil,
   He will guard your soul.
8. The Eternal will guard your going out and your coming in
   from now and until forever.

This is one of the best-loved and most familiar of Psalms. The Hebrew text is particularly well known by the Jewish community because of a variety of melodies to which it can be sung – including the solemn but melodic 'liturgical' one and a rather jolly, rhythmic Israeli one. In fact it lends itself to such simple, repeating melodies as it has a symmetrical structure, consisting of four sets of two verses each. The same sort of structure can be found in Psalm 114, particularly since verses 5 and 6 are minor transformations of verses 3 and 4, giving the Psalm a unity of content as well as form. (The same applies to Psalm 126, which is also sung to a simple melody, and which really consists of eight 'sense units' even though it is only divided into six verses.)

We can already see our phrase, 'Maker of heaven and earth', at the end of verse 2, but before we get to it, we need to look at the structure of the passage that precedes it.

The Psalm begins with a question which we can take as 'real', a genuine request for an answer, or, perhaps more likely, as 'rhetorical', because the answer is already assumed:

1. I lift up my eyes to the mountains,
    whence will come my help?
2. My help is from the Eternal,
    Maker of heaven and earth.

But why does he look to the mountains? Do they represent a source of danger (human enemies on the heights, the 'gods' who inhabit the 'high places') from whom help is needed? Or are they the place to which he looks because help may be expected to come from there, because that is where God is to be encountered, as at Sinai?

The answer to the Psalmist's question is to be found in the first part of verse 2, and indeed it is presented as a kind of chiastic reversal of the question:

> *mei'áyin   yavo   ezri*
>   *x*
> *ezri   mei'im   adonay*

whence	will come	my help
	x	
my help	(comes) from	the Eternal

The Hebrew is quite tightly constructed, with '*ezri*', 'my help', coming at the end of v. 1 and the beginning of v. 2. Similarly the question '*mei'áyin*', 'from where?' is matched for similarity of sound by the word '*mei'im*', literally 'from with'. It is even possible to read the whole of these two sentences as standing in a chiastic relationship to each other:

> *essa   einay   el-heharim*   *mei'áyin   yavo   ezri*
>   *x*
> *ezri   mei'im   adonay*   *oseh   shamáyim   va'árets*

> I will lift up my eyes to the mountains,
>> whence will come my help?
>> my help is from the Eternal,
> Maker of heaven and earth.

The 'turning to the mountains' is balanced against our phrase 'Maker of heaven and earth' (with a possible play on the words *essa*, 'I lift up', and *oseh*, 'who makes, Maker'). The fact that God creates heaven and earth stills the Psalmist's anxiety. This could still work however we understand the point of the opening question. If he sees the hills as the source of danger, then God as their creator could protect him from any danger that may come from them. Alternatively, the tops of mountains are the points where heaven and earth come closest together, and indeed where they meet when God comes down to earth:

> Eternal, bow your heavens and come down!
> Touch the mountains so that they smoke! (Ps. 144.5)

Having established this statement of faith in the first person – 'this is what my tradition teaches about God and this is what I also experience' – the Psalmist develops the idea of how God provides this help, describing God's qualities in the third person and addressing the individual listener or reader in the second person singular.

The key word that describes God's actions is the root *shamar*, 'to guard or keep', versions of which come six times in the following six verses. The same word is used of the task given to Adam in the garden of Eden, '*l'ovdah ul'shomrah*', 'to work/serve/tend it and to *guard/keep* it' (Gen. 2.15). But it also appears in the Deuteronomy version of the Ten Commandments where we are to 'keep' (presumably 'preserve' and 'observe' in this case) the Sabbath day (Deut. 5.12). The particular phrase, '*shomer yisrael*', 'Guardian of Israel', in verse 4, becomes a title of God that is used in medieval Jewish liturgical poems which appeal to God, 'Guardian of Israel, guard the remnant of Israel'. But as we shall see, the repetition of the verb in the closing verses builds towards a powerful, rhythmic, rolling climax of certainty.

We begin with our feet very firmly on the earth:

> 3. He will not allow your foot to slip,
>   your guardian does not slumber.

4. See, He neither slumbers nor sleeps,
   the guardian of Israel.

Your foot shall not stumble – an image of walking that dominates
the rest of the Psalm, returning specifically in verse 8, God guarding
your 'going out and coming in'. (The same image is developed very
powerfully in Ps. 91.11–13:

> For He commands His messengers for you,
> to guard you in all your ways.
> They bear you in their palms
> lest you strike your foot on the stone.
> You will tread on the lion and the adder,
> trample the young lion and serpent.)

Unlike a human guardian, Israel's guardian does not slumber or sleep
(v. 4). This new statement, though comforting, seems unrelated to
what has gone before. The image may be related to that of the
watchman of a city who does his rounds at night and has to stay
awake (Song of Songs 3.3; 5.7), a technical use of our word *shomer*.
It also reminds us of the way the prophet Elijah taunted the prophets
of Baal when no fire came down from heaven to burn up their
offerings – 'call louder than that! for he is a god! Perhaps he is
meditating or is busy or on a journey. Perhaps he is sleeping and
needs to be woken up!' (1 Kings 18.27). We will see how this image,
that God neither slumbers nor sleeps, will also be picked up again
in the Psalm.

So who is this guardian who does not sleep? Verse 5 gives an
emphatic reply by placing the name of God as the first word of the
next two phrases:

> *adonay   shomrécha*
> *adonay   tsil'cha   al-yad   yeminécha*

> *The Eternal* is your guardian!
> *The Eternal* is your shade at your right hand!

The image of God being a 'shade at your right hand' presumably
derives from military usage. The right side of the body is unprotected
by a shield held in the left hand, so the person who stands to your
right protects you from attack on that side. Presumably the same
idea stands behind the English phrase 'right-hand man', which has
also moved from the strictly military sense, the comrade who stood

A Rabbi Reads the Psalms

at your right side to protect it, to a metaphorical usage. (For other uses of the word *tsel*, 'shade', in this military sense of protection, see Num. 14.9; Jer. 48.45 and Lam. 4.20.)

But this use of the word 'shade' leads the Psalmist to bring in yet another image that effectively ties together the different strands he has prepared.

> By day the sun will not strike you,
> nor the moon by night. (v. 6)

The 'shield' at your right hand becomes literally 'shade' and protection from the sun's rays. It also protects you from the light of the moon. Israel knew of other dangers that came by night (Ps. 91.5), and commentators have suggested that Israel, like other nations in the Ancient Near East, feared the light of the moon. But perhaps this is more of a literary conceit, balancing the use here of the 'sun'. In fact, we should note that here there is another poetic device in operation. There are a number of phrases in Hebrew made up of pairs of words that are linked by being opposites. We are already dealing with one in this chapter, 'heaven and earth', but similar are 'day and night', 'sun and moon', 'good and bad'. (In all these cases the combined form may simply mean the two elements that are named, but may also imply some 'totality' that is included between the two extremes that they represent. We will see the implications of this later on in this chapter.) Because such phrases come together so frequently, it is often a device of the poet to split them and share them between the two half-lines of his poem – and verse 6 is a marvellous example, where 'day' and 'sun' are placed in the first half and 'night' and 'moon' in the second. In the same way 'heaven and earth' are neatly divided in the song of Moses in Deuteronomy 32.1:

> Give ear, O *heavens*, and I will speak;
> let the *earth* hear the words of my mouth.

Whether or not Israel was scared of the moonlight, our verse helps explain the emphasis on their guardian 'not sleeping' – God is alert to protect you at all times of day and night. Beyond even this is the attribute with which we began, for it is the Eternal who created the vault of heaven, the place of sun and moon, so who better than God to protect you from them? Perhaps here there is even a reminiscence of the creation, for 'days' existed before there were even a sun and moon.

> Who made the heaven by understanding
> 'for His faithful love endures forever'
> who spread out the earth on the waters
> 'for His faithful love endures forever'
> who made the great lights
> 'for His faithful love endures forever'
> the sun to rule by day
> 'for His faithful love endures forever'
> the moon and stars to rule by night
> 'for His faithful love endures forever'. (Ps. 136.5–8)

Nothing on earth can make your foot slip; no power in the heaven can harm you. With these two domains firmly established within God's control, the last two verses reach a general conclusion and move there, as already mentioned, by the rhythmic repetition of the verb *shamar*.

> 7. *The Eternal* will guard you from all evil,
>   He will guard your soul.
> 8. *The Eternal* will guard your going out and your coming in
>   from now and until forever.

> *adonay   yishmor'cha   mikol   ra*
> *yishmor   et   nafshècha*
> *adonay   yishmor   tset'cha   uvoécha*
> *me'attah   v'ad-olam*

This repetition of the form *yishmor* has a very special effect, reinforcing and at the same time rolling over us like waves of supportive sound. Technically the verse belongs to a kind of unclassifiable variation of parallelism. We have looked at the problem in the chapter on biblical poetry, cases where only one element really repeats itself but the general rhythmic feel and the advancing of a particular idea through repetition and development have a special poetic quality. I was delighted to discover that this particular example is classified as 'stair-like parallelism' or *anadiplosis* (rising and doubling). It is always nice to be able to sprinkle one's vocabulary with such exotic terms – I cherish this one alongside such other gems of Hebrew grammar as 'the epenthetic *nun*', the 'pleonastic *vav*' and the 'enclitic *mem*'.

Perhaps it is important to point out that some of the terms in verse 7 are rather difficult to translate into English. The Hebrew *ra* means 'bad', in the sense of 'harmful' or 'unpleasant', as well as the more specific usage as 'evil'. As we have noted above, it is often linked with its opposite *tov*, 'good'. Hence the combination, as in the case of the 'tree of the knowledge of good and evil' (Gen. 2.17), can stand for all the things that lie between these two extremes, both in a moral and non-moral sense. In fact, in 2 Samuel 14.17, David is complimented on knowing 'good and evil', and the phrase is subsequently expressed (v. 20) as 'everything on earth'. Thus the meaning of the word *ra* is determined by the context – so that in this Psalm the word 'harm' may be a better translation than 'evil'. (In the same way *tov*, 'good', can mean good behaviour, that which is morally correct, but also material benefit, 'blessing', the 'good' that God bestows, and many other nuances.) Similarly the word *nefesh*, the 'soul' that God will guard, has a range of meanings from one's 'life', to one's 'self' or even 'appetite/desire' as well as a more intangible idea of 'soul' or 'life force'. The general tenor of the Psalm would suggest that in this case neither 'evil' nor 'soul' are appropriate translations, rather – 'the Eternal will guard you from all *harm* and will guard your *life*'. But this does not exclude the possibility of those other dimensions of the terms entering in.

Even the closing phrase, 'from now and until forever', may also be a form of commentary on 'Maker of heaven and earth'. The permanence of heaven and earth is used as a guarantee of their reliability as witness to events (Deut. 30.19; 32.1; Isa. 1.2). 'Heaven' is also used as a kind of synonym for the word *olam*, 'enduring time', in Psalm 89.3 and 119.89 and for the similar *la'ad*, 'forever' in Psalm 89.30.

> I will establish his seed forever
> and his throne as the days of the heavens.

If we sum up the possible meanings of our phrase in this Psalm, the following points emerge. The Psalmist who turns to the mountains for help or as a source of danger finds comfort from the God who created them. The earth cannot trip his feet nor the sun or moon harm him because God made the earth and the vault of heaven.

The eternal existence of heaven and earth reinforces the idea of the enduring nature of this help throughout all time.

Nevertheless, before leaving this Psalm, it is worth nothing that the Rabbinic tradition, no less than other prophetic writings and biblical texts, was prepared to question the certainties expressed here. On the verse 'see, He neither slumbers nor sleeps, the guardian of Israel' the Midrash on Psalms comments:

> But is there such a thing as sleep in heaven? Surely not! In heaven there is no sleep, nor is there sitting. As scripture says, 'I saw in the visions of my head upon my bed, and behold, a wakeful one and a holy one came down from heaven' (Dan. 4.10), and says also 'The matter is by the decree of the wakeful ones' (4.14). In these verses, the word 'wakeful' proves that there is no sleep in heaven. Why, then, does the Psalmist make a point of saying that He that keepeth thee does not slumber? Because it would appear from the troubles which come upon the children of Israel in this world that the Holy One, blessed be He, was asleep, if one dare speak thus. Indeed Asaph did say: 'Awake, why sleepest Thou, O Lord?' (Ps. 44.24).

PSALM 124

1. *A Pilgrim Song. David's.*
   'If the Eternal had not been for us,'
   – let Israel repeat it,
2. 'If the Eternal had not been for us,
   when there arose against us man,
3. then alive they would have swallowed us
   in their burning rage at us;
4. then the waters would have overwhelmed us,
   a torrent sweeping over our souls;
5. then sweeping over our souls
   would be the cruel waters.'
6. Blessed is the Eternal
   who did not make us a prey to their teeth.
7. Our soul is like a bird
   escaped from the fowler's trap.
   The trap itself is smashed
   and we have escaped.

8. Our help is in the name of the Eternal
   Maker of heaven and earth.

I find this a quite extraordinary Psalm. Like the previous one it plays
most powerfully with the pattern of repeating words or phrases and
thus advancing a particular idea while sustaining a powerful rhythm.
In the translation I have tried again to follow the Hebrew word
order which leads to some English peculiarities. But even a literal
translation cannot capture the intensity and rhythm of the original
and the cumulative effect of the repetitions. Look at the way the
Psalmist creates a tension from the outset with his repeated con-
ditional phrase – 'If the Eternal had not been for us . . .' We feel the
fear that must have been experienced in that moment when all might
have been lost – in the seconds before the wave broke over them,
before the predators' jaws closed, before the trap snapped shut! The
two Hebrew words that open verses 1–2 and 3–5 are very inad-
equately translated by 'if' and 'then'. They need the two syllables
of the Hebrew to give them substance, and even the sounds of the
Hebrew terms seem to reinforce the two emotions, the wonderment
of the 'if' – *lulei*, and the sharper and more definite 'then' – *azai*.

lulei	*adonay*	*shehayah*	*lánu*	*yomár-na*	*yisrael*
lulei	*adonay*	*shehayah*	*lánu*	*b'kum aléinu*	*adam*
azai	*chayyim*	*b'laúnu*	*bacharot*	*appam*	*bánu*
azai	*hammáyim*	*sh'tafúnu*	*nachlah*	*avar*	*al-nafshéinu*
azai	*avar*	*al-nafshéinu*	*hammáyim*	*hazzeidonim*	

It even contains a couple of rhymes, rare in biblical poetry, between
chayyim, 'alive', and *hammáyim*, 'the waters', followed respectively
by *b'laúnu*, 'swallowed' and *sh'tafúnu* (accent on the first 'u' – 'ooo'
in each case).

These repetitions suggest, as the Psalmist demands at the outset,
that his words indeed be repeated by the community. Which implies
that the Psalm may well have been read antiphonally between two
choirs or a leader and the congregation. Certainly it lends itself to
some such way of chanting or singing it, even if this demand is only
a literary device of the writer to proclaim the importance of what is
being said.

One other translation point needs to be noted. At the end of verse 2
comes emphatically the word '*adam*'. This term is the one used to

designate the first human being (Gen. 1.26), with a wordplay on the word for 'ground', *adamah*, from which he was formed, and serves as his 'name' as well – though it is important to bear in mind that this initial creature had to be split to form two complementary parts before recognizable human beings, man and woman, appeared. It is used generally in the Bible to mean 'humanity', but very often it is used in the sense of 'mortal man', or even the lowest kind of human being, in contrast to the word *ish* that implies someone who has substance, identity and their own will. Here it seems to play a double role – first, the menace that 'men' represent to each other, the dangers they pose when they use violent means; but there is also an implicit contrast, coming as the very last word of the sentence with the subject of the opening of the sentence – the Eternal. Only the *Eternal* could achieve such a victory over overwhelming human odds – however powerful they may be. In the end, compared to God, they are only '*adam*'.

Like the previous Psalm, this one links our phrase, 'Maker of heaven and earth' with the concept of God as our source of help, and indeed uses the same word – '*ezréinu*', '*our* help', compared with '*ezri*', '*my* help' (121.1, 2). Here, however, it comes as the concluding thought of the Psalm (v. 8) and not the opening.

If we now look at the overall structure of the Psalm we will see how our phrase functions within it. The Psalm divides up quite clearly into two main sections, verses 1–5 and 6–7, with verse 8 providing a general conclusion. This division is underlined by placing the name of God (YHWH, *adonay*, the Eternal) at the beginning of each section; '*lulei adonay*' in verse 1; '*baruch adonay*' ('blessed be/is the Eternal') in verse 6. Each part also contains a metaphor for the danger in which Israel found itself – overwhelming waters, a trapped bird escaping. Moreover, the key word '*nafshéinut*', 'our soul/life', is found in the second part of each section (vv. 4, 7).

Verses 1–3 state the circumstances of danger in which Israel found itself, under threat from foes who, in the heat of their anger, might have swallowed Israel alive. As mentioned above they are simply designated as *adam*, 'man'. But at this point the first metaphor breaks in, that of waters engulfing them (vv. 4–5), which develops the image of being physically overwhelmed. However, the image of being devoured (swallowed up alive) recurs in verse 6, where gratitude is more directly expressed to God for rescuing them:

6. Blessed is the Eternal
   who did not make us a prey to their teeth.

If we examine the two intervening verses we see that they also are
built according to our now familiar chiastic pattern:

azai hammáyim sh'tafúnu   *nachlah avar al-nafshéinu*

                                x

azai avar al-nafshéinu   *hammáyim hazzeidonim*

4. then the waters would have overwhelmed us,
   a torrent sweeping over our souls;
5. then sweeping over our souls
   would be the cruel waters.

The chiastic repetition of 'waters' (*máyim*) and of the phrase 'sweeping over our souls' ('*avar al-nafshéinu*') reinforces the sense of
overwhelming engulfment. Professor Nehama Leibowitz, in a short
study of this Psalm, influenced by Ludwig Strauss, points to the way
the word order reinforces this feeling. She translates:

Then alive they had swallowed us,
When their wrath was kindled against us,
Then the waters had overwhelmed us,
The torrent had gone over our souls,
Then had gone over our souls
The raging waters.

   Three times the waters overwhelm us, but we, our souls, stand
up to them, survive and still exist as an object of their wrath at
the end of the verse. Each line ends with 'us' or 'our souls', and
only at the end of the sixth line does the phrase 'the raging waters'
exist. For we have been swallowed up and nothing exists anymore
but they, the waters that 'had gone over our souls'.[1]

If we designate verses 1–3 as the A part of this section (relating
God's relationship to the danger Israel faced at human hands), then
verses 4–5 are the B part, a powerful metaphor of the overwhelming
nature of that danger.

   In the second section, verse 6 is a shortened equivalent to A,
blessing the Eternal who did *not* let them be devoured by the human
adversaries. In a parallel to B, verse 7 brings another metaphor,

similarly drawn from nature, but this time expressing Israel's escape.
Like the first section B, it too is composed as a chiastic structure:

nafshéinu k'tsippor niml'tah   mippach yokshim

x

happach   nishbar va'anáchnu   nimlátnu

7. Our soul is like a bird
    escaped from the fowler's trap.
    The trap itself is smashed
    and we have escaped.

The effect of both metaphors is to dramatize the danger Israel faced
and the significance of her escape. The overwhelming waters become
replaced by the image of a bird flying free from its snare. The
'swallowing' by their enemies, another image of engulfment, is
replaced by the futile snapping of their teeth (v. 6), for Israel is no
longer deep within the throat but only at the surface of the mouth,
the trap that closes on nothing (v. 7).

With the final verse comes a summation and interpretation of the
experience.

8. Our help is in the name of the Eternal
    Maker of heaven and earth.

In this Psalm the sense of 'heaven and earth' seems to be that these
are the media in which God's creatures live, the threefold division
of nature: sky, earth and waters, a division going back to the creation
story in Genesis 1 that is frequently noted in Psalms (8.7–9; 69.35;
96.11f.; 135.6). To the human menace on earth (v. 2f., 6) are added
images of danger from waters, and of the freedom of a bird in the
skies. The soul that was nearly pulled down forever into the waters
below escapes instead into the air. God as 'Maker of heaven and
earth' can rescue Israel from danger posed by or within (literally or
metaphorically) all three of these domains.

PSALM 115

1. Not to us, Eternal, not to us,
    but to Your name give glory,
    for Your faithful love, for Your truth.

2. Why do the nations say:
   'Where, now, is their God?'
3. But our God is in heaven,
   all that pleases Him, He does.
4. Their idols are silver and gold,
   the work of the hands of man.
5. A mouth is theirs, but they do not speak,
   eyes are theirs, but they do not see.
6. Ears are theirs, but they do not hear,
   a nose is theirs, but they do not smell.
7. With their hands they do not feel,
   with their feet they do not walk;
   they make no sound in their throat.
8. Like them shall be those who make them,
   all who trust in them.
9. Israel trust in the Eternal –
   'their help and their shield is He'.
10. House of Aaron, trust in the Eternal –
    'their help and their shield is He'.
11. Those who fear the Eternal, trust in the Eternal –
    'their help and their shield is He'.
12. The Eternal remembers us! May He bless . . .
    May He bless the house of Israel!
    May He bless the house of Aaron!
13. May He bless those who fear the Eternal,
    the small together with the great!
14. May the Eternal give increase to you,
    to you and your children!
15. Blessed are you to the Eternal,
    Maker of heaven and earth.
16. The heavens are the heavens of the Eternal
    but the earth He gave to the children of man.
17. None who are dead praise God,
    nor all who go down into silence.
18. But we bless God
    from now and for evermore.
    Praise God!

This Psalm plays a significant role in Jewish life as it is part of the group of Psalms (113–118) known collectively as the 'Hallel'. The verb means 'praise' and appears frequently within this group in the term '*hallelu-yah!*', 'praise God'. They are read and chanted during the major Jewish festivals and sections of them have melodies suited to the particular festival.

Our phrase, 'Maker of heaven and earth', occurs in verse 15, and is linked to the description of God as the source of blessing. But the Psalm itself starts with an emphatic statement of denial, one which is puzzling both in its content and the intensity of its expression. It effectively presents the reader with a riddle at the very outset of the Psalm so that throughout the rest of the text we are looking for an explanation.

> *lo lánu adonay lo lánu*
> *ki l'shimcha tein kavod*
> *al-hasd'cha al-amittêcha*

The opening also presents a number of translation problems. The Hebrew *lo* simply means 'not', but *lánu* can be translated as 'to us', 'for us' or even 'because of us'. Hence a variety of explanations arises: one assumes that the Psalmist, in a cultic context, is insisting that it is not the congregation that is being honoured by the ritual but God, reading the opening as a kind of self-deprecation; a counterview suggests that what is at stake here is God's honour in the eyes of the nations, so that 'it is not because of us but for the sake of Your reputation . . .'

I once caught part of a television lecture by Leonard Bernstein, one of the Norton Lectures he gave at Harvard on music, this time touching on the theme of Semantics. In exploring forms of musical composition he cited the opening of this Psalm as an example of antithesis, like the closing verses 'the dead shall not praise You . . . but we shall bless God', which he felt was the metaphor that informs the whole Psalm.

As a curious aside it is worth noting that the opening phrase '*lo lánu*' is so striking that, presumably via Yiddish, it has entered the Dutch language! The phrase Lou Loene (pronounced, 'lau loonê') means 'I can't be bothered with it!'

The closing phrase, 'for Your faithful love, for Your truth' is another variation on the theme we have already explored of God's attributes, first listed in Exodus 34.6–7. Here, again, the Psalmist has taken the conventional pair *chésed ve'emet* and split them. Paradoxically, by omitting the word 'and' that we would expect to link them together, their strong identity with each other is stressed – Your faithful love which is 'true', that is, 'reliable', 'to be trusted'. In the same way that other 'conventional phrases' may be split up, so this phrase is also divided between the two parts of a sentence in Psalm 92.3:

> *l'haggeed   babbóqer   chasdécha*
> *ve'emunat'cha   balleilot*

> To tell in the morning Your faithful love,
> and your faithfulness every night.

Here the word *emunah*, 'faith/faithfulness' or 'trust', replaces the word *emet*, 'truth', though both are derived from the same root *amen*, that which is 'firm', 'reliable', and can be 'affirmed' – by responding 'amen'.

God's 'name' is here related to the enduring nature of God's faithful love, the word *chésed* being the essential binding force in the covenant between God and Israel. Given the challenging question that the nations are about to pose in the following verse, 'where now is their God!?', this evocation of God's faithful love becomes more pressing. It is God's seeming absence in times of trial that calls forth such an assertion – if we, by our behaviour, may have done something to estrange ourselves from You, nevertheless, if the covenant has any meaning, we can rely on You to remain loyal. Such a reading would tip the translation of the opening phrase in the direction of 'not for our sakes but for the sake of Your name . . .' But we will see that a quite different view can also emerge, which is an important reminder that there is no 'one correct reading', particularly in such an evocative text.

Perhaps it is useful at this point to look at the end of the Psalm where we might expect some part of the opening riddle to be resolved. Here we find Bernstein's other example of antithesis, but it is also worth pointing out the return of the 'we' of the speaker. In fact it is quite strongly asserted with the personal pronoun *anáchnu*, preceded by the letter *vav*, usually translated as 'and', but here as a strongly adversative '*but!*'

> *lo   hammetim   y hallelu-yah*
> *v'lo   kol-yordei   dumah*
> *va'anáchnu nevarech yah*
> *mei'attah v'ad-olam*
> *hallelu-yah*

17. None who are dead praise God,
    nor all who go down into silence.
18. But we bless God
    from now and for evermore.
    Praise God!

In contrast to the risk of our receiving (undeserved) praise, as suggested in verse 1, the closing verses put the emphasis the correct way round – we, the living, will bless God. Thus these negative and positive expressions of giving due honour to God form a kind of bracket (the technical term is 'inclusio') around the Psalm.

The second verse poses another question, though it is possible to read it as a rhetorical statement: 'How absurd of the nations to say . . .'

2. Why do the nations say:
   'Where, now, is their God?'
3. But our God is in heaven,
   all that pleases Him, He does.

As is often the case in the Bible, even a simple phrase may be loaded with a lot of background assumptions. The statement, 'all that pleases Him, He does' crops up a few other times and may go back to an old legal formula that pre-dates the Bible.[2] When someone purchased something the sense of ownership was expressed by stating that he could now do with it everything that he wished. Something of that is conveyed in Psalm 135.6:

All that pleased him, the Eternal did,
in heaven and on earth,
in the seas and all the deeps.

From ownership, and hence complete control over something, it is only a slight step to asserting the freedom of the 'owner' to do whatever he or she wishes. Here the implication seems to be that everything is in God's hands – which could be a statement of resignation, or an acknowledgement that God's ways are mysterious and not to be explained by us, and possibly even a hint at a protest at feeling abandoned by God in a time of trouble.

Once again to pick up a 'technical' point, verse 3 mentions 'heaven', *shamáyim*, and the same word reappears shortly before the end of the Psalm (vv. 15–16), where our phrase occurs. Given the 'inclusio' linking the opening and closing verses and this use of heaven as a possible 'key word', we may be looking once again at a concentric structure to the Psalm as a whole.

The next section (vv. 4–8) contains a condemnation of the gods of the nations, the idols with human appearance but lacking in any human abilities, let alone divine ones.

4. Their idols are silver and gold,
   the work of the hands of man.
5. A mouth is theirs, but they do not speak,
   eyes are theirs, but they do not see.
6. Ears are theirs, but they do not hear,
   a nose is theirs, but they do not smell.
7. With their hands they do not feel,
   with their feet they do not walk;
   they make no sounds in their throat.
8. Like them shall be those who make them,
   all who trust in them.

This form of attack is found again in Psalm 135.15–18 in almost identical language, but it is a familiar theme in prophetic writings (Isa. 44.9–20; 47.6f.; Jer. 10.1–9; Hab. 2.18f.).

What is emphasized is that their idols are the works of 'man' (v. 4), which reminds us of the denial in verse 1, give not to man, and his works, the glory due to God (whose 'works' are the whole of heaven and earth). In fact the verb *asah*, to 'make' or 'do' (hence 'works') seems to be another key word – what God 'does' or 'makes' (v. 3, 15) has substance, reality and endurance, but what men 'make' (vv. 4, 8) lack the one essential quality of life.

Idols are dumb, blind and deaf; they can neither smell nor feel; their arms and legs do not function, no sound is emitted by their throat. They look like men, but are less than men – they are inanimate, effectively dead – which reminds us of our closing verses about the dead and 'those who go down into silence' who cannot praise God. Those who make them become like them. In fact, to return to our opening verse, we may have here one answer to the riddle. In what circumstances do people praise themselves? When they create idols in their own image which they worship. 'Not to us, Eternal, not to us, but to Your name give honour.' Thus the Psalmist is working with two sets of contrasting concepts: God and idols; the living and the dead.

The critique of idols here is often seen as oversimplistic. Self-evidently such artefacts have no physical reality – but surely they are only representative of something beyond them, a spiritual reality that their worshippers are really seeking to address. This crude kind of mockery recurs in later Rabbinic tradition in the story of Abraham's argument with his father. His father used to manufacture idols for the local populace. One day Abraham, who had already discovered the one God behind all things, smashed all but one of the idols in his father's shop, the largest, and left the hammer in its hand. When his horrified father asked what had happened, Abraham explained that the biggest idol had smashed the others. To which his father pointed out that idols could not do such things since they were only made of wood or stone. Abraham replied that if only his father's ears could hear what his mouth was saying!

It is clear that there is a strong iconoclastic streak running through these various prophetic and other denunciations. It is as if the very idea of attempting to depict God through some sort of material representation was such a scandal and seemed such a diminution of God's transcendent reality that it was totally unacceptable, even if some symbolic idea lay behind it. Incidentally the same applies even to the use of the 'name' of God which similarly had to be protected from being 'instrumentalized'. In other cultures, to know the 'secret' name of a person or a god meant to exercise control over them. When Moses tries to learn God's name (Ex. 3.13–15) he is met with evasions. Jewish tradition forbids the saying aloud of the four-letter name of God, hence the substitution of the word *adonay*, 'Lord'. The proper name was only to be pronounced once a year – on the holiest day (the Day of Atonement), by the holiest person in the community (the High Priest) in the holiest of places, the Holy of Holies in the Temple.

Nevertheless the question remains as to whether the Psalmist here is working on such a simplistic level in his condemnation of these idolatrous artefacts. Perhaps on one level he is addressing the general problem of anthropomorphism which is also an essential part of Israel's attempt to understand and relate to God. In the Hebrew Bible God does have a voice, does see and hear, and does use hands. But the God who acts in such ways must still remain invisible and uncontrollable, and Israel must live with this unbearable and incomprehensible paradox, however great is the price in suffering and however much the 'nations' may mock a God that no one can see – 'our God is in heaven'. The attack on the idols reinforces the view that despite lacking all these tangible 'organs', God is intensely present and has all these essential attributes.

Before attempting to see yet another dimension to this section we need to look at the one that follows. The bridge between them is the verb *batach*, 'to trust': they 'trust' in idols (v. 8), Israel must 'trust' in the Eternal (v. 9).

> 9. Israel trust in the Eternal –
>   'their help and their shield is He'.
> 10. House of Aaron, trust in the Eternal –
>   'their help and their shield is He'.
> 11. Those who fear the Eternal, trust in the Eternal –
>   'their help and their shield is He'.
> 12. The Eternal remembers us! May He bless . . .
>   May He bless the house of Israel!
>   May He bless the house of Aaron!
> 13. May He bless those who fear the Eternal,
>   the small together with the great!
> 14. May the Eternal give increase to you,
>   to you and your children!

If we recognize in this Psalm a concentric structure, then verses 9–14 are 'geographically' the equivalent of verses 4–8. They have no content in common and their form appears at first glance to be entirely different. But the frequent repetition of phrases within the latter verses is equivalent to the long list of the inadequacies of the idols in the former. That is to say, both sections depend on the cumulative effect of repetition (either of an idea or of formulaic phrases) for their impact. Here the threefold division of those addressed (Israel, the House of Aaron and those who fear the Eternal) represent the true relationship between people and God that should be universally present – not just Israel but all who come into the category of those who 'fear/revere God'. They trust in the Eternal, their help, and God comes to bless them. There is a reciprocal relationship, repeated three times in each case, to show its mutuality and certainty, between two living entities, human beings and the real God. This stands in stark contrast to the dead idols and their 'dead' worshippers. Corresponding to the seven negatives of verses 4–8 are the three expressions of help and the fourfold blessings of verses 9–14. In contrast to the idolaters who are as dead as their idols, Israel lives on to receive blessings in generations to come (v. 14). Thus if verses 4–6 concern earthly 'things', shaped like men, that aspire to heavenly powers, then verses 9–14 speak of heavenly blessings that come to earthly creatures. The two passages are effectively inverted images of each other.

We have already noted above that verses 15–16 contain our phrase and correspond to verses 2–3 in their assertion that God is in heaven.

15. Blessed are you to the Eternal,
    Maker of heaven and earth.
16. The heavens are the heavens of the Eternal
    but the earth He gave to the children of man.

Our formula 'Maker of heaven and earth' takes on a totally new meaning because of its expansion in verse 16 and in the light of what has gone before. Whereas elsewhere 'heaven and earth' may imply a unity, the totality of creation, here they are taken apart to indicate two domains, two separate spheres of interest: the heavens that belong to God and the earth that belongs to human beings. The heavens belong to God, and God alone is the source of all things. Human beings are to live their life on earth, acknowledging that the source of that life is the God of heaven. But the boundary between the two domains must not be crossed. The idols that human beings make are an attempt to make an image of God, to usurp the ruler of heaven. But they are less even than human beings themselves, and just as they are dead, so do those who worship them become less than human – and the dead do not praise. Thus our formula here is used to differentiate the two realms, heaven and earth, and to indicate the boundary that lies between them.

And yet the boundary can be crossed, if an appropriate acknowledgement is made. The Rabbis noticed an apparent contradiction between verse 16 of our Psalm and Psalm 24.1:

To the Eternal is the earth and its fullness,
the inhabited world and all who dwell in it.

The verse from Psalm 24 claims that the earth belongs to God and the one from Psalm 115 that it belongs to human beings! How to resolve this contradiction? One applies before we recite a blessing, the other after we have recited it. That is to say, before we partake of anything we have to acknowledge that it comes from God, and this we do in Jewish tradition by the recital of a blessing. Thus a blessing in this case is not intended to make something 'special' or 'holy', but rather, paradoxically, to 'desacralize' it, to move it from the heavenly domain of God's ownership to the earthly domain which allows us to partake of it. The boundary can be crossed, but on God's terms, not ours.

Before leaving this Psalm there is one more comment to introduce. It comes from a study of the Psalm by the American Bible scholar Chanan Brichto.[3] He suggests that the Psalm is a comment on the aesthetic hubris of the makers of idols, worshipping their own creation and artistry. By extension such aesthetic pretensions can apply to literary creativity, including the composition of our Psalm itself! For the literary artist does create worlds and characters that live in the imagination and interpretation of others – including the images we need to depict 'God' for ourselves. The Psalm loops back on itself – 'not to us, Eternal, not to us, but to Your name give glory'. The riddle with which we began returns to challenge us.

PSALM 146

1. Praise God!
   Praise, my soul, the Eternal!
2. I will praise the Eternal all my life.
   I will sing to my God while I yet am.
3. Do not trust in princes,
   in any human being who has no power to save.
4. His breath departs, he returns to his ground,
   on that day perish all his plans.
5. Happy the one for whom the God of Jacob is his help
   whose hope is in the Eternal his God;
6. the Maker of heaven and earth,
   the sea and all within them;
   who guards the truth forever,
7. who does justice for the oppressed,
   who gives bread to the starving.
   The Eternal releases those who are bound.
8. The Eternal opens the eyes of the blind.
   The Eternal raises those bent low.
   The Eternal loves the righteous.
9. The Eternal guards strangers,
   supporting the orphan and widow,
   but distorting the way of the wicked.

10. The Eternal will rule forever,
    your God, O Zion, from age to age!
    Praise God!

It is far harder to evaluate this Psalm than the previous three. Its structure is not so clear-cut and the particular function of our phrase within the context of the whole (v. 6) is not so obvious.

The Psalm is the first of a series of five Psalms which close the Psalter, each beginning and ending with Hallelu-yah, 'Praise God!' They contain praises of God in various forms and lists of divine qualities. Our Psalm also shares with Psalm 145 a first-person intro-duction that praises God, which seems to belong to a conventional opening (see, for example, the call to 'bless the Eternal, O my soul' of Psalms 103 and 104) prior to launching into a more general theme.

The remainder of the Psalm may be divided into two main parts: verses 3–4 warn against trusting in princes, presumably any kind of leaders, whose power is limited by their mortality; whereas verses 5–9 extol the merits of God as a more reliable source of help. The last verse is a doxology reminiscent of the end of the Song at the Sea (Ex. 15.18), leading into the closing 'Hallelu-yah!'

The unevenness of construction becomes more apparent when we examine in greater detail verses 3–4.

al-tivt'chu   vin'divim   b'ven-adam   she'ein   lo   t'shuah

                                x

teitsei   rucho   yashuv   l'admato   bayyom   hahu   avdu   esht'notav

3. Do not trust in princes,
   in any human being who has no power to save.
4. His breath departs, he returns to his ground,
   on that day perish all his plans.

Two wordplays suggest a partial chiastic structure to the verses. The most obvious is that between *adam*, 'man/human being' and *admato*, 'ground' – do not trust in the *adam* who returns to the *adamah* from which he came. However, it is possible that a parallel wordplay is intended between 'princes', *n'divim* (in the form *vin'divim*, 'and princes') and the statement that their help 'perishes', *avdu*, when most needed. In addition there is an assonance between *vin'divim* and *b'ven-adam* (literally 'the son of adam/man'), and possibly a further play between *teshuah*, 'the power to save', and *esht'notav*, a word which appears only here in the Bible as a noun, and probably means 'concern', rather than mere 'thoughts' or 'plans'. (The same sense occurs in Jonah 1.6 where the verb appears: 'Perhaps God will think (favourably) about us so that we do not perish'.)

The combined effect of these wordplays is a powerful reinforcement of the overt meaning. Not only are princes and men powerless to help because of their limited lifespan, but they are intrinsically unreliable by their very nature, made of mere 'ground' and 'perishable'; not only can they offer no tangible 'help', even their very desire to help is transient.

In contrast to this tightly constructed and densely woven pair of verses, the following catalogue of God's attributes seems a far looser stringing together of phrases with no apparent pattern to the sequence. However, the first two verses (5–6) are more clearly built as a direct contrast to verses 3–4.

The contrast is stated in verse 5:

> 5. Happy the one for whom the God of Jacob is his help
>   whose hope is in the Eternal his God;

If this contrasts with verse 3 in naming God as the legitimate help to turn to, as opposed to the unreliable help available from mere human beings, then similarly verse 6 parallels verse 4 in describing the attributes of God as a source of help (as opposed to their failings):

> 6. the Maker of heaven and earth,
>   the sea and all within them;
>   who guards the truth forever.

In contradistinction to human beings who return to their dust is the God who created the very dust from which human beings came. Unlike human beings, whose desire to help may never go beyond wishful thinking, God's 'truth' (*emet*), 'faithfulness' and 'reliability' are eternal.

Having stated these contrasts the Psalmist goes on to list more generally the attributes of God in common with the other Psalms in this section. If there is an overriding theme to these it lies within the area of *mishpat*, which means 'justice' in the fullest sense of restoring the correct balance or order of things, the harmonious, regulated interaction between human beings and between humanity and nature. (For this broader sense of *mishpat* see Isa. 28.23–29 and Jer. 8.7.) Indeed the sequence from verses 7–9 seems to follow the

pattern of undoing wrongs (providing justice for the oppressed, feeding the hungry, releasing the bound, giving sight to the blind, straight-
ening the bowed) before moving into the positive aspect of giving
due love to the 'righteous' (*tsaddik* also carries the connotation
of the 'innocent' party in a court case) and protecting in advance
those at risk, the stranger, orphan and widow. Justice concludes,
necessarily, with the punishment of those who pervert it.

Is this list of attributes influenced in any way by our phrase?
It is possible that it may be because of other elements associated
frequently in Psalms with the image of *shamáyim*, 'heaven'. Heaven
is where God dwells (Ps. 2.4; 11.4; 18.14; 73.25; 115.3; 123.1) and
from where God observes the earth and the ways of human beings
(11.4; 14.2 = 53.3; 33.13; 102.20). God's throne is to be found
there (11.4; 103.19) and from there God judges (76.9–10) and rules
(103.19). Thus it is possible that God's role as a 'judge', the restorer
of the harmony of things, beyond the transient promises of princes
and mere mortals, is developed in the Psalm in relation to our phrase
– God, the Maker of heaven and earth, who keeps the truth forever.

Something of these elements may have also influenced the choice
of the closing verse.

> 10. The Eternal will rule forever,
> your God, O Zion, from age to age!
> Praise God!

God who guards the truth forever, whose throne is in heaven, will
rule forever. The association with Zion will be explored further in
the last Psalm of this series.

Before moving on, though, I cannot resist quoting a Midrash on
this Psalm. It depends upon a Rabbinic view of the *ger*, 'the stranger'.
In the Hebrew Bible, the term referred to the 'resident alien', someone who had settled in the Israelite community and was entitled to
most civil rights. With the transformation of Judaism into an exilic
religious community in the later period, the 'political' sense of the
term became transformed into a 'religious' one. The *ger tsédek*
became the 'righteous gentile' = convert. Most Rabbinic utterances
about converts are favourable, with Ruth becoming the ideal model,
but there are occasional expressions of anxiety or even hostility
towards them. In contrast the following is a beautiful expression of
welcome, admiration and love for those who join themselves to
Israel, though perhaps it was needed precisely because of the fears

that some had expressed about those who wished to become part of the Jewish people.

The Lord preserveth the strangers (Ps. 146.9). The Holy One, blessed be He, greatly loves converts. What parable fits here? That of a king who had a flock. Every day it used to go out and feed in the pasture and come back in the evening. One time a stag joined the flock, walking along with the goats and the ewes and feeding with them. He would come back with the flock, and when it would go out to feed, he would go with it. The king was told, 'A stag goes with the flock and feeds with it, every day going out and coming back with it.' And the king came to love the stag exceedingly. When the stag went out into the pasture, the king would command the shepherd, saying to him: 'Take special care of this stag! Let no one strike him.' And when the stag came back with the flock, the king would command his friend concerning him: 'Give him to eat and to drink.' And the king loved the stag more and more. The shepherd said to the king: 'My lord king, many are the he-goats, many the she-goats, many the ewes and many the lambs thou hast, but thou dost not command me to take special care of them. But the stag – every day thou givest me commands about him.' The king replied: 'As for the flock, it feeds in its usual way. But stags, they live in the wilderness. It is not their way to come into inhabited land, among men. This stag did come in, however, and found a place among us. Shall we not show our appreciation of him for having left the great wide wilderness, the place where stags and hinds feed, for having abandoned them and coming among us? We must show our appreciation of him.'

Even so does the Holy One, blessed be He, say: 'I must show My great appreciation of the stranger who has left his family and his father's house and has come to Me.' Therefore, I command concerning him: *Love ye therefore the stranger* (Deut. 10.19); *And a stranger shalt thou not wrong* (Ex. 22.20). Hence it is said *The Lord preserveth the strangers. (Midrash Psalms* 146.8)

PSALM 134

1. *A Pilgrim Song*
   Come! bless the Eternal,
   all servants of the Eternal,
   who stand every night in the house of the Eternal.
2. Raise your hands [to the] holy place
   and bless the Eternal.
3. May the Eternal bless you from Zion,
   the Maker of heaven and earth.

Though the shortest of our five Psalms, this one has the clearest context and on the face of it is the simplest. It belongs, like its companion piece Psalm 135, with which it shares a number of phrases, to the Jerusalem Temple. If Psalm 135 speaks of the servants of the Eternal who stand in the Temple by day, our Psalm speaks of those who serve during the night hours (1 Chron. 9.33).

Verse 1 is matched almost exactly by Psalm 135.1, assuming that the call to 'praise' (*halal*) and to 'bless' (*barach*) God are interchangeable in this particular context (as would also appear to be the case in Ps. 145 vv. 1 and 2).

Verse 2 seems to describe how the ritual was to be performed – in reciting the blessing they should raise their hands towards the 'holy', presumably the innermost part of the sanctuary, the 'Holy of Holies'.

Verse 3. The actual formula of blessing used in this verse is the inversion of that found in Psalm 135.21:

19. House of Israel, bless the Eternal!
    House of Aaron, bless the Eternal!
20. House of Levi, bless the Eternal!
    Those who fear the Eternal, bless the Eternal!
21. 'Blessed is the Eternal from Zion
    who dwells in Jerusalem!
    Praise God!'

In Psalm 135 it is God who is to be blessed/praised according to the command issued in the two previous verses. It is also evident here that just as 'House of Aaron' and 'House of Levi' represent the priests and Levites who served in the Temple, and 'House of Israel' stands for the rest of the Israelite community, so 'those who fear the Eternal' seems to affirm the existence of a group of non-Israelites who nevertheless have a recognized status and place within the ritual. It remains unclear whether they were 'visitors' who came from afar to worship Israel's God, or were themselves already people who had decided to join the Israelite community with full 'political' and 'religious' rights – 'Your people, my people; your God, my God' (Ruth 1.16).

In this form, in Psalm 135, the blessing is both an affirmation and a way of ensuring God's continuing presence on Zion.

To return to verse 3, the version here invokes God's blessing on the worshippers. The actual blessing seems to consist of only three words, 'May the Eternal bless you from Zion', before continuing with the rather awkward transition to our formula, 'Maker of heaven and earth'. However, it is possible that the Psalmist is only quoting here the opening phrase of a somewhat longer blessing. We are familiar with the priestly blessing that is quoted in Numbers 6.24–26, the text of which has been found on a silver 'amulet' that dates back to the sixth century BCE.

> May the Eternal bless you and guard you.
> May the Eternal turn the light of His face to you and be gracious to you.
> May the Eternal lift up his face [in favour] to you and give you peace.

But even closer is the formula to be found in Psalm 128.5–6 which may indeed be the fuller text of which only the opening is cited here:

> 5. May the Eternal bless you from Zion,
>   and may you see the good of Jerusalem
>   all the days of your life!
> 6. May you [live to] see the children of your children!
>   Peace be upon Jerusalem!

Nevertheless the question remains as to the meaning of our phrase in connection with this blessing formula. Part of the answer would seem to lie in the significance of the Jerusalem Temple. Though God dwells in heaven, while the Temple exists, God is manifest upon Zion.

> Out of Zion, the perfection of beauty,
> God has shined forth . . .
> He called to the heaven above and to the earth
> that He might judge His people . . .
> And the heavens declare His righteousness
> for God, He is judge. (Ps. 50.2, 4, 6)

Here God appears as judge of his people; elsewhere in connection with Zion God is seen as the instructor and judge of the nations (Isa. 2.3–4); from Zion will come salvation for his people (Ps. 53.7). However, none of these associations seems to fit the specific context of blessing of our Psalm. But Psalm 135 contains a variation on our phrase which we have already noted earlier in our discussion of the sentence: [But our God is in heaven,] all that pleases Him, He does.

> 5. For I know that the Eternal is great
>   and our Lord is above all gods.
> 6. All that pleased Him, the Eternal did,
>   in heaven and on earth,
>   in the seas and all the deeps.

The rituals that take place in the Temple, the sacrifices, prayers and blessings performed by the priests, have cosmic consequences. While God is present there, the God who created and who owns both heaven and earth, the blessings that flow from the Temple help sustain the earth and indeed the entire cosmic order.

MAKER OF HEAVEN AND EARTH

For the purpose of this study I have assumed that the phrase 'Maker of heaven and earth' was somehow available to all the different composers of these Psalms as part of the currency of religious language. In each case it must have seemed appropriate to include it in the Psalm, though we can never know how consciously the writer was seeking to develop from it a different nuance. Nevertheless, the range of meanings is quite broad.

For the composer of Psalm 121, God, as creator of heaven and earth, can protect human beings on earth from stumbling on the ground itself, and from the sun and moon which God has placed in the heavens. These become, by extension, any natural hazards that might endanger us.

In Psalm 124 it is dangers from human enemies that are evoked, and here the metaphors of engulfing waters and of a bird escaping into the sky emphasize the threefold division of God's creation: sky, earth and water. In this extended metaphor, as their creator, God can likewise protect human beings from dangers present within these domains.

Psalm 115 has a quite different emphasis. Here heaven and earth are defined as the two realms which must be kept apart – a problem examined in the stories of the sons of God and the daughters of man in Genesis 6.1–4 and in the tower of Babel (Gen. 11.1–9). Idols, images of God in human form, symbolize the danger of human beings attempting to cross the barrier. But it may be that the whole issue of artistic representation of any sort and its relationship to human creativity is also being examined.

Psalm 146 explores God's attribute of justice which is particularly associated with God's dwelling in heaven. The contrast is made between the transience of human life, therefore of human attempts at securing justice, and the eternally reliable justice of God.

Finally, Psalm 134 may be evoking the entire cosmos which is to be the recipient of blessings recited by the faithful servants of God at the sanctuary in Zion.

This exploration helps to remind us that no formula or conventional phrase in the Bible can be taken for granted, or removed from its context, if we want to understand its meaning. Whether the biblical writers were motivated by an artistic fascination with the many dimensions of language, or by a religious desire to celebrate God's gift of speech, no phrase remains a mere convention; it is always a potential source of creativity.

I began this chapter by evoking the memory of Rabbi William Braude and in the original version I ended with a quotation from one of his essays. There he was writing about the authors of the Midrash, the Rabbis who sought to find a multiplicity of meanings in the texts that they considered to be the revealed word of God. But I noted then that the same words could apply to the composers of the Psalms who also seemed to delight in the discovery of new dimensions to the language and phrases of their own tradition. Here he refers to the *peshat*, the 'plain' or 'commonsense' meaning of a text. As a master of the art of interpretation and translation, his words apply not only to the great Rabbis of the Midrashic tradition but to his own contribution to our knowledge:

> Surely scripture, whether its author was an artist or, as I would say *the* Artist, provides a thousand and more entrance-ways for the man whose heart is alert and whose eyes are open to *peshat*'s unending depths.[4]

11

A Thousand Years in Your Sight: Psalm 90

I was first attracted to this Psalm because of a strange pun that linked the opening and closing words. The Psalm itself is a profound and moving reflection of the transience of human life and it grapples with the quest for 'meaning' and 'purpose' in our existence. But it was the pun that first puzzled and challenged me to look closer, so let us start there and see how it draws us into a further exploration.

1. *Psalm 90. A Prayer of Moses, the Man of God*
   Lord, You have been our home from generation to generation.
2. Before the mountains were born,
   or the earth and world were formed in travail,
   even from everlasting to everlasting You are God.
3. You return human beings to the dust
   yet You say, 'Return, you mortals!'
4. For a thousand years in Your sight
   are but as a yesterday when it is past,
   a passing hour in the night.
5. You sweep them away,
   They are like sleep.
   In the morning they grow like grass,
6. in the morning it flourishes and grows,
   in the evening it fades and withers.
7. For we are consumed in Your anger,
   terrified by Your rage.
8. You have set our sins before You,
   our hidden ones before the light of Your face.
9. For all our days pass away in Your wrath.
   We end our days like a sigh.
10. The days of our years are seventy years,
    eighty years with strength,

but they are troubled with grief and emptiness;
for it is speedily gone and we fly away.

11. Who knows the power of Your anger?
Your wrath matches the fear of You.

12. So teach us to measure our days
that we acquire a heart of wisdom.

13. Return, O Eternal, how long!
Take pity on Your servants!

14. Satisfy us in the morning with Your faithful love
that we may rejoice and be glad all our days.

15. Make us glad according to the days You afflicted us,
the years we saw evil.

16. Let Your deeds be seen by Your servants
and Your glory upon their children.

17. Let the pleasantness of the Lord our God be upon us.
Establish for us the work of our hands;
the work of our hands, establish it.

First the pun! It is to be found, as we have already seen in other Psalms, in an 'inclusio', one that links together verses 2 and 17. The former reads:

2. *adonay ma'on attah hayyíta lánu b'dor vador*
Lord, You have been our home from generation to generation.

In both verses 2 and 17 the word used for God is *adonay* – not the customary 'substitute' reading for the tetragrammaton, YHWH, but the full set of consonants, *álef, dálet, nun, yod*, that spell the word *adon*, 'Lord', itself. That in itself should lead us to link the two verses, particularly as the tetragrammaton only otherwise appears once, in verse 13. In verse 2 God is described as being our *ma'on*, a word variously translated as 'dwelling place', 'shelter' or 'refuge'. Ibn Ezra draws our attention to the blessing Moses gave to the tribe of Asher (Deut. 33.27) – in a Psalm that is itself ascribed to Moses:

m'onah elohei kédem
The God of eternity is your dwelling place.

Therefore *ma'on* seems to be an appropriate and understandable term. But when we get to verse 17, the Psalmist requests:

vihi no'am adonay elohéinu aléinu
Let the pleasantness of the Lord our God be upon us.

It is the word 'pleasantness' that seems somehow out of place. The same root gives us the name 'Naomi'. But 'pleasantness' is a rather weak, let alone puzzling, term to invoke here, and the problem is reflected in the different suggestions offered to translate it: 'graciousness', 'favour', 'loveliness', 'delightfulness'. But if they 'fit' the English they may not accurately reflect the Hebrew. The one other place where it appears, also linked with the name of God, is Psalm 27.4:

> One thing I ask of the Eternal,
> that I will seek,
> to dwell in the House of the Eternal all the days of my life
> to gaze upon the 'pleasantness' of the Eternal
> and to visit in His Temple.

Here the term makes more sense and it may well be that some relationship exists between the usages of the term in these two Psalms. But it remains odd in Psalm 90 until we recognize that *no'am* is an anagram of our opening word *ma'on*; in fact it is the identical consonants reversed. It is then only a short step to realize that whereas the opening speaks about us dwelling *in* the *ma'on* of God, in the past, we look to God's *no'am* being upon us in the future. Both sentences speak of being 'contained', 'secure' within God's presence, and project this experience in time either backwards into the past or forward into the future. The slight awkwardness of the term *no'am* is explained by the necessity, or literary conceit, of this pun. It makes sense, of course, but it has pushed this word to the boundaries of its meaning.

This 'inclusio' suggests that the entire Psalm, which deals with the transience of human life, is framed by a sense of a timeless past and future, as well as some kind of security that can be found in the presence of God. It gives a structure and perspective for the exploration that will now ensue within the Psalm itself.

The problem of 'time' is directly addressed in the first two verses which have a chiastic structure:

> *adonay   ma'on   attah   hayíta   lánu   b'dor   vador*
> *b'térem   harim   yulládu*
> *vat'choleil   érets   v'teiveil*
> *uma'olam   ad-olam   attah   el*

1. Lord, You have been our home from generation to generation.
2. Before the mountains were born,
   or the earth and world were formed in travail,
   even from everlasting to everlasting You are God.

God has been our home from 'generation to generation' – here time is measured by the passing of human generations, a biological measurement that already hints that generations come and go, but God remains eternal. There follows a paradoxical image – the mountains which are permanent features of the world and the very earth itself are described with human terms for procreation: *yulládu*, 'born'; *vat'choleil*, literally, 'writhing', a term used of 'birthpangs'. The material world itself had a beginning, a physical birth, one witnessed and caused by God, before human beings ever came into existence. Then comes the parallel to 'generation to generation', the phrase 'from everlasting to everlasting'. But in this case any 'biological' association is lost, *olam* being a more abstract term for a long period of time, from before the earth even came into existence (Proverbs 8.23). ('Historical' time is usually limited by four generations, forward and backward in time from the speaker.)

But what can be born can also die so that mortality is already implied in these two verses in anticipation of its blunt description in verse 3:

tashev   enosh   ad-dakka   vattómer   shúvu   v'nei-adam

3. You return human beings to the dust
   yet You say, 'Return, you mortals!'

The root *'shuv* which appears here twice is one of the key words of this Psalm and one which has a variety of meanings, all of which can be brought into play here. Its first meaning is to 'turn', but that allows it to incorporate a number of physical actions – to turn around, turn back, return – as well as the figurative sense of 'turning from evil actions' (Jonah 3.10) and hence a 'spiritual' turning about, a return to the right path or to God. Its first appearance in this verse suggests that it is a paraphrase of the Genesis view (3.19) that human beings (*adam*) were created from the 'ground', *adamah* to which they return when they die. But instead of the expected term *'aphar'*, 'dust' ('for dust you are and to dust you return'), we have the term *dakka* from a root meaning to 'grind' or 'crush'. Hence it can mean 'dust' in the sense of something that has been ground down into fine particles, or in a figurative sense, a person who is 'crushed', 'contrite', 'humble in spirit' (Isa. 57.15), 'broken in heart' (Ps. 34.19). So the verse can mean, 'You return human beings back to the dust from which they came', a statement of objective reality; or 'You force human beings into a state of contrition', which has a stronger emotive content. Since we would have expected the Genesis term *'aphar'* for dust in this phrase, the use of *'dakka'* suggests that a deliberate play on the two meanings is intended.

Incidentally it was once my privilege to invite to speak at Leo Baeck College Dr W. E. Shewell-Cooper, a remarkable horticulturalist and organic gardener, a committed Christian who was fascinated with studying the plant life of the Bible. He had an eight acre garden around his home where he experimented with organic gardening techniques. (I went to visit him one Sunday with my in-laws from Germany who were farmers, and he told me off for disturbing his day of rest. I pointed out that I could not come on Saturday because that was *my* day of rest! We agreed to disagree.) At the College he spoke with enormous enthusiasm about composting and explained that the biblical term *aphar* should not be translated as 'dust', because that implied something lifeless. Instead he preferred the term 'humus': 'Humus thou art and to humus thou shalt return.' As he puts it in his book:[1]

> [It is] the compost heap which produces the right organic matter which will provide the necessary humus in the soil and *this* is vital. Humus has been described as the 'blood' of the soil, thus no humus, and the soil is dead.

I came away wondering whether he thought that the only purpose of the birth and life of human beings was so that on our death we could provide useful nourishment for the soil! If that is to parody his views, I apologize, because he was a serious religious believer so perhaps I had misread his understanding of the transcendent value of human life. But I am grateful to him for awakening me to the 'life' in a piece of soil, and as a result of meeting him our family became committed to 'composting' organic waste long before it became fashionable.

But to return to our Psalm, *dakka* contains precisely that sense of something so pulverized that all life is crushed out of it, the very opposite of 'humus'. Which leads us to the problem of understanding the second part of our verse, where the verb *shuv* recurs. When God speaks, is it to say: 'Return, O children of Adam [to the dust from which you came'], thus simply reinforcing the message of the previous part of the verse? Or is it instead an appeal to the one who is contrite: 'Return to Me', or as the derived term *teshuvah* is usually translated, 'repent'? Both options are equally possible and so this verse penetrates to the very heart of the problem posed by the Psalm. Is human life a mere episode, we come from 'dust' and return to it, because that is the nature of existence or the 'will of God', depending on how one views things? Or is human life, and the suffering that leads to 'a contrite heart', part of a drama in which we are continually being called to return to God, so that our life can have some kind of meaning and fulfilment, can indeed experience something of the eternity that is the reality of God? Or is it simply that we swing between these two perceptions, reading our life sometimes as destiny and sometimes as mere fate? The Psalm clearly comes down on the side of the quest for religious meaning as it develops its argument, but at this stage both options are open.

Incidentally, the meaning we choose to find in the latter part of this verse depends almost entirely on how we read the letter *vav* at the beginning of the word *vattómer*, 'You say', because the *vav*, as well as its grammatical role in establishing the tense of the verb, can mean a simple 'and', thus furthering the idea of the earlier part, or an adversative 'but!', allowing for God to call us back instead of sending us further away.

The third occurrence of *shuv* is in verse 13, where the Psalmist reverses the situation and calls to God to 'turn', or 'turn back' or 'return' and take pity on 'Your servants'. Here it is the human feeling of being abandoned by God that is being addressed, as yet another nuance of the word is evoked. But also the mutual responsibility of God and Israel is being asserted. If the speaker is saying here, 'Return to us!', then, at least by this stage of the Psalm, we can reread the words of God as a similar plea to human beings: 'Return to Me!'

The examination of the 'quality' of life continues with the next section. For measured against the 'eternity' of God's existence, 'a thousand years', our own seems like no more than a night that has passed, or even less than that, a 'watch', one of the subdivisions of the night for those on guard duty, perhaps the smallest unit of time they could measure. (The same sort of contrast between 'a thousand', the largest unit of time they could imagine, and a single 'lifespan' in terms of the four generations an individual might know, is found also in the Ten Commandments, Ex. 20.5–6.)

The 'thousand years' described here leads to a marvellous piece of Midrashic interpretation. In the Garden of Eden, God had warned Adam about the fruit of the tree of the knowledge of good and evil: 'on the day you eat from it you shall surely die!' (Gen. 2.17). But Adam did not die on that day! Because the 'day' in question was God's day, which lasts for one thousand years by human reckoning. Because he could see into the future Adam knew that one day King David would be born but that he was destined to die very young, so he lent him 70 years from his own lifespan so that he could fill his normal quota, as our Psalm itself expresses it: 'The days of your years are seventy years' (v. 10). That explains why Adam died at the age of 930 (Gen. 5.5).

Verses 5 and 6 explore the transience of human life through two, or possibly three images. Most clear is that of grass that springs up 'in the morning', but by evening fades and dies. The second one is that of a mere night's sleep – which is actually time outside of time, since we are not even conscious of it. (Rabbi David Kimchi explains the verse to mean that our life is like a dream, for when we awake nothing of the dream remains real.)

The first term in verse 5, '*z'ramtam*', is less easy to understand. The root *zaram* seems to mean to pour out, flood – as in floods of rain but also, in one case (Ezek. 23.20), a seminal emission. So the commonest interpretation of this image is that of our being swept away as by a flood of water. However, with the help of a slight emendation, Professor Harry Torczyner, who later settled in Israel and wrote under the name Tur Sinai, proposed the magnificent 'an emission from the bladder are they'! Professor Winton Thomas follows the same line with 'emission of seed in sleep are they'. Neither of these readings seems particularly convincing.

Perhaps what is intentional here is the staccato effect of the opening of verse 4 – as if mimicking the sudden interruption that death brings unexpectedly to our lives: '*z'ramtam sheinah yih'yu*', 'You sweep them away! Sleep they are!'

In my Notes on this Psalm I have recorded an observation by my then student Rabbi Fred Morgan that these verses too are chiastically constructed.

5. You sweep them away.
   They are like sleep.
   In the morning they grow like grass,
6. in the morning it flourishes and grows,
   in the evening it fades and withers.

The outer framework emphasizes transience and death – swept away, like sleep, withering and fading. (The closing word of this part, *v' yavesh*, 'withers', 'dries up', is also an anagram of *shuv*, 'return', with the two consonants reversed. It is hard to know if this is intentional, but it would reinforce the idea of our 'returning' to the dust, dried up, brittle and falling apart.) The inner sentences express the hopefulness and freshness of the morning when they blossom.

The Psalmist now moves from the length of our life (vv. 4–6) to its nature and quality (vv. 7–9).

7. For we are consumed in Your anger,
   terrified by Your rage.
8. You have set our sins before You,
   our hidden ones before the light of Your face.
9. For all our days pass away in Your wrath.
   We end our days like a sigh.

The familiar chiastic form emerges here once again, the outer structure describing God's anger and our fear (We), the inner part explaining why this is so in terms of our sins that stand before God's face (You).

It is a very dark picture. On one level it is a simple observation of human experience and reality – that we have no control over the major factors that enter our life and especially the way in which, or time when, it ends. We live with that fear. That we spend our life alienated from God, failing to live up to what we could or should be, is a common religious position, different faiths being more or less generous in the provisions they make for restoring what is considered the right relationship to God. Interestingly Rabbi David Kimchi takes the 'we' of this section to refer to Israel in exile – that is why we are living under God's anger, our sins constantly before God's eyes. Abraham Ibn Ezra seems to be attempting to bridge the gap between the 'objective' evaluation of human experience and the problem of finding a proper theological explanation of suffering and death. He surprisingly and daringly adds an 'as if' to his paraphrase of verse 7:

> As if You are angry with us. That is why our days end!

This is the second way in which the Psalmist has tried to show our lives through two different perspectives – that of human beings and that of God. First came the comparison of our thousand years against God's 'day', now comes the attempt to view the quality of our life from God's perspective.

God	*Human Beings*
Timelessness	Timebound
Worth	Sin/worthlessness

But we are still at this stage only part way through the Psalmist's analysis, and he will now change his perspective again.

> 10. The days of our years are seventy years,
>   eighty years with strength,
>   but they are troubled with grief and emptiness;
>   for it is speedily gone and we fly away.
> 11. Who knows the power of Your anger?
>   Your wrath matches the fear of You.

From seeing our years from God's perspective, we now turn back to our own human experience – a life of a limited period, one full of trouble and grief, that nevertheless passes all too quickly. (Some of the medieval Jewish commentators addressed the question posed to them: How could Moses have written this Psalm since he lived to be 120 years old? Their answer, that Moses is here speaking about the generality of humanity!)

The closing part of verse 11 is somewhat unclear: '*u'ch' yirat'cha evratécha*', literally, 'and as the fear of You Your anger'. Rashi tried to explain it:

> In such a short life as this who can acquire for himself a heart to understand the strength of Your anger and to fear You? And as for You, as is the fear of You, so is Your anger.

Rabbi David Kimchi gives this verse a brilliant reading:

> Who can guard himself from Your anger and how great is Your anger for we see that as much as is the fear of you in a person, so is Your anger upon them. That is to say, whoever fears You

more, so much more will be Your anger upon him when he sins
a little, as did Moses [when he struck the rock and was punished
by being unable to enter the Promised Land, Num. 20.12–13] . . .
and as was the case with the sons of Aaron [struck down for
bringing 'strange fire' to the altar] (Lev. 10.3). From those close
to Me I expect proper holiness!

We can now see how the Psalmist has constructed this central part
of his argument:

4–6 Transience of life	God's perspective
7–9 Value of life	God's perspective
10 Transience of life	Human perspective
11 Value of life	Human perspective

Since this dual perspective is being acted out against the question
of the value of human life we can show what is going on with a
further diagram:

PAST

Timelessness   Time

PRESENT

Worth   Worthlessness

FUTURE

How are these different polarities to be resolved? The answer is, in
part, to acquire a 'heart of wisdom'.

limnot   yaméinu   kein   hoda
v'navee   l'vav   chochmah

12. So teach us to measure our days
    that we acquire a heart of wisdom.

Ibn Ezra reads this to mean that when we acknowledge that our days
are few in number we will get a wise heart. But perhaps the thrust
of the Psalm so far is to indicate that through wisdom we are able
not merely to count our days but 'measure' them, seek their value,
somewhere between God's and our own human perspective upon
them.

Rashi discusses the adjective *kein*, which comes from a root meaning to 'establish', and is often translated as 'so' – as in the Genesis
story: 'and it was so!' (Gen. 1.7, 9, 11, etc.). He notes that it has

the numerical value of 70 (*kaf* = 20, *nun* = 50). This would lead to the translation: 'To count our days, 70, teach us!'

But 'wisdom' alone is not enough. Here the broader framework of the Psalm, the fact that it is couched throughout in the 'we' form rather than the singular 'I', comes to the fore. It is presumably for this reason that Radak has consistently read it in terms of the experience of Israel in exile – for now comes the plea to God to 'return' to 'Your servants'. But with the introduction of that now familiar term *chésed*, 'faithful love', in verse 14, the broader framework of the covenant is evoked.

13. Return, O Eternal, how long!
    Take pity on Your servants!
14. Satisfy us in the morning with Your faithful love
    that we may rejoice and be glad all our days.
15. Make us glad according to the days You afflicted us,
    the years we saw evil.
16. Let Your deeds be seen by Your servants
    and Your glory upon their children.

The 'morning' that had given the false illusion of a fresh new growth, only to wither in the evening (vv. 5–6), is now to be strengthened by God's *chésed*. The 'eternal' covenant (with a 'thousand generations' (Ex. 34.7)) now intertwines with the transient life of the individual or community, giving it a different kind of permanence. And not only permanence but also joy, enough to replace the sorrow and travail of a life without God. Here the Jewish commentators divide. Some see in this text a messianic promise – the morning of redemption and salvation which is the morning following the night of trouble, sighing and blackness, i.e. exile (Rashi). Others read it in terms of our personal lives – If You treat us with Your *chésed* in our youth when You teach us the straight way, then we will rejoice all our days, even in our old age (Abraham Ibn Ezra).

Yet again this section is chiastically arranged. This time there are two elements in the 'inner' part, a new time of joy in our lives, but one that will last for the 'days' that are equivalent to the past days in which we saw evil. Around it is the return of God to his faithful servants, showing mercy upon them because of their suffering in the past, but also displaying new deeds for those 'servants' in the present and even greater glory for their children. We are moving our focus from the present into the future.

Which leads us into verse 17 and the final resolution of the tensions the Psalmist has explored, between time and timelessness, worthlessness and worth – the moment when what we do and what God wills for us coincide.

> 17. Let the pleasantness of the Lord our God be upon us.
>   Establish for us the work of our hands;
>   the work of our hands, establish it.

Let God's 'pleasantness' be upon us – 'favour', 'agreement', 'approval'? And support us for the work that we seek to do, and support that work itself.

The 'symmetry' within the Psalm is quite extraordinary – as one might expect in a Psalm composed with 'wisdom', *chochmah*, which in its first sense in Hebrew means 'craftsmanship'. God's call to us to *shuv* (v. 3), to return to God, is matched by our plea to God to return to us (v. 13). Our lives are examined as they appear to us and to God. The *ma'on*, 'refuge', we have experienced in God in the past is to be restored in a new way in the future, when we live within the *no'am*, 'favour', of God. The days of suffering we experienced in the past, in God's anger, are to be replaced by days of joy. Just as we are to experience that change in our own personal lives, so the closeness to God of past generations will again be experienced by our future ones.

12

'But Surely . . .': A Meditation on Psalm 73

For the final Psalm it seemed appropriate to move beyond the analysis of a text into some kind of interpretation. Psalm 73 lends itself to a more meditative kind of treatment, particularly because of the inner drama that it describes. The following analysis was sparked off by reading an essay on it by Martin Buber and it allowed me the opportunity to incorporate a few passages from spiritual thinkers and teachers that continue to speak to me. After so much analysis it is right to try a kind of synthesis.

In the following translation I have tried to indicate, by translating words consistently, some of the 'key words' that interact with each other. I have also divided up the Psalm on the basis of the 'character' that is at the centre of the discussion: the 'wicked'/'they'; the 'I' of the writer; and 'God'.

1. *A Psalm of Asaph*
   But surely God is good to Israel!
   to those who are pure in heart!

2. But as for me, my foot came close to stumbling,
   my steps almost gave way,
3. for I was envious of the arrogant
   when I saw the peace of the wicked.
4. For they suffer no pangs,
   their bodies are perfectly sound.
5. They are not troubled like the rest of humanity,
   nor plagued like other people.
6. So pride is their necklace,
   they clothe themselves in violence.
7. Their eyes bulge out of fatness,
   the insolence of their heart overflows.

8. They scoff and speak of evil,
   speaking of oppression from above.
9. They set their mouth against the heavens
   and their tongue struts through the earth.
10. So His people turn towards them,
    drinking their words to the full.
11. And they say: 'How can God know?
    Is there knowledge in the Most High?
12. Look! Such are the wicked,
    always at ease and growing in power!'

13. But surely for nothing have I kept my heart clean
    and washed my hands in innocence.
14. For I am plagued all day long,
    tormented morning after morning.
15. Yet if I had said, 'I will speak thus!'
    I would have betrayed a generation of Your children.
16. But when I strove to know what this meant
    it was always troublesome to my eyes.
17. Until I entered into the sanctuaries of God
    and understood their end.

18. Surely You set them on a slippery path,
    hurl them into utter ruin.
19. How they are destroyed in a moment,
    utterly swept away by terrors!
20. Like a dream to one suddenly awake, O Lord,
    You despise these phantoms when You arise.

21. When my heart was soured
    and I was pierced with inner pain,
22. I was stupid and did not know;
    I was a beast before You.
23. But as for me, I am always before You,
    You have grasped my right hand.
24. You will guide me with Your counsel
    and afterwards receive me in glory.
25. Whom else have I in heaven?
    And having You, I want no one on earth.

26. My flesh and my heart may waste away
    but the rock of my heart and my portion forever is God.

27. For see, those far from You perish.
    You make an end to those who betray You.
28. But as for me, the nearness of God is my good.
    I have made the Lord God my refuge
    that I might tell of all Your works.

'But surely, nevertheless . . . !' Dramatically our Psalm begins –
despite appearances, despite experience, despite history – 'God is
good to Israel'. Whether the Psalmist responds here to Israel's biblical experience of exile, or looks to some other event that shows the
agonizing contradictions between the hopes and the fate of the people
of God – 'God is good to Israel'.

The writer begins with what should logically be the end, the
conclusion that the Psalm itself painfully works towards. So this
creates a tension, changing with a single 'but' what might otherwise
seem a simply pious belief into an affirmation that can only be
reached after struggle and self-doubt. So we might imagine an audience, in the aftermath of destruction, questioning, confused and
uncertain – less about God's justice, for that remains an ultimate
mystery, than about our own desire or need to link ourselves to God,
about our own faith, if 'God does not know, the Most High is not
concerned' (v. 11).

Again it must be made clear that it is not the success or failure
of the wicked that is ultimately at stake here – but rather the reactions
of the person of faith to these disconcerting realities. Our Psalm
stands, as it were, within brackets (yet another 'inclusio'), for just
as it opens with the word 'good', so it closes with it as well: 'But
as for me, the nearness of God is my *good* . . .' (v. 28). The 'good'
the poet finds personally is that same 'good' that Israel experienced
– to be near to God; and the whole Psalm turns upon the mystery
of that inner struggle between being near to or distant from God.

Even the continuation of the first verse explores this idea: 'to those
who are pure in heart'. At first glance this phrase seems almost
elitist. Whether 'Israel' is characterized as the 'pure in heart' among
the nations, or the Psalmist speaks of the 'righteous' among Israel
itself, it seems to say that God's goodness is reserved for some
special class of saints or pietists to which the author presumably

belongs. And indeed we know the term 'pure in heart' from Psalm
24 where it is one of the qualities needed so as to stand in the
presence of God (Ps. 24.3–4). Yet already the Midrash on Psalms
reads it differently, seeing the background of the Psalm as a time of
oppression and suffering, and interpreting the 'good' that God brings
as these very afflictions that Israel suffers.

> Good for them in what way? Do not read 'for the pure in heart'
> but 'to purify the heart', that is 'to purify the heart of the righ-
> teous'. (*Midrash Psalms* 73.1)

Purity of heart in this view is not a static thing – nor is it some
guaranteed result of piety or religious affiliation. Rather it is the
painful process of self-discovery and self-refinement – perhaps trig-
gered, as the Midrashist suggests, by the experience of suffering.
We can hear the voice of Natalia Ginzburg returning to her old home
in Turin after the war, having lost her husband, a victim of the Nazis
in a Roman prison:

> The war is over and people have seen a lot of homes knocked
> down and now they don't feel safe in their own homes any more,
> in the way they used to feel safe and snug in them once. Something
> has happened that they can't get over and years will go by but
> they will never get over it. So we have lamps lit on our tables
> again and vases of flowers and portraits of our loved ones, but
> we don't believe in any of these things any more because once
> we had to abandon them without warning or scrape around point-
> lessly for them in the rubble . . .
>
> When you have been through it once, the experience of evil is
> never forgotten. Anybody who has seen homes knocked down
> knows only too well what fragile blessings vases of flowers and
> paintings and clean white walls are . . . But we do not go defence-
> less against this fear. We have a toughness and resilience which
> others before us never knew . . . We are forced to go on dis-
> covering an inner calm that is not born of carpets and vases of
> flowers . . .
>
> There is not one of us who at sometime or other has not dreamed
> of being able to bed down on something soft and comfortable,
> be soothed, be master of some kind of certainty, some faith or
> other, and rest. But now the old certainties have all been shattered,
> and faith has never been just a resting place . . . But we are bound

to this anguish of ours and deep down glad of our destiny as men.[1]

'And faith has never been just a resting place.' It is this awareness that leads Martin Buber in his commentary on our Psalm[2] to write:

> The questioner [whom the Psalmist here answers] had drawn from the fact that things go ill with Israel the conclusion that therefore God is not good to Israel. But only one who is not pure in heart draws such a conclusion. One who is pure in heart, one who becomes pure in heart, cannot draw any such conclusion. For he experiences that God is good to him. But this does not mean that God rewards him with his goodness. It means, rather, that God's goodness is revealed to him who is pure in heart: he experiences this goodness. Insofar as Israel is pure in heart, becomes pure in heart, it experiences God's goodness . . .
>
> The state of the heart determines whether a man lives in the truth, in which God's goodness is experienced, or in the semblance of truth, where the fact that it 'goes ill' with him is confused with the illusion that God is not good to him.
>
> The state of the heart determines. That is why 'heart' is the dominant key word in this Psalm, and recurs six times'. (p. 200)

But before we can live comfortably with this assertion we must experience the struggle of the Psalmist.

2. But as for me, my foot came close to stumbling,
   my steps almost gave way,
3. for I was envious of the arrogant
   when I saw the peace of the wicked.

Who these wicked are is not certain for we have no clear historical context. Are they Israel's conquerors, strutting about in their new dominion? Or are they contemporaries of the Psalmist among Israel, those with similar rank, who nevertheless abuse their power and influence to their own ends rather than using them for the service of God and their community? Something of this latter view is suggested by the comparison made within the Psalm itself – for the Psalmist speaks of their power to move the people by their arrogant words (vv. 10–11), whereas if the writer spoke in public his own feelings of doubt, he would have 'betrayed the generation of Your children' (v. 15).

Yet this portrayal of the success of the wicked, with all the obscurity of some of the phrases, reveals more than angry concern and powerful rhetoric. It displays an obsessive interest, a luscious detailing of their smugness and sleekness, their callousness and pride that moves uneasily from righteous passion to a semi-conscious envy, that the Psalmist will personally have to face and come to terms with.

As so often before it is the repetition of a word or phrase that spotlights the inner message or motivation. Here the internal problem he faces focuses upon his conviction that they are untouched by problems that worry other people. As we first read the sentence (v. 5), 'They are not *troubled* like the rest of humanity, nor *plagued* like other people', the root *amal* with its double sense of 'labour/ toil' and 'trouble/distress' suggests that all the daily burdens of work and struggle to survive are not theirs. Similarly they are not 'plagued' (*naga*); the disasters that befall ordinary people seem not to come upon them. Yet both these words recur with regards the state of the Psalmist himself: 'for I am *plagued* (*naga*) all day long' (v. 14), 'and when I strove to know what this meant, it was always *trouble-some* (*amal*) to my eyes' (v. 16).

In a subtle way, these descriptions of the inner torments of the Psalmist force us to re-examine his critique of the wicked. For not only are they not burdened by the external 'struggles' and 'disasters' of normal people, but it seems that they are untouched by painful moral and ethical choices, they are not troubled by conscience or duty, as is the Psalmist. And here the writer betrays the core of the problem. One part of it is expressed by the founder of Chasidism, the Baal Shem Tov:

> Sinners are mirrors. When we see faults in them, we must realize that they only reflect the evil in us.

Or in terms of a modern Jewish master of the unconscious:

> We hate the criminal and deal severely with him because we view in his deed, as in a distorting mirror, our own criminal instincts. (Sigmund Freud)

For we would secretly love to be pagans, and somewhere inside we resent the rigorous self-refining that God demands of us. It is the recognition and honest acknowledgement of this inner tension that gives us the strength to work with it and turn it to other goals. As the Midrash reworks the passage in Genesis 4.7:

'Sin couches at the door; its urge is towards you, but you can master it.' Do not read 'but you', instead read 'that you' – 'Its urge is towards you *that* you master it, it longs for you to master it.' (*Genesis Rabbah* 22.6)

It is this struggle that the Psalmist seems to be undergoing, though on the surface it is the success of the wicked alone that disturbs him. This is what is revealed in his cry of despair, the second great 'but!' in the Psalm (vv. 12–13): 'Look! such are the wicked, always at ease, amassing wealth! *But* I have kept my heart pure for nothing, washing my hands in innocence!' We recognize here the tragedy of his struggle, but also within it an element of evasion familiar to us all, the one we use to avoid admitting to ourselves that the problem lies not 'out there' in the things that others do or do not do, but 'in here', within us. It is neatly told by C. S. Lewis in his *The Screwtape Letters*. Screwtape, the senior devil, supervising Wormwood, an apprentice devil, guides him in how to use his newly converted Christian 'patient's' first visits to church as a weapon against him.

When he gets to his pew and looks round him he sees just that selection of his neighbours whom he has hitherto avoided. You want to lean pretty heavily on those neighbours ... Provided that any of those neighbours sing out of tune, or have boots that squeak, or double chins, or odd clothes, the patient will quite easily believe that their religion must therefore be somehow ridiculous ...

I have been writing hitherto on the assumption that the people in the next pew afford no *rational* ground for disappointment. Of course if they do – if the patient knows that the woman with the absurd hat is a fanatical bridge-player or the man with the squeaky boots a miser or extortioner – then your task is so much easier. All you then have to do is to keep out of his mind the question 'If I being what I am, can consider that I am in some sense a Christian, why should the different vices of those people in the next pew prove that their religion is mere hypocrisy and convention?' You may ask whether it is possible to keep such an obvious thought from occurring even to a human mind. It is, Wormwood, it is![3]

So our Psalmist is trapped, as he painfully describes it – bearing on

his outside the physical suffering he daily endures while the wicked
are at ease; and internally torn apart by the self-doubt about God's
justice. He is caught in that closed circle of self-contemplation and
self-pity from which there is no direct way out. It is similar to that
perverse relishing of one's own sin and guilt that the Chasidic master
Yitzchak Meir of Ger describes and warns against:

> One who talks about and reflects on the evil he did is thinking
> evil, and what one thinks, therein is one caught ... Stir filth this
> way or that, and it is still filth ... In the time I brood, I could be
> stringing pearls for the joy of heaven. This is what is written:
> 'Depart from evil and do good' (Ps. 34.15) – turn wholly from
> evil, do not brood over it, but do good. You have done wrong?
> Then balance it by doing right.

It is that radical leap out of himself that the Psalmist needed, and
which he found through turning away from the endless contemplation
of the wicked and of his own distress to the encounter with God:
'Until I entered the sanctuaries of God and understood their end'
(v. 17).

The use of the term 'sanctuaries' (from the root *kódesh*, 'holy')
is surprising. In the Hebrew it is expressed in a plural form,
mikd'shei, and some scholars believe this form to be no more than
a standard Hebrew usage for describing important buildings – and
that here the Temple is meant. Others see it as the 'heavenly' sanctuary, or, as Buber suggests, 'the sphere of God's holiness, the holy
mysteries of God. Only to him who draws near to these is the true
meaning of the conflict revealed.'[4]

Yet what is it he finds? Again Buber warns us not to see here the
description of

> a future state of affairs of a quite different kind, in which 'in the
> end' things go well with the good and badly with the bad; in the
> language of modern thought the meaning is that the bad do not
> truly exist, and their 'end' brings about only this change, that
> they now inescapably experience their nonexistence, the suspicion
> of which they had again and again succeeded in dispelling. Their
> life was 'set in slippery places'; it was so arranged as to slide
> into the knowledge of their own nothingness; and when this finally
> happens, in a moment, the great terror falls upon them and they
> are consumed with terror. Their life has been a shadow structure

in a dream of God's. God awakes, shakes off the dream, and disdainfully watches the dissolving shadow image.[5]

Something similar to this is expressed at the end of Psalm 1.

> For the Eternal knows the way of the righteous, but the way of the wicked shall perish.

It is not God who destroys them even – it is their own way itself that leads to their end.

But we cannot escape from the internal psychological nature of the Psalmist's problem, whatever the fate of the wicked may be. For, in a curious reversal of fortune, he, the man whose steps almost slipped, now contemplates the slippery path on which the wicked really walk. And if they vanish in a moment 'consumed by terrors', they who boasted that 'God does not know, the Most High is not concerned', what secret fears of his own depart here with them? How far are they really his own rebellious fantasies that vanish 'like a dream when one awakes'? For those who boast that God does not know may be longing for God 'to know' and prove them wrong. While those who are angered by the boast of the scoffers may believe deep down inside that their words are true, or wish that they were.

> The heart is deceitful above all things, and desperately corrupt; who can know it? (Jer. 17.9)

Again these inner dimensions are hinted at by repetitions in the text itself. For formerly his disgust for the wicked was expressed by saying: 'They have set their mouth against *heaven*, and their tongue walks through the *earth*' (v. 9). But in the personal resolution, these phantoms have utterly vanished: 'Whom [else] have I in *heaven*? And having You, I want no one on *earth*' (v. 25).

Perhaps this explains the vehemence of the final exclamation of self-criticism: 'When my heart was soured within me, and I was pierced by inner pain, *I was stupid and I did not know*; I was a beast before You' (vv. 21–22). We can feel with him that familiar pain of shame and embarrassment that comes with the sudden knowledge of our own folly or religious failure. It is that moment we cannot avoid when we recognize the truth about what we have done, even though, until then, we had pretended to ourselves it was something harmless and innocent. Yet with these words it is not only the realization of some ultimate justice of God's that the Psalmist comes to understand, but it is also possible that a part of Israelite liturgical tradition has suddenly come alive to the writer in a new way. From the Sabbath evening Psalm 92, we recognize the phrase: 'A stupid man does not know,' and its continuation

> and a fool does not understand this,
> that when the wicked flourish they are like grass
> and when all workers of evil spring up,
> it is to be destroyed forever. (Ps. 92.7–8)

That God's justice will finally triumph he has experienced for himself, and so on an outer level has resolved the problem of the seeming triumph of evil that disturbed him. But a deeper answer is also found in the reworking of another verse from that same Psalm:

> For see Your enemies, Eternal, for see Your enemies perish
> *ki   hinneih   oivécha   yovéidu* (Ps. 92.10)

becomes in his version

> *ki   hinneih   r'cheikécha   yovéidu*
> for see, those far from You perish!

This seems to describe the writer's own situation of remoteness and distance from God that has suddenly, and painfully, been acknowledged.

Or was God really that far from the Psalmist? So it seemed when gazing enviously at the wicked – and resenting the time spent trying to keep a pure heart. Perhaps till that moment the Psalmist had been responding like the man in the story told by Herman Wouk:

> The past can be cancelled by a true cry from the heart to God and a return to His law. This holds not only for the annual reckoning, but to the last hour a man lives; so my grandfather taught me.
>
> He had in his Bronx apartment a lodger less learned than himself, and much fiercer in piety. One day when we were studying the laws of repentance together, the lodger burst from his room. 'What!' he said. 'The atheist guzzles whisky and eats pork and wallows with his women all his life long, and then repents the day before he dies and stands guiltless? While I spend a lifetime trying to please God?' My grandfather pointed to the book. 'So it is written,' he said gently. – 'Written!' the lodger roared. 'There are books and there are books!' And he slammed back into his room.

The lodger's outrage seemed highly logical. My grandfather pointed out afterwards that cancelling the past does not turn it into a record of achievement. It leaves it blank, a waste of spilled years. A man had better return, he said, while time remains to write a life worth scanning. And since no man knows his death day, the time to get a grip on his life is the first hour when the impulse strikes him.[6]

The Psalmist, unlike the lodger, now understood this truth. 'A lifetime trying to please God!' is the same cry as the Psalmist's despairing: 'But I have kept my heart pure for nothing, washing my hands in innocence!' (v. 13). Neither faith nor piety are guarantees that we will receive a reward we can recognize – but their effort is not lost. It is when we look for the reward that we do not see it – as expressed in another Chasidic story:

A man complained to Rabbi Bunam: 'The Talmud (Erubin 13a) tells us that when a man runs away from honours, honours run after him. Now I have run away from honours, but no honours pursue me!' 'The reason,' explained the Rabbi, 'is that you keep looking backwards.'

But when we look beyond the reward to the source of our lives, to the 'sanctuaries of God', then we realize what we have truly earned. When the Psalmist's obsession with the evil of others, and his own self-pity, fell away, his real relation to God became crystal clear.

But I am always with You, You hold my right hand ... My flesh and my heart may fail – God is the rock of my heart and my portion forever ... For me, the nearness of God is my good; I have made the Lord God my refuge, that I may tell of all Your works.' (vv. 23, 26, 28)

When the Psalmist breaks through the nightmare of doubt and secret envy, it is this truth he recognizes:

O Eternal, my whole desire is for You
Even though I cannot bring it to my lips.

When far from You, I die while yet in life;
But if I cling to You I live, though I should die.

(Judah Halevi)

But there remains no simple 'happy end'. It is not just the conclusion of the Psalm we are left with, but the whole of it, the record of the struggle. For it is the struggle that is our task when each day the same doubts assail us, when each day it is difficult to see that 'God is good to Israel' and each day demands the further 'purifying of the heart'. We are encouraged by the Psalmist's experience to know that there is the possibility of resolution, but the scoffers within and without must also be heard. For the Psalm begins with 'But . . . !' and it is to that 'nevertheless' that the person of faith repeatedly comes to seek the nearness of God.

In the words of the Chasidic master Levi Yitschak of Berditchev:

> I do not beg You to reveal to me the secret of Your ways – I could not bear it. But show me one thing; show it to me more clearly and more deeply; show me what this, which is happening at this very moment, means to me, what it demands of me, what You, Eternal One of the world, are telling me by way of it. Ah, it is not why I suffer, that I wish to know, but only whether I suffer for Your sake.

Epilogue

Shabbat Morning Sermon at the 35th Jewish–Christian Bible Week, 13–20 July 2003

The Rabbis must have recognized the need to establish a new category of religious literature when they came to consider the Psalms. The Psalms were clearly human compositions. Many were written to accompany the regular worship that took place within the Temple, so they must have been acceptable to God. The solution they came up with was to invoke the *ruach ha-qodesh*, the 'holy spirit'. Thus the Psalms were not directly revealed by God, but God had inspired the authors to write them, using all their human creativity.

The word *ruach* has a number of meanings. In the Bible it is firstly a term for the 'wind', that invisible force, outside of human control, that comes and goes without any obvious reason. One can see how it can be used to represent the mysterious presence of an invisible God. At the same time *ruach* is understood as 'spirit', that mysterious life force within us, the breath of life that disappears with our death.

Any number of biblical references come to mind. The *ruach elohim*, the 'spirit of God' hovering over the waters at the time of the creation. In the Torah reading for this *shabbat* from Parashat Pinchas we discover another use of the word. Moses is told that he will soon die and he appeals to God to appoint a successor so that the people are not left like sheep without a shepherd. So Moses addresses God as '*elohey ha-ruchot l'khol basar*' (Num. 27.16), 'the God of the spirits of all flesh'. Only God who knows the inner spirit of each person alive would be able to select the right person to take on the role of leading the people.

Yet *ruach* is also used in an attempt to understand certain psychological phenomena, particularly the sudden emotional changes that can take place within someone. The Bible understands these as being the result of an external force that enters into that person. When Samson confronts the Philistines in battle, the *ruach adonay*, the 'spirit of the Eternal', descends upon him and he is victorious (Judg. 14.19). On the other hand, the destructive moods that fall upon King Saul are described as a *'ruach elohim ra'ah'*, 'an evil spirit from God' (1 Sam. 16.16, 23). When David played and sang for Saul the evil *ruach* left him.

I would like to introduce another image that also seems to reflect the same sense of divinely ordained but arbitrary forces acting on human beings. The image is that of the pillar of cloud that accompanied the children of Israel on their journey through the wilderness. Whenever the cloud moved on, the children of Israel would break camp and follow it, and whenever the cloud settled, there the children of Israel would camp. I think it was Werner Pelz many years ago at one of the earliest Bible Weeks who asked the question: What would happen if you did not follow the cloud when it moved on? His answer: You would be left behind alone in the wilderness. Both of these images, that of the *ruach* and of the 'cloud', suggest that it is part of our task to be sensitive to their presence in our lives, but also to recognize when they have moved on and look to find them again.

I began to think of this idea because of one of the Psalm verses we have read this week. In the centre of Psalm 5 is a sentence that clearly belonged to the Temple service: *'va'ani b'rov hasd'kha avo veitekha, eshtachaveh el-heikhal-qod'sh'kha b'yir'atekha'*, 'as for me, through Your great loving-kindness, I enter Your House, I prostrate myself before Your Holy Temple, in awe of You.' The Temple was the place where the *ruach* could be encountered, where the cloud settled, where the presence of God was to be found. That is why it could inspire so many Psalms of petition, of thanksgiving, of joy. Tragically, according to the biblical record, the very power of the Temple in the imagination of the people led to its destruction. The people turned it into something magical, a guarantee of their safety. Surely God could never let it be destroyed. It was the tragic fate of the prophet Jeremiah to challenge that magical belief. He mocked those who chanted *'heikhal adonay, heikhal adonay, heikhal adonay'*, 'the Temple of the Eternal, the Temple of the Eternal, the Temple of the Eternal'. The Temple fell and in time so did the Second Temple. But even as the Second Temple fell, there was something there to replace it. Prayer took the place of sacrifices. The synagogue became an alternative place where Jews could worship God, where the *ruach* could be found. So the verse from our Psalm was also relocated. It became one of the opening verses of our daily morning prayers. Through the greatness of God's lovingkindness we enter this other *bayit*, this other house, the house of prayer.

Is the synagogue a holy place? It is certainly not holy in the same way as the Temple. No cloud settles upon it. If it becomes holy, it is because of the *ruach ha-qodesh*, the spirit of holiness, that is brought into it, the holy deeds that are performed there. Through them it can indeed become a Temple to God; without them it is simply another piece of real estate.

I have taken us on this long examination of the language of *ruach* because there is another *bayit*, another 'house', that is particularly dear to all of us who are here today, and very much in our thoughts. It is a house that we have also been privileged to enter *b'rov hasdekha*, because of the 'loving-kindness of God'. It is this house, the Hedwig Dransfeld Haus, that has been a holy place for many of us for significant parts of our life. We carry memories and emotions which are unique to each of us, yet which form part of the extraordinary story of what this house has witnessed and what so many people have brought to it. It is all those who have come here who have brought the *ruach* that we have been privileged to experience and to share.

This week we have been confronted with the shocking reality that this house, this special *bayit*, is in serious financial difficulties and may close. It may be that a rescue plan will still save it at the last moment. It has certainly had to face financial crises for as long as I have known it. We must do what we can to save it. But if our best efforts do not succeed, then we have a different responsibility. For the *ruach* that was here must not be allowed to die. When the cloud moved on, the people moved on with it. The Temple fell, but the *ruach* found a new place in the synagogue. Wherever the programmes that have had their home here may end up, we must ensure that the *ruach* of this place is there too – the love and friendships, the honesty and the piety, the imagination and the courage that renewed our own spirit each time we came.

Elohay ha-ruchot l'khol basar – may the God of the spirits of all flesh give us the strength to preserve the *ruach*, the holy spirit, of this house, and carry the living memory of all we have gained here into our lives and out into the world.

Notes

1 Why Another Book on the Psalms?

1. Joshua Trachtenberg, *Jewish Magic and Superstition: A Study in Folk Religion*, Meridian Books, The World Publishing Company, Cleveland and The Jewish Publication Society of America, Philadelphia, 1961, p. 107.
2. M. Grunwald and Kaufmann Kohler, 'Bibliomancy', *The Jewish Encyclopedia*, Funk & Wagnall, New York, 1903, Vol. 2, pp. 203–4.

2 Biblical Poetry for Beginners

1. Luis Alonso Schökel, *A Manuel of Hebrew Poetics*, Editrice Pontificio Istituto Biblico, Rome, 1988; Robert Alter, *The Art of Biblical Poetry*, Basic Books, New York, 1985; Harold Fisch, *Poetry With A Purpose: Biblical Poetics and Interpretation*, Indiana University Press, Bloomington and Indianapolis, 1990; James L. Kugel, *The Idea of Biblical Poetry: Parallelism and Its History*, Yale University Press, New Haven and London, 1981; M. O'Connor, *Hebrew Verse Structure*, Eisenbrauns, Winona Lake, Indiana, 1980; Wilfred G. E. Watson, *Classical Hebrew Poetry: A Guide to its Techniques*, Journal for the Study of the Old Testament Supplement Series 26, JSOT Press, Sheffield, 1984 – a very helpful, 'hands on' approach to studying the biblical text.
2. See the discussion by Professor Alonso Schökel in *A Manual of Hebrew Poetics*, pp. 8–10.
3. Jonathan Magonet, *A Rabbi Reads the Bible*, second edition, SCM Press, 2004 (originally published as *A Rabbi's Bible*), pp. 73–74.
4. Jonathan Magonet, *Bible Lives*, SCM Press, 1992, pp. 23–32.
5. Jan Fokkelman, *Narrative Art in Genesis: Specimens of Stylistic*

and Structural Analysis. Van Gorcum, Assen/Amsterdam, 1975. Reprinted with new introduction Sheffield Academic Press, Sheffield, 1991.

3 David Sings the Blues – On Concentric Psalms: Psalms 145 and 92

1. Jonathan Magonet, 'Some Concentric Structures in Psalms', *The Heythrop Journal: A Quarterly Review of Philosophy and Theology*, Vol. 23, 4 October 1982, pp. 365–76.
2. Jonathan Magonet, *Bible Lives*, SCM Press, 1992, pp. 20–22.
3. 'Psalms and the Life of Faith: A Suggested Typology of Function', *JSOT* 17, June 1980, pp. 3–32.
4. H. Gunkel, *Die Psalmen*, ed. 5, Göttingen, 1929, reprinted 1968, p. 610.
5. M. Buttenwieser, *The Psalms*, New York, 1938, reprinted 1969, p. 849.
6. W. O. E. Osterley, *The Psalms*, London, 1955, p. 572.
7. Magonet, 'Some Concentric Structures in Psalms', pp. 369–71.
8. Harold Fisch, *Poetry With A Purpose: Biblical Poetics and Interpretation*, Indiana University Press, Bloomington and Indianapolis, 1988, pp. 126–35.

4 Through Rabbinic Eyes: Psalm 23

1. Aubrey R. Johnson, *The Vitality of the Individual in the Thought of Ancient Israel*, Cardiff, 1949, pp. 10ff.
2. Nehama Leibowitz, *Leader's Guide to the Book of Psalms*, Hadassah Education Department, 1971, p. 39.
3. Daniel Jeremy Silver, 'The Twenty-Third Psalm: A Modern Rabbinic Commentary', *Journal of Reform Judaism*, Spring 1978, pp. 45–53, 49f.
4. M. Buttenwieser, *The Psalms*, New York, 1938, reprinted 1969, p. 552.

5   Rewriting Tradition: Psalm 25

1. Peter C. Craigie, *Psalms 1–50, Word Biblical Commentary 19*, Word Publishing, 1983, p. 217.

6   A Stairway to Paradise: On Psalm 19

1. Artur Weiser, *The Psalms (Old Testament Library)*, SCM Press, 1962, p. 197.
2. Mitchell Dahood, *Psalms (The Anchor Bible)*, Vol. I, Doubleday & Co, New York, 1968, p. 121.
3. Revd Dr A. Cohen, *The Psalms With Hebrew Text and English Translation*, The Soncino Press, 1944, p. 53.
4. H. Tur Sinai, *P'shuto Shel Miqra*, Kiryat Sefer, Jerusalem, 1962, Vol. 4:1, p. 36. What was presumably an earlier version of this is quoted by my late Bible teacher Dr Ellen Littmann in an article, 'An Interpretation of Psalm 19', in *The Synagogue Review* December 1960, pp. 93–95. She gives as the source H. Torczyner, *The Riddle In The Bible*, pp. 148–49.
5. Amos Chacham, *Sefer Tehillim (Da'at Miqra)*, 2 Vols, Mossad Harav Kook, Jerusalem, 1979, Vol. 1, p. 102.
6. D. J. A. Clines, 'The Tree of Knowledge and the Law of Yahweh (Psalm XIX)', *Vetus Testamentum*, 24 (1974), pp. 8–14.
7. Gordon M. Freeman, *The Heavenly Kingdom*, University Press of America, 1986.

7   Why Have You Forsaken Me? Psalm 22

1. See his comments on Psalm 19 (p. 85) and the reference there to his commentary on Psalms, note 5.
2. William G. Braude, *The Midrash on Psalms*, Yale Judaica Series, Vol. XIII, 2 Vols, Yale University Press, New Haven, Connecticut, 1959.

8   Did My Mother Conceive Me in Sin? Psalm 51

1. Artur Weiser, *The Psalms (OTL)*, SCM Press, 1962, p. 405.
2. *The Jerusalem Bible*, Darton, Longman & Todd, 1966, p. 833, Ps 51 note c.

3. Meir Weiss, *The Bible From Within: The Method of Total Trans-lation*, The Magnes Press, The Hebrew University, Jerusalem, 1984, p. 126.

9 'The Musical!': Psalm 118

1. In the chapter 'From a Narrow Place: A New Year Sermon' in my book *Talking to the Other: Jewish Interfaith Dialogue with Christians and Muslims*, I. B. Tauris, 2003, pp. 192–8.

10 Maker of Heaven and Earth – A Text in Context: Psalms 115, 121, 124, 134, 146

1. Nehama Leibowitz, *Leader's Guide to the Book of Psalms*, Hadassah Education Department, 1971, p. 49.
2. Avi Hurvitz, 'The History of a Legal Formula *kol 'asher hafets 'asah* (Psalms 115.3; 135.6)', *Vetus Testamentum*, 23, 3 (1982), pp. 257–67.
3. Chanan Brichto, 'The Beauty of Japhet and the Tents of Shem – An Exegesis of Psalm 115', *Journal of Reform Judaism*, 29, 3 (1982), pp. 26–32.
4. W. G. Braude, 'Midrash as Deep Peshat', *Studies in Judaica, Karaitica and Islamica Presented to Leon Nemoy on his Eightieth Birthday*, Ramat Gan, 1982, p. 38.

11 A Thousand Years in Your Sight: Psalm 90

1. W. E. Shewell-Cooper, *God Planted a Garden: Horticulture in the Bible*, Arthur James, 1977, p. 213.

12 'But Surely . . .': A Meditation on Psalm 73

1. Natalia Ginzburg, 'A Son of Man', *European Judaism*, Vol. 6, no. 2, Summer 1972, pp. 7ff.
2. Martin Buber, 'The Heart Determines', *Biblical Humanism: Eighteen Studies*, Schocken Books Inc, New York/MacDonald & Co, London, 1968, pp. 199–210.
3. C. S. Lewis, *The Screwtape Letters: Letter from a Senior to a Junior Devil*, Collins, Fontana Books, 1955, pp. 16, 18.

4. Buber, 'The Heart Determines', p. 204.
5. Buber, 'The Heart Determines', p. 204.
6. Herman Wouk, *This Is My God*, Jonathan Cape, 1960, p. 88.

Glossary

(*indicates a term appearing elsewhere in this Glossary)

Adonay   Literally, 'Lord', the term used in Jewish tradition as a substitute for pronouncing aloud the tetragrammaton, the four-letter name of God, YHWH. Translated in this book as The Eternal.

Emet   Hebrew term: 'Truth'. It is derived from the root *amen* that indicates something 'firm' and 'reliable'. Hence we say 'amen' when we wish to record our acceptance of what has just been said. Hence 'truth' is something that can be relied on. From the same root comes the word *emunah*, 'faith' or 'belief'.

Chanan   Hebrew term: To be gracious, hence 'to show favour'.

Chasid, Chasidic   Chasidism is a popular pietistic and mystical movement that developed in Eastern Europe in the eighteenth century.

Chésed   Hebrew term: It stands for the binding force of love and loyalty within a covenant relationship. It is often translated as 'loving-kindness' or 'mercy', but it is best understood in terms of 'faithful love'.

Genesis Rabbah   *Midrashic commentary on the biblical Book of Genesis. Before the tenth century.

Ibn Ezra, Abraham   (1089–1140)   Spanish Rabbi, poet, Bible commentator, philosopher, grammarian and physician. He travelled widely throughout North Africa and Europe, including visits to London and Oxford.

Judah Halevi   (c. 1075–1141)   Spanish Hebrew poet, philosopher and physician. Author of *The Kuzari*.

Kavod   Hebrew term: From a root meaning 'heavy', 'weight', it suggests the 'weight' or 'significance' people ascribe to you – hence 'glory', 'presence' or 'self'.

Kimchi, Rabbi David (RaDaK) (*c.* 1160-*c.* 1235)   Rabbi, grammarian and biblical commentator in Provence. His work was studied in Christian circles and influenced indirectly Martin Luther's Bible translation.

Leviticus Rabbah   *Midrashic commentary on the Book of Leviticus.

Melech   Hebrew term: King.

Midrash   Explanation. From the root *darash* meaning 'to seek out', or 'search'. The term used for Rabbinic interpretation of the Hebrew Bible. There are a number of Midrashic collections on various books of the Bible, including a tenth-century collection commenting on the Psalms.

Midrash Psalms   Homiletical   *Midrash on the Book of Psalms, tenth century. Also called Midrash Schocher Tov.

Mishnah   (Learning) Legal work consisting of Rabbinic decisions and interpretations of the *Torah, and forming the basis of the *Talmud. Compiled by Judah HaNasi in the second century CE. It represents the 'Oral' Law as opposed to the 'Written' Law, i.e. the Torah.

Néfesh   Hebrew term: Related to a word meaning to breathe, it stands for the 'soul', 'life force', 'self', 'life' itself and 'appetite'.

Pesachim   (Passover) Tractate of the *Mishnah and in the *Talmud in the order *Mo'ed* (Seasons) dealing with the laws of Passover.

rachum   Hebrew term: Derived from the word *rechem*, 'womb', it means to be loving, compassionate, generous and merciful.

Rashi   (Rabbi Solomon ben Isaac) (1040–1105) French Rabbi and leading scholar of his age. His commentary accompanied the first printed edition of the Hebrew Bible.

Talmud   (Teaching) Compilation of the commentaries of the Rabbis on the *Mishnah from the second to the fifth centuries, covering both religious and civil matters. A mixture of laws, customs, discussions, stories and *obiter dicta*, it became the foundation of Jewish practice throughout the world.

Targum   The Aramaic translation of the Hebrew Bible.

Tehillim   Hebrew term: From the root *halal*, 'to praise', it is the term used for the Book of Psalms. The same root gives the term 'Halleluyah', 'Praise God'.

Torah   (Teaching) The Five Books of Moses (Pentateuch). The term is also used to mean the whole of the Bible and subsequent Jewish teaching.

Yalkut Shimeoni   A collection of *midrashim on the Hebrew Bible compiled by Simeon of Frankfurt in the thirteenth century.

zachar   To remember, in the sense of calling something back into existence. In one grammatical form it means to 'call out' or 'speak out'.

Appendix:

Hebrew Texts of the Psalms

Because this book is basically in English, it would
be confusing at this point to print the Hebrew
Psalms from the back forward as they would
appear in the Hebrew Bible. They therefore follow
the English pattern.

Psalm 19

1   לַמְנַצֵּחַ מִזְמוֹר לְדָוִד:

2   הַשָּׁמַיִם מְסַפְּרִים כְּבוֹד־אֵל וּמַעֲשֵׂה יָדָיו מַגִּיד הָרָקִיעַ:

3   יוֹם לְיוֹם יַבִּיעַ אֹמֶר וְלַיְלָה לְּלַיְלָה יְחַוֶּה־דָּעַת:

4   אֵין־אֹמֶר וְאֵין דְּבָרִים בְּלִי נִשְׁמָע קוֹלָם:

5   בְּכָל־הָאָרֶץ | יָצָא קַוָּם וּבִקְצֵה תֵבֵל מִלֵּיהֶם
לַשֶּׁמֶשׁ שָׂם־אֹהֶל בָּהֶם:

6   וְהוּא כְּחָתָן יֹצֵא מֵחֻפָּתוֹ יָשִׂישׂ כְּגִבּוֹר לָרוּץ אֹרַח:

7   מִקְצֵה הַשָּׁמַיִם | מוֹצָאוֹ וּתְקוּפָתוֹ עַל־קְצוֹתָם
וְאֵין נִסְתָּר מֵחַמָּתוֹ:

8 תּוֹרַת יְהוָה תְּמִימָה מְשִׁיבַת נָפֶשׁ
עֵדוּת יְהוָה נֶאֱמָנָה מַחְכִּימַת פֶּתִי:

9 פִּקּוּדֵי יְהוָה יְשָׁרִים מְשַׂמְּחֵי־לֵב
מִצְוַת יְהוָה בָּרָה מְאִירַת עֵינָיִם:

10 יִרְאַת יְהוָה | טְהוֹרָה עוֹמֶדֶת לָעַד
מִשְׁפְּטֵי־יְהוָה אֱמֶת צָדְקוּ יַחְדָּו:

11 הַנֶּחֱמָדִים מִזָּהָב וּמִפַּז רָב וּמְתוּקִים מִדְּבַשׁ וְנֹפֶת צוּפִים:

12 גַּם־עַבְדְּךָ נִזְהָר בָּהֶם בְּשָׁמְרָם עֵקֶב רָב:

13 שְׁגִיאוֹת מִי־יָבִין מִנִּסְתָּרוֹת נַקֵּנִי:

14 גַּם מִזֵּדִים | חֲשֹׂךְ עַבְדֶּךָ אַל־יִמְשְׁלוּ־בִי
אָז אֵיתָם וְנִקֵּיתִי מִפֶּשַׁע רָב:

15 יִהְיוּ לְרָצוֹן | אִמְרֵי־פִי וְהֶגְיוֹן לִבִּי לְפָנֶיךָ יְהוָה צוּרִי
וְגֹאֲלִי:

Psalm 22

1 לַמְנַצֵּחַ עַל־אַיֶּלֶת הַשַּׁחַר מִזְמוֹר לְדָוִד:

2 אֵלִי אֵלִי לָמָה עֲזַבְתָּנִי רָחוֹק מִישׁוּעָתִי דִּבְרֵי שַׁאֲגָתִי:

3 אֱלֹהַי אֶקְרָא יוֹמָם וְלֹא תַעֲנֶה וְלַיְלָה וְלֹא־דוּמִיָּה לִי:

4 וְאַתָּה קָדוֹשׁ יוֹשֵׁב תְּהִלּוֹת יִשְׂרָאֵל:

5 בְּךָ בָּטְחוּ אֲבֹתֵינוּ בָּטְחוּ וַתְּפַלְּטֵמוֹ:

6 אֵלֶיךָ זָעֲקוּ וְנִמְלָטוּ בְּךָ בָטְחוּ וְלֹא־בוֹשׁוּ:

7 וְאָנֹכִי תוֹלַעַת וְלֹא־אִישׁ חֶרְפַּת אָדָם וּבְזוּי עָם:

8 כָּל־רֹאַי יַלְעִגוּ לִי יַפְטִירוּ בְשָׂפָה יָנִיעוּ רֹאשׁ:

9 גֹּל אֶל־יְהוָה יְפַלְּטֵהוּ יַצִּילֵהוּ כִּי חָפֵץ בּוֹ:

10 כִּי־אַתָּה גֹחִי מִבָּטֶן מַבְטִיחִי עַל־שְׁדֵי אִמִּי:

11 עָלֶיךָ הָשְׁלַכְתִּי מֵרָחֶם מִבֶּטֶן אִמִּי אֵלִי אָתָּה:

12 אַל־תִּרְחַק מִמֶּנִּי כִּי־צָרָה קְרוֹבָה כִּי־אֵין עוֹזֵר:

13 סְבָבוּנִי פָּרִים רַבִּים אַבִּירֵי בָשָׁן כִּתְּרוּנִי:

14 פָּצוּ עָלַי פִּיהֶם אַרְיֵה טֹרֵף וְשֹׁאֵג:

15 כַּמַּיִם נִשְׁפַּכְתִּי וְהִתְפָּרְדוּ כָּל־עַצְמוֹתָי הָיָה לִבִּי כַּדּוֹנָג נָמֵס בְּתוֹךְ מֵעָי:

16 יָבֵשׁ כַּחֶרֶשׂ | כֹּחִי וּלְשׁוֹנִי מֻדְבָּק מַלְקוֹחָי וְלַעֲפַר־מָוֶת תִּשְׁפְּתֵנִי:

17 כִּי סְבָבוּנִי כְּלָבִים עֲדַת מְרֵעִים הִקִּיפוּנִי כָּאֲרִי יָדַי וְרַגְלָי:

18 אֲסַפֵּר כָּל־עַצְמוֹתָי הֵמָּה יַבִּיטוּ יִרְאוּ־בִי:

19 יְחַלְּקוּ בְגָדַי לָהֶם וְעַל־לְבוּשִׁי יַפִּילוּ גוֹרָל:

20 וְאַתָּה יְהוָה אַל־תִּרְחָק אֱיָלוּתִי לְעֶזְרָתִי חוּשָׁה:

21 הַצִּילָה מֵחֶרֶב נַפְשִׁי מִיַּד־כֶּלֶב יְחִידָתִי:

22 הוֹשִׁיעֵנִי מִפִּי אַרְיֵה וּמִקַּרְנֵי רֵמִים עֲנִיתָנִי:

23 אֲסַפְּרָה שִׁמְךָ לְאֶחָי בְּתוֹךְ קָהָל אֲהַלְלֶךָּ:

24 יִרְאֵי יְהוָה | הַלְלוּהוּ כָּל־זֶרַע יַעֲקֹב כַּבְּדוּהוּ
וְגוּרוּ מִמֶּנּוּ כָּל־זֶרַע יִשְׂרָאֵל:

25 כִּי לֹא־בָזָה וְלֹא שִׁקַּץ עֱנוּת עָנִי
וְלֹא־הִסְתִּיר פָּנָיו מִמֶּנּוּ וּבְשַׁוְּעוֹ אֵלָיו שָׁמֵעַ:

26 מֵאִתְּךָ תְהִלָּתִי בְּקָהָל רָב נְדָרַי אֲשַׁלֵּם נֶגֶד יְרֵאָיו:

27 יֹאכְלוּ עֲנָוִים | וְיִשְׂבָּעוּ יְהַלְלוּ יְהוָה דֹּרְשָׁיו
יְחִי לְבַבְכֶם לָעַד:

28 יִזְכְּרוּ | וְיָשֻׁבוּ אֶל־יְהוָה כָּל־אַפְסֵי־אָרֶץ
29 וְיִשְׁתַּחֲווּ לְפָנֶיךָ כָּל־מִשְׁפְּחוֹת גּוֹיִם:

30 כִּי לַיהוָה הַמְּלוּכָה וּמֹשֵׁל בַּגּוֹיִם:

31 אָכְלוּ וַיִּשְׁתַּחֲווּ | כָּל־דִּשְׁנֵי־אֶרֶץ לְפָנָיו יִכְרְעוּ כָּל־יוֹרְדֵי עָפָר
וְנַפְשׁוֹ לֹא חִיָּה:

32 זֶרַע יַעַבְדֶנּוּ יְסֻפַּר לַאדֹנָי לַדּוֹר:

33 יָבֹאוּ וְיַגִּידוּ צִדְקָתוֹ לְעַם נוֹלָד כִּי עָשָׂה:

Psalm 23

מִזְמוֹר לְדָוִד 1
יְהוָה רֹעִי לֹא אֶחְסָר׃

בִּנְאוֹת דֶּשֶׁא יַרְבִּיצֵנִי 2
עַל־מֵי מְנֻחוֹת יְנַהֲלֵנִי׃

נַפְשִׁי יְשׁוֹבֵב 3
יַנְחֵנִי בְמַעְגְּלֵי־צֶדֶק לְמַעַן שְׁמוֹ׃

גַּם כִּי־אֵלֵךְ בְּגֵיא צַלְמָוֶת לֹא־אִירָא רָע 4
כִּי־אַתָּה עִמָּדִי שִׁבְטְךָ וּמִשְׁעַנְתֶּךָ הֵמָּה יְנַחֲמֻנִי׃

תַּעֲרֹךְ לְפָנַי ׀ שֻׁלְחָן נֶגֶד צֹרְרָי 5
דִּשַּׁנְתָּ בַשֶּׁמֶן רֹאשִׁי כּוֹסִי רְוָיָה׃

אַךְ ׀ טוֹב וָחֶסֶד יִרְדְּפוּנִי כָּל־יְמֵי חַיָּי 6
וְשַׁבְתִּי בְּבֵית־יְהוָה לְאֹרֶךְ יָמִים׃

Psalm 25

1 לְדָוִד
אֵלֶיךָ יְהוָה נַפְשִׁי אֶשָּׂא׃

2 אֱלֹהַי בְּךָ בָטַחְתִּי אַל־אֵבוֹשָׁה אַל־יַעַלְצוּ אֹיְבַי לִי׃

3 גַּם כָּל־קֹוֶיךָ לֹא יֵבֹשׁוּ יֵבֹשׁוּ הַבּוֹגְדִים רֵיקָם׃

4 דְּרָכֶיךָ יְהוָה הוֹדִיעֵנִי אֹרְחוֹתֶיךָ לַמְּדֵנִי׃

5 הַדְרִיכֵנִי בַאֲמִתֶּךָ ׀ וְלַמְּדֵנִי כִּי־אַתָּה אֱלֹהֵי יִשְׁעִי
אוֹתְךָ קִוִּיתִי כָּל־הַיּוֹם׃

6 זְכֹר־רַחֲמֶיךָ יְהוָה וַחֲסָדֶיךָ כִּי מֵעוֹלָם הֵמָּה׃

7 חַטֹּאות נְעוּרַי ׀ וּפְשָׁעַי אַל־תִּזְכֹּר כְּחַסְדְּךָ זְכָר־לִי־אַתָּה
לְמַעַן טוּבְךָ יְהוָה׃

8 טוֹב־וְיָשָׁר יְהוָה עַל־כֵּן יוֹרֶה חַטָּאִים בַּדָּרֶךְ׃

9 יַדְרֵךְ עֲנָוִים בַּמִּשְׁפָּט וִילַמֵּד עֲנָוִים דַּרְכּוֹ׃

10 כָּל־אָרְחוֹת יְהוָה חֶסֶד וֶאֱמֶת לְנֹצְרֵי בְרִיתוֹ וְעֵדֹתָיו׃

11 לְמַעַן־שִׁמְךָ יְהוָה וְסָלַחְתָּ לַעֲוֹנִי כִּי רַב־הוּא׃

12 מִי־זֶה הָאִישׁ יְרֵא יְהוָה יוֹרֶנּוּ בְּדֶרֶךְ יִבְחָר׃

13 נַפְשׁוֹ בְּטוֹב תָּלִין וְזַרְעוֹ יִירַשׁ אָרֶץ׃

14 סוֹד יְהוָה לִירֵאָיו וּבְרִיתוֹ לְהוֹדִיעָם׃

15 עֵינַי תָּמִיד אֶל־יְהוָה כִּי הוּא־יוֹצִיא מֵרֶשֶׁת רַגְלָי:

16 פְּנֵה־אֵלַי וְחָנֵּנִי כִּי־יָחִיד וְעָנִי אָנִי:

17 צָרוֹת לְבָבִי הִרְחִיבוּ מִמְּצוּקוֹתַי הוֹצִיאֵנִי:

18 רְאֵה עָנְיִי וַעֲמָלִי וְשָׂא לְכָל־חַטֹּאותָי:

19 רְאֵה־אוֹיְבַי כִּי־רָבּוּ וְשִׂנְאַת חָמָס שְׂנֵאוּנִי:

20 שָׁמְרָה נַפְשִׁי וְהַצִּילֵנִי אַל־אֵבוֹשׁ כִּי־חָסִיתִי בָךְ:

21 תֹּם־וָיֹשֶׁר יִצְּרוּנִי כִּי קִוִּיתִיךָ:

22 פְּדֵה אֱלֹהִים אֶת־יִשְׂרָאֵל מִכֹּל צָרוֹתָיו:

Psalm 51

1 לַמְנַצֵּחַ מִזְמוֹר לְדָוִד:

2 בְּבוֹא־אֵלָיו נָתָן הַנָּבִיא כַּאֲשֶׁר־בָּא אֶל־בַּת־שָׁבַע:

3 חָנֵּנִי אֱלֹהִים כְּחַסְדֶּךָ כְּרֹב רַחֲמֶיךָ מְחֵה פְשָׁעָי:

4 הֶרֶבה [הֶרֶב] כַּבְּסֵנִי מֵעֲוֹנִי וּמֵחַטָּאתִי טַהֲרֵנִי:

5 כִּי־פְשָׁעַי אֲנִי אֵדָע וְחַטָּאתִי נֶגְדִּי תָמִיד:

6 לְךָ לְבַדְּךָ ׀ חָטָאתִי וְהָרַע בְּעֵינֶיךָ עָשִׂיתִי
לְמַעַן תִּצְדַּק בְּדָבְרֶךָ תִּזְכֶּה בְשָׁפְטֶךָ:

7 הֵן־בְּעָווֹן חוֹלָלְתִּי וּבְחֵטְא יֶחֱמַתְנִי אִמִּי:

8 הֵן־אֱמֶת חָפַצְתָּ בַטֻּחוֹת וּבְסָתֻם חָכְמָה תוֹדִיעֵנִי:

9 תְּחַטְּאֵנִי בְאֵזוֹב וְאֶטְהָר תְּכַבְּסֵנִי וּמִשֶּׁלֶג אַלְבִּין:

10 תַּשְׁמִיעֵנִי שָׂשׂוֹן וְשִׂמְחָה תָּגֵלְנָה עֲצָמוֹת דִּכִּיתָ:

11 הַסְתֵּר פָּנֶיךָ מֵחֲטָאָי וְכָל־עֲוֹנֹתַי מְחֵה:

12 לֵב טָהוֹר בְּרָא־לִי אֱלֹהִים וְרוּחַ נָכוֹן חַדֵּשׁ בְּקִרְבִּי:

13 אַל־תַּשְׁלִיכֵנִי מִלְּפָנֶיךָ וְרוּחַ קָדְשְׁךָ אַל־תִּקַּח מִמֶּנִּי:

14 הָשִׁיבָה לִּי שְׂשׂוֹן יִשְׁעֶךָ וְרוּחַ נְדִיבָה תִסְמְכֵנִי:

15 אֲלַמְּדָה פֹשְׁעִים דְּרָכֶיךָ וְחַטָּאִים אֵלֶיךָ יָשׁוּבוּ:

16 הַצִּילֵנִי מִדָּמִים ׀ אֱלֹהִים אֱלֹהֵי תְּשׁוּעָתִי
תְּרַנֵּן לְשׁוֹנִי צִדְקָתֶךָ:

17 אֲדֹנָי שְׂפָתַי תִּפְתָּח וּפִי יַגִּיד תְּהִלָּתֶךָ:

18 כִּי ׀ לֹא־תַחְפֹּץ זֶבַח וְאֶתֵּנָה עוֹלָה לֹא תִרְצֶה:

19 זִבְחֵי אֱלֹהִים רוּחַ נִשְׁבָּרָה
לֵב־נִשְׁבָּר וְנִדְכֶּה אֱלֹהִים לֹא תִבְזֶה:

20 הֵיטִיבָה בִרְצוֹנְךָ אֶת־צִיּוֹן תִּבְנֶה חוֹמוֹת יְרוּשָׁלָ͏ִם:

21 אָז תַּחְפֹּץ זִבְחֵי־צֶדֶק עוֹלָה וְכָלִיל
אָז יַעֲלוּ עַל־מִזְבַּחֲךָ פָרִים:

Psalm 73

1 מִזְמוֹר לְאָסָף
אַךְ טוֹב לְיִשְׂרָאֵל אֱלֹהִים לְבָרֵי לֵבָב:

2 וַאֲנִי כִּמְעַט נָטָיוּ רַגְלָי כְּאַיִן שֻׁפְּכוּ אֲשֻׁרָי:

3 כִּי־קִנֵּאתִי בַּהוֹלְלִים שְׁלוֹם רְשָׁעִים אֶרְאֶה:

4 כִּי אֵין חַרְצֻבּוֹת לְמוֹתָם וּבָרִיא אוּלָם:

5 בַּעֲמַל אֱנוֹשׁ אֵינֵמוֹ וְעִם־אָדָם לֹא יְנֻגָּעוּ:

6 לָכֵן עֲנָקַתְמוֹ גַאֲוָה יַעֲטָף־שִׁית חָמָס לָמוֹ:

7 יָצָא מֵחֵלֶב עֵינֵמוֹ עָבְרוּ מַשְׂכִּיּוֹת לֵבָב:

8 יָמִיקוּ | וִידַבְּרוּ בְרָע עֹשֶׁק מִמָּרוֹם יְדַבֵּרוּ:

9 שַׁתּוּ בַשָּׁמַיִם פִּיהֶם וּלְשׁוֹנָם תִּהֲלַךְ בָּאָרֶץ:

10 לָכֵן | יָשׁוּב עַמּוֹ הֲלֹם וּמֵי מָלֵא יִמָּצוּ לָמוֹ:

11 וְאָמְרוּ אֵיכָה יָדַע־אֵל וְיֵשׁ דֵּעָה בְעֶלְיוֹן:

12 הִנֵּה־אֵלֶּה רְשָׁעִים וְשַׁלְוֵי עוֹלָם הִשְׂגּוּ־חָיִל:

13 אַךְ־רִיק זִכִּיתִי לְבָבִי וָאֶרְחַץ בְּנִקָּיוֹן כַּפָּי:

14 וָאֱהִי נָגוּעַ כָּל־הַיּוֹם וְתוֹכַחְתִּי לַבְּקָרִים:

15 אִם־אָמַרְתִּי אֲסַפְּרָה כְמוֹ הִנֵּה דוֹר בָּנֶיךָ בָגָדְתִּי:

16 וָאֲחַשְּׁבָה לָדַעַת זֹאת עָמָל הוּא בְעֵינָי:

17 עַד־אָבוֹא אֶל־מִקְדְּשֵׁי־אֵל אָבִינָה לְאַחֲרִיתָם:

18 אַךְ בַּחֲלָקוֹת תָּשִׁית לָמוֹ הִפַּלְתָּם לְמַשּׁוּאוֹת:

19 אֵיךְ הָיוּ לְשַׁמָּה כְרָגַע סָפוּ תַמּוּ מִן־בַּלָּהוֹת:

20 כַּחֲלוֹם מֵהָקִיץ אֲדֹנָי בָּעִיר | צַלְמָם תִּבְזֶה:

21   כִּי יִתְחַמֵּץ לְבָבִי וְכִלְיוֹתַי אֶשְׁתּוֹנָן:

22   וַאֲנִי־בַעַר וְלֹא אֵדָע בְּהֵמוֹת הָיִיתִי עִמָּךְ:

23   וַאֲנִי תָמִיד עִמָּךְ אָחַזְתָּ בְּיַד־יְמִינִי:

24   בַּעֲצָתְךָ תַנְחֵנִי וְאַחַר כָּבוֹד תִּקָּחֵנִי:

25   מִי־לִי בַשָּׁמָיִם וְעִמְּךָ לֹא־חָפַצְתִּי בָאָרֶץ:

26   כָּלָה שְׁאֵרִי וּלְבָבִי צוּר־לְבָבִי וְחֶלְקִי אֱלֹהִים לְעוֹלָם:

27   כִּי־הִנֵּה רְחֵקֶיךָ יֹאבֵדוּ הִצְמַתָּה כָּל־זוֹנֶה מִמֶּךָּ:

28   וַאֲנִי | קִרְבַת אֱלֹהִים לִי־טוֹב שַׁתִּי | בַּאדֹנָי יְהוִֹה מַחְסִי לְסַפֵּר כָּל־מַלְאֲכוֹתֶיךָ:

1 תְּפִלָּה לְמֹשֶׁה אִישׁ־הָאֱלֹהִים
אֲדֹנָי מָעוֹן אַתָּה הָיִיתָ לָּנוּ בְּדֹר וָדֹר:

2 בְּטֶרֶם | הָרִים יֻלָּדוּ וַתְּחוֹלֵל אֶרֶץ וְתֵבֵל וּמֵעוֹלָם עַד־עוֹלָם
אַתָּה אֵל:

3 תָּשֵׁב אֱנוֹשׁ עַד־דַּכָּא וַתֹּאמֶר שׁוּבוּ בְנֵי־אָדָם:

4 כִּי אֶלֶף שָׁנִים בְּעֵינֶיךָ כְּיוֹם אֶתְמוֹל כִּי יַעֲבֹר
וְאַשְׁמוּרָה בַלָּיְלָה:

5 זְרַמְתָּם שֵׁנָה יִהְיוּ בַּבֹּקֶר כֶּחָצִיר יַחֲלֹף:

6 בַּבֹּקֶר יָצִיץ וְחָלָף לָעֶרֶב יְמוֹלֵל וְיָבֵשׁ:

7 כִּי־כָלִינוּ בְאַפֶּךָ וּבַחֲמָתְךָ נִבְהָלְנוּ:
שַׁתָּ עֲוֹנֹתֵינוּ לְנֶגְדֶּךָ עֲלֻמֵנוּ לִמְאוֹר פָּנֶיךָ:

8 כִּי כָל־יָמֵינוּ פָּנוּ בְעֶבְרָתֶךָ כִּלִּינוּ שָׁנֵינוּ כְמוֹ־הֶגֶה:

9 יְמֵי־שְׁנוֹתֵינוּ בָהֶם שִׁבְעִים שָׁנָה וְאִם בִּגְבוּרֹת | שְׁמוֹנִים שָׁנָה
וְרָהְבָּם עָמָל וָאָוֶן כִּי־גָז חִישׁ וַנָּעֻפָה:

10 מִי־יוֹדֵעַ עֹז אַפֶּךָ וּכְיִרְאָתְךָ עֶבְרָתֶךָ:

11 לִמְנוֹת יָמֵינוּ כֵּן הוֹדַע וְנָבִא לְבַב חָכְמָה:

12 שׁוּבָה יְהוָה עַד־מָתָי וְהִנָּחֵם עַל־עֲבָדֶיךָ:

13 שַׂבְּעֵנוּ בַבֹּקֶר חַסְדֶּךָ וּנְרַנְּנָה וְנִשְׂמְחָה בְּכָל־יָמֵינוּ:

14 שַׂמְּחֵנוּ כִּימוֹת עִנִּיתָנוּ שְׁנוֹת רָאִינוּ רָעָה:

15 יֵרָאֶה אֶל־עֲבָדֶיךָ פָעֳלֶךָ וַהֲדָרְךָ עַל־בְּנֵיהֶם:

16 וִיהִי | נֹעַם אֲדֹנָי אֱלֹהֵינוּ עָלֵינוּ וּמַעֲשֵׂה יָדֵינוּ כּוֹנְנָה עָלֵינוּ
וּמַעֲשֵׂה יָדֵינוּ כּוֹנְנֵהוּ:

1 מִזְמוֹר שִׁיר לְיוֹם הַשַּׁבָּת:

2 טוֹב לְהֹדוֹת לַיהֹוָה וּלְזַמֵּר לְשִׁמְךָ עֶלְיוֹן:

3 לְהַגִּיד בַּבֹּקֶר חַסְדֶּךָ וֶאֱמוּנָתְךָ בַּלֵּילוֹת:

4 עֲלֵי־עָשׂוֹר וַעֲלֵי־נָבֶל עֲלֵי הִגָּיוֹן בְּכִנּוֹר:

5 כִּי שִׂמַּחְתַּנִי יְהֹוָה בְּפָעֳלֶךָ בְּמַעֲשֵׂי יָדֶיךָ אֲרַנֵּן:

6 מַה־גָּדְלוּ מַעֲשֶׂיךָ יְהֹוָה מְאֹד עָמְקוּ מַחְשְׁבֹתֶיךָ:

7 אִישׁ־בַּעַר לֹא יֵדָע וּכְסִיל לֹא־יָבִין אֶת־זֹאת:

8 בִּפְרֹחַ רְשָׁעִים | כְּמוֹ עֵשֶׂב וַיָּצִיצוּ כָּל־פֹּעֲלֵי אָוֶן לְהִשָּׁמְדָם עֲדֵי־עַד:

9 וְאַתָּה מָרוֹם לְעֹלָם יְהֹוָה:

10 כִּי הִנֵּה אֹיְבֶיךָ | יְהֹוָה כִּי־הִנֵּה אֹיְבֶיךָ יֹאבֵדוּ יִתְפָּרְדוּ כָּל־פֹּעֲלֵי אָוֶן:

11 וַתָּרֶם כִּרְאֵים קַרְנִי בַּלֹּתִי בְּשֶׁמֶן רַעֲנָן:

12 וַתַּבֵּט עֵינִי בְּשׁוּרָי בַּקָּמִים עָלַי מְרֵעִים תִּשְׁמַעְנָה אָזְנָי:

13 צַדִּיק כַּתָּמָר יִפְרָח כְּאֶרֶז בַּלְּבָנוֹן יִשְׂגֶּה:

14 שְׁתוּלִים בְּבֵית יְהֹוָה בְּחַצְרוֹת אֱלֹהֵינוּ יַפְרִיחוּ:

15 עוֹד יְנוּבוּן בְּשֵׂיבָה דְּשֵׁנִים וְרַעֲנַנִּים יִהְיוּ:

16 לְהַגִּיד כִּי־יָשָׁר יְהֹוָה צוּרִי וְלֹא־עַוְלָתָה בּוֹ:

Psalm 115

1 לֹא לָנוּ יְהוָה לֹא לָנוּ כִּי־לְשִׁמְךָ תֵּן כָּבוֹד
עַל־חַסְדְּךָ עַל־אֲמִתֶּךָ:

2 לָמָּה יֹאמְרוּ הַגּוֹיִם אַיֵּה־נָא אֱלֹהֵיהֶם:

3 וֵאלֹהֵינוּ בַשָּׁמָיִם כֹּל אֲשֶׁר־חָפֵץ עָשָׂה:

4 עֲצַבֵּיהֶם כֶּסֶף וְזָהָב מַעֲשֵׂה יְדֵי אָדָם:

5 פֶּה־לָהֶם וְלֹא יְדַבֵּרוּ עֵינַיִם לָהֶם וְלֹא יִרְאוּ:

6 אָזְנַיִם לָהֶם וְלֹא יִשְׁמָעוּ אַף לָהֶם וְלֹא יְרִיחוּן:

7 יְדֵיהֶם | וְלֹא יְמִישׁוּן רַגְלֵיהֶם וְלֹא יְהַלֵּכוּ לֹא־יֶהְגּוּ
בִּגְרוֹנָם:

8 כְּמוֹהֶם יִהְיוּ עֹשֵׂיהֶם כֹּל אֲשֶׁר־בֹּטֵחַ בָּהֶם:

9 יִשְׂרָאֵל בְּטַח בַּיהוָה עֶזְרָם וּמָגִנָּם הוּא:

10 בֵּית אַהֲרֹן בִּטְחוּ בַיהוָה עֶזְרָם וּמָגִנָּם הוּא:

11 יִרְאֵי יְהוָה בִּטְחוּ בַיהוָה עֶזְרָם וּמָגִנָּם הוּא:

12 יְהוָה זְכָרָנוּ יְבָרֵךְ יְבָרֵךְ אֶת־בֵּית יִשְׂרָאֵל
יְבָרֵךְ אֶת־בֵּית אַהֲרֹן:

13 יְבָרֵךְ יִרְאֵי יְהוָה הַקְּטַנִּים עִם־הַגְּדֹלִים:

14 יֹסֵף יְהוָה עֲלֵיכֶם עֲלֵיכֶם וְעַל־בְּנֵיכֶם:

15 בְּרוּכִים אַתֶּם לַיהוָה עֹשֵׂה שָׁמַיִם וָאָרֶץ:

16 הַשָּׁמַיִם שָׁמַיִם לַיהוָה וְהָאָרֶץ נָתַן לִבְנֵי־אָדָם:

17 לֹא הַמֵּתִים יְהַלְלוּ־יָהּ וְלֹא כָּל־יֹרְדֵי דוּמָה:

18 וַאֲנַחְנוּ | נְבָרֵךְ יָהּ מֵעַתָּה וְעַד־עוֹלָם הַלְלוּ־יָהּ:

Psalm 118

1 הוֹדוּ לַיהוָה כִּי־טֶוֹב כִּי לְעוֹלָם חַסְדּוֹ:

2 יֹאמַר־נָא יִשְׂרָאֵל כִּי לְעוֹלָם חַסְדּוֹ:

3 יֹאמְרוּ נָא בֵית־אַהֲרֹן כִּי לְעוֹלָם חַסְדּוֹ:

4 יֹאמְרוּ נָא יִרְאֵי יְהוָה כִּי לְעוֹלָם חַסְדּוֹ:

5 מִן־הַמֵּצַר קָרָאתִי יָּהּ עָנָנִי בַמֶּרְחָב יָהּ:

6 יְהוָה לִי לֹא אִירָא מַה־יַּעֲשֶׂה לִי אָדָם:

7 יְהוָה לִי בְּעֹזְרָי וַאֲנִי אֶרְאֶה בְשֹׂנְאָי:

8 טוֹב לַחֲסוֹת בַּיהוָה מִבְּטֹחַ בָּאָדָם:

9 טוֹב לַחֲסוֹת בַּיהוָה מִבְּטֹחַ בִּנְדִיבִים:

10 כָּל־גּוֹיִם סְבָבוּנִי בְּשֵׁם יְהוָה כִּי אֲמִילַם:

11 סַבּוּנִי גַם־סְבָבוּנִי בְּשֵׁם יְהוָה כִּי אֲמִילַם:

12 סַבּוּנִי כִדְבוֹרִים דֹּעֲכוּ כְּאֵשׁ קוֹצִים
בְּשֵׁם יְהוָה כִּי אֲמִילַם:

13 דַּחֹה דְחִיתַנִי לִנְפֹּל וַיהוָה עֲזָרָנִי:

14 עָזִּי וְזִמְרָת יָהּ וַיְהִי־לִי לִישׁוּעָה:

15 קוֹל | רִנָּה וִישׁוּעָה בְּאָהֳלֵי צַדִּיקִים
יְמִין יְהוָה עֹשָׂה חָיִל:

16 יְמִין יְהוָה רוֹמֵמָה יְמִין יְהוָה עֹשָׂה חָיִל:

17 לֹא אָמוּת כִּי־אֶחְיֶה וַאֲסַפֵּר מַעֲשֵׂי יָהּ:

18 יַסֹּר יִסְּרַנִּי יָּהּ וְלַמָּוֶת לֹא נְתָנָנִי:

19 פִּתְחוּ־לִי שַׁעֲרֵי־צֶדֶק אָבֹא־בָם אוֹדֶה יָהּ:

20 זֶה־הַשַּׁעַר לַיהוָה צַדִּיקִים יָבֹאוּ בוֹ:

21 אוֹדְךָ כִּי עֲנִיתָנִי וַתְּהִי־לִּי לִישׁוּעָה:

22 אֶבֶן מָאֲסוּ הַבּוֹנִים הָיְתָה לְרֹאשׁ פִּנָּה:

23 מֵאֵת יְהֹוָה הָיְתָה זֹּאת הִיא נִפְלָאת בְּעֵינֵינוּ:

24 זֶה־הַיּוֹם עָשָׂה יְהֹוָה נָגִילָה וְנִשְׂמְחָה בוֹ:

25 אָנָּא יְהֹוָה הוֹשִׁיעָה נָּא אָנָּא יְהֹוָה הַצְלִיחָה נָּא:

26 בָּרוּךְ הַבָּא בְּשֵׁם יְהֹוָה בֵּרַכְנוּכֶם מִבֵּית יְהֹוָה:

27 אֵל ׀ יְהֹוָה וַיָּאֶר לָנוּ

אִסְרוּ־חַג בַּעֲבֹתִים עַד קַרְנוֹת הַמִּזְבֵּחַ:

28 אֵלִי אַתָּה וְאוֹדֶךָ אֱלֹהַי אֲרוֹמְמֶךָ:

29 הוֹדוּ לַיהֹוָה כִּי־טוֹב כִּי לְעוֹלָם חַסְדּוֹ:

Psalm 121

1 שִׁיר לַמַּעֲלוֹת
אֶשָּׂא עֵינַי אֶל־הֶהָרִים מֵאַיִן יָבֹא עֶזְרִי:

2 עֶזְרִי מֵעִם יְהוָה עֹשֵׂה שָׁמַיִם וָאָרֶץ:

3 אַל־יִתֵּן לַמּוֹט רַגְלֶךָ אַל־יָנוּם שֹׁמְרֶךָ:

4 הִנֵּה לֹא־יָנוּם וְלֹא יִישָׁן שׁוֹמֵר יִשְׂרָאֵל:

5 יְהוָה שֹׁמְרֶךָ יְהוָה צִלְּךָ עַל־יַד יְמִינֶךָ:

6 יוֹמָם הַשֶּׁמֶשׁ לֹא־יַכֶּכָּה וְיָרֵחַ בַּלָּיְלָה:

7 יְהוָה יִשְׁמָרְךָ מִכָּל־רָע יִשְׁמֹר אֶת־נַפְשֶׁךָ:

8 יְהוָה יִשְׁמָר־צֵאתְךָ וּבוֹאֶךָ מֵעַתָּה וְעַד־עוֹלָם:

Psalm 124

שִׁיר הַמַּעֲלוֹת לְדָוִד 1
לוּלֵי יְהֹוָה שֶׁהָיָה לָנוּ יֹאמַר־נָא יִשְׂרָאֵל׃

לוּלֵי יְהֹוָה שֶׁהָיָה לָנוּ בְּקוּם עָלֵינוּ אָדָם׃ 2

אֲזַי חַיִּים בְּלָעוּנוּ בַּחֲרוֹת אַפָּם בָּנוּ׃ 3

אֲזַי הַמַּיִם שְׁטָפוּנוּ נַחְלָה עָבַר עַל־נַפְשֵׁנוּ׃ 4

אֲזַי עָבַר עַל־נַפְשֵׁנוּ הַמַּיִם הַזֵּידוֹנִים׃ 5

בָּרוּךְ יְהֹוָה שֶׁלֹּא נְתָנָנוּ טֶרֶף לְשִׁנֵּיהֶם׃ 6

נַפְשֵׁנוּ כְּצִפּוֹר נִמְלְטָה מִפַּח יוֹקְשִׁים 7
הַפַּח נִשְׁבָּר וַאֲנַחְנוּ נִמְלָטְנוּ׃

עֶזְרֵנוּ בְּשֵׁם יְהֹוָה עֹשֵׂה שָׁמַיִם וָאָרֶץ׃ 8

Psalm 134

1 שִׁיר הַמַּעֲלוֹת
הִנֵּה | בָּרְכוּ אֶת־יְהוָה כָּל־עַבְדֵי יְהוָה
הָעֹמְדִים בְּבֵית־יְהוָה בַּלֵּילוֹת:

2 שְׂאוּ־יְדֵכֶם קֹדֶשׁ וּבָרְכוּ אֶת־יְהוָה:

3 יְבָרֶכְךָ יְהוָה מִצִּיּוֹן עֹשֵׂה שָׁמַיִם וָאָרֶץ:

Psalm 145

1 תְּהִלָּה לְדָוִד
אֲרוֹמִמְךָ אֱלוֹהַי הַמֶּלֶךְ וַאֲבָרֲכָה שִׁמְךָ לְעוֹלָם וָעֶד:

2 בְּכָל־יוֹם אֲבָרֲכֶךָּ וַאֲהַלְלָה שִׁמְךָ לְעוֹלָם וָעֶד:

3 גָּדוֹל יְהוָה וּמְהֻלָּל מְאֹד וְלִגְדֻלָּתוֹ אֵין חֵקֶר:

4 דּוֹר לְדוֹר יְשַׁבַּח מַעֲשֶׂיךָ וּגְבוּרֹתֶיךָ יַגִּידוּ:

5 הֲדַר כְּבוֹד הוֹדֶךָ וְדִבְרֵי נִפְלְאוֹתֶיךָ אָשִׂיחָה:

6 וֶעֱזוּז נוֹרְאֹתֶיךָ יֹאמֵרוּ וּגְדוּלָּתְךָ אֲסַפְּרֶנָּה:

7 זֵכֶר רַב־טוּבְךָ יַבִּיעוּ וְצִדְקָתְךָ יְרַנֵּנוּ:

8 חַנּוּן וְרַחוּם יְהוָה אֶרֶךְ אַפַּיִם וּגְדָל־חָסֶד:

9 טוֹב־יְהוָה לַכֹּל וְרַחֲמָיו עַל־כָּל־מַעֲשָׂיו:

10 יוֹדוּךָ יְהוָה כָּל־מַעֲשֶׂיךָ וַחֲסִידֶיךָ יְבָרֲכוּכָה:

11 כְּבוֹד מַלְכוּתְךָ יֹאמֵרוּ וּגְבוּרָתְךָ יְדַבֵּרוּ:

12 לְהוֹדִיעַ | לִבְנֵי הָאָדָם גְּבוּרֹתָיו וּכְבוֹד הֲדַר מַלְכוּתוֹ:

13 מַלְכוּתְךָ מַלְכוּת כָּל־עֹלָמִים וּמֶמְשֶׁלְתְּךָ בְּכָל־דּוֹר וָדוֹר:

14 סוֹמֵךְ יְהוָה לְכָל־הַנֹּפְלִים וְזוֹקֵף לְכָל־הַכְּפוּפִים:

15 עֵינֵי־כֹל אֵלֶיךָ יְשַׂבֵּרוּ וְאַתָּה נוֹתֵן־לָהֶם אֶת־אָכְלָם בְּעִתּוֹ:

16 פּוֹתֵחַ אֶת־יָדֶךָ וּמַשְׂבִּיעַ לְכָל־חַי רָצוֹן:

17 צַדִּיק יְהוָה בְּכָל־דְּרָכָיו וְחָסִיד בְּכָל־מַעֲשָׂיו:

18 קָרוֹב יְהוָה לְכָל־קֹרְאָיו לְכֹל אֲשֶׁר יִקְרָאֻהוּ בֶאֱמֶת:

19 רְצוֹן־יְרֵאָיו יַעֲשֶׂה וְאֶת־שַׁוְעָתָם יִשְׁמַע וְיוֹשִׁיעֵם:

20 שׁוֹמֵר יְהוָה אֶת־כָּל־אֹהֲבָיו וְאֵת כָּל־הָרְשָׁעִים יַשְׁמִיד:

21 תְּהִלַּת יְהוָה יְדַבֶּר־פִּי וִיבָרֵךְ כָּל־בָּשָׂר שֵׁם קָדְשׁוֹ
לְעוֹלָם וָעֶד:

Psalm 146

1 הַלְלוּ־יָהּ
הַלְלִי נַפְשִׁי אֶת־יְהוָה:

2 אֲהַלְלָה יְהוָה בְּחַיָּי אֲזַמְּרָה לֵאלֹהַי בְּעוֹדִי:

3 אַל־תִּבְטְחוּ בִנְדִיבִים בְּבֶן־אָדָם | שֶׁאֵין לוֹ תְשׁוּעָה:

4 תֵּצֵא רוּחוֹ יָשֻׁב לְאַדְמָתוֹ בַּיּוֹם הַהוּא אָבְדוּ עֶשְׁתֹּנֹתָיו:

5 אַשְׁרֵי שֶׁאֵל יַעֲקֹב בְּעֶזְרוֹ שִׂבְרוֹ עַל־יְהוָה אֱלֹהָיו:

6 עֹשֶׂה | שָׁמַיִם וָאָרֶץ אֶת־הַיָּם וְאֶת־כָּל־אֲשֶׁר־בָּם
הַשֹּׁמֵר אֱמֶת לְעוֹלָם:

7 עֹשֶׂה מִשְׁפָּט | לָעֲשׁוּקִים
נֹתֵן לֶחֶם לָרְעֵבִים יְהוָה מַתִּיר אֲסוּרִים:

8 יְהוָה | פֹּקֵחַ עִוְרִים יְהוָה זֹקֵף כְּפוּפִים
יְהוָה אֹהֵב צַדִּיקִים:

9 יְהוָה | שֹׁמֵר אֶת־גֵּרִים
יָתוֹם וְאַלְמָנָה יְעוֹדֵד וְדֶרֶךְ רְשָׁעִים יְעַוֵּת:

10 יִמְלֹךְ יְהוָה | לְעוֹלָם אֱלֹהַיִךְ צִיּוֹן לְדֹר וָדֹר
הַלְלוּ־יָהּ:

Index of Biblical Verses